J. C. FISCHER AND HIS DIARY
OF INDUSTRIAL ENGLAND 1814-51

J. C. FISCHER AS A JOURNEYMAN IN DRESDEN, 1793
By courtesy of Georg Fischer A. G., Schaffhausen

J. C. Fischer and his Diary of Industrial England 1814-51

W. O. HENDERSON

FRANK CASS & CO. LTD.
1966

Published in 1966 by Frank Cass & Co. Ltd.
10 Woburn Walk, London W.C.1

Printed in Northern Ireland by
W. & G. Baird, Ltd.
Belfast

ACKNOWLEDGMENTS

THE AUTHOR is indebted to several scholars
—K. Schib, R. Gnade, and Hans Boesch—
—who have written on Johann Conrad
Fischer and his diaries. He thanks Herr Merz,
Herr Reiffer, and Herr Buss for much assistance in his research particularly when he
visited Schaffhausen on two occasions to work
in the archives of the firm of Georg Fischer.
Some articles which have appeared in the
Zeitschrift für die Gesamte Staatswissenschaft
and in *Tradition* are reprinted by permission
of the editors of these journals. Several illus-
trations, reproduced by permission of the
Georg Fischer Aktiengesellschaft, have
appeared in publications of the firm. The
maps have been drawn by Mr. Alan Hodgkiss
of the University of Liverpool. The author
thanks Dr. Chaloner, Mr. B. M. Ratcliffe and
Dr. Aldcroft for reading the proofs of the
book and Mrs. J. Lochett for her invaluable
help in typing the manuscript.

W. O. H.

CONTENTS

ix

B

LIST OF ILLUSTRATIONS

Industrial Switzerland[1]

It was surprising that so small and so remote a country as Switzerland should have played such an important part in the industrial revolution on the Continent in the nineteenth century. Nature had not endowed her with the resources which appeared to be essential for the development of manufactures on a large scale. Important basic raw materials were lacking since Switzerland had no coal[2] and little iron ore. Her population was too small—only 1,687,000 in 1817—to provide a substantial home market for mass produced goods. Her centres of trade were far from the ports which linked the Continent with those parts of the world from which 'colonial goods' could be obtained. Communications between different parts of Switzerland were difficult, particularly in the winter, owing to the mountainous nature of the country and the poor roads. In the 1780s for example Basel and Schaffhausen were linked only by narrow lanes badly in need of repair, and there were no bridges across the Wutach and the Steinach.[3] The mutual jealousies of the 25 territorial units into which the little country was divided seriously hampered the exchange of goods between one part of Switzerland and another. Prior to the civil war of 1847 there existed numerous internal customs barriers as well as vexatious tolls on the roads, bridges and rivers.[4] It was not until the introduction of a new constitution in 1848 that Switzerland had a central government which possessed the administrative apparatus and the financial resources which were needed to foster the expansion of manufactures. And the high tariffs of Switzerland's neighbours made it difficult for her to develop her export trade.

On the other hand there were factors which promoted industrial expansion in Switzerland. The people were hardworking and thrifty. High standards of workmanship had been attained in the eighteenth century by such craftsmen as the watchmakers of Geneva and the silkweavers of Zürich. Since three languages were spoken in the country the Swiss had close cultural ties with their German, French and Italian neighbours. Circumstances encouraged the Swiss to become proficient linguists. The central location of Switzerland on the highways of Europe attracted transit trade. The valleys of the Rhine and the Rhône linked Switzerland with France and Germany, while Napoleon's road over the Simplon facilitated commerce with Italy. Certain frontier towns, such as Geneva, Basel and Schaffhausen, were favourably located from the point of view of developing trade with France and Germany. Before the outbreak of the French revolution, Switzerland had for many years been at peace, while her neighbours had been at war. Foreign funds were attracted to Switzerland which had a well developed banking system in the eighteenth century. By 1790 the city of Berne had invested over £440,000 in London while the city of Zürich held £50,000 of Bank of England stock. Some of the capital held by Swiss bankers was later made available to industry. And the Continental System gave Swiss industries— particularly textiles—a breathing space free from English competition in which to introduce modern machinery.

The Swiss made the most of their limited industrial resources and commercial opportunities and exploited to the full the factors favourable to the expansion of manufactures. Since their homeland was so small they travelled abroad to gain experience and they studied industrial developments in Britain and on the Continent. They built up industries capable of exporting goods to neighbouring countries. Swiss costs were often high since raw materials had frequently to be imported and finished goods had to be exported. To make up for this the Swiss concentrated on the manufacture of products requiring a high degree of skill such as watchmaking, machine-making, precision engineering and chemicals.[5] In such products the 'value added' to the raw materials by the manufacturing process was considerable. In the absence of coal the Swiss made the most of their resources of water power.[6] The Swiss took full advantage of the location of their industries near the frontiers of France, Germany, Italy and Austria so as to sell their products abroad. And when high tariffs had to be surmounted on the Continent the Swiss showed initiative and energy in opening up more distant markets overseas. F. C. Zellweger observed in 1825 that circumstances were forcing Swiss merchants to widen their horizons. 'Nos commerçants se voient obligés d'élargir leurs horizons . . . Nos relations directes avec les pays immenses du Nord et du Sud de l'Amérique sont déjà si étendues, que la diminution de nos exportations en Europe nous touche à peine'.

When John Bowring visited Switzerland in 1836 a well informed Swiss told him that the success of his countrymen in industry was due to '(a) Free trade, which enables us to buy all that we want in the cheapest markets without import duty worth mentioning, (b) our light taxes which affect but very slightly the working classes, (c) the low price of labour . . ., (d) efficient capitals and the low rate of interest (3 to $3\frac{1}{2}$ per cent) resulting from the simplicity and efficiency of the laws relating to mortgages and credit, (e) the intelligence, prudence and economy of our manufacturers, who although they do not hastily and without reflection undertake new enterprises, pursue their object with energy and perseverance, (f) the aptitude of our population for manufacturing occupation, and their laborious habits of which the higher classes set the example.'[8]

A number of Swiss entrepreneurs built up great businesses in the nineteenth century. Many of them started from small beginnings and saved their own initial capital or borrowed money from relatives. The versatility of some of the early Swiss entrepreneurs was remarkable. Philipp Suchard not only established a great chocolate concern but operated steamers on Lake Neuchâtel and the Rhine, exploited asphalt in the Val de Travers and took a leading part in establishing Swiss settlers in New York State. Alfred Escher promoted railways and founded insurance companies. Hans Caspar Escher and Salomon von Wyss began as cotton spinners and ended as builders of textile machinery. Johann Conrad Fischer was in some respects typical of the entrepreneurs who laid the foundations of Switzerland's prosperity.

[1] For the industrial development of Switzerland see: Swiss Board of Trade, *Volkswirtschaft, Arbeitsrecht, und Sozialversicherung der Schweiz* (Einsiedeln, 1925); British Iron and Steel Federation, *The Swiss Iron and Steel Industry* (1953); John Bowring, *Report on the Commerce and Manufacturies of Switzerland* (*Parliamentary Papers*, 1836, Vol. XCV, p. 60); Emil Frey, 'Die schweizerische Handelspolitik der letzten Jahrzehnte' (in *Die Handelspolitik der wichtigeren Kulturstaaten;* Vol. XLIX of the *Schriften des Vereins für Sozialpolitik*, 1892); Bernard de Cérenville, *Le système continental et la Suisse* (1906); T. Geering and R. Hotz, *Wirtschaftskunde der Schweiz* (1910); A. Jenny-Trümpy, *Die schweizerische Baumwollindustrie* (1909); W. E. Rappard, *Le révolution industrielle et les origines de la protection légale du travail en Suisse* (1914); H. Nabholz, L. von Muralt, R. Feller and E. Bonjour, *Geschichte der Schweiz*, Vol. II (1938), Book 4, ch. ix and Book 6, ch. xi; W. Waldvogel, *Les relations économiques entre la Grande Bretagne et la Suisse* (1922); Albert Hauser, *Schweizerische Wirtschafts- und Sozialgeschichte von den Anfängen bis zur Gegenwart* (1961); W. Bodmer, *Die Entwicklung der schweizerischen Textilwirtschaft* . . .(1960).

[2] In the middle of the nineteenth century J. C. Fischer was paying £3 10s a ton for coal imported from St. Etienne.

[3] Karl Schib (editor), *Johann Conrad Fischer 1773–1854: Tagebücher* (1954), p. 677. This book is cited as Fischer's *Tagebuch*.

[4] 'Previous to the new constitution obtained by Switzerland in 1848 . . . the cantons were harassed by the multitude of federal and local tolls and regulations, partly arising out of the last general concordat of 1821 and partly arising out of the mutual jealousy of the cantons' (Tooke and Newmarch, *History of Prices*, (edition of 1828, Vol. V, p. 463).

[5] 'A mesure que les marchés voisins nous ont été fermés, nous avons vu s'accroître chez nous la fabrication des articles de qualité supérieure qui, travaillés avec plus de soin, et en même temps d'un poids plus léger, se prêtaient que d'autres à frayer au loin de nouvelles voies au commerce.' (*Rapport de la commission fédéral d'experts en matière de commerce* (1844), p. 177, quoted by W. E. Rappard, *loc. cit.*, p. 199).

[6] As early as 1798 J. K. Escher told the Swiss Grand Council that 'in the waterfalls of its many streams Switzerland possesses sources of power of incalculable value. If we can harness this source of power to industry our achievements will be prodigious and will be greater than those of other nations however many steam engines they may possess.' This was probably Hans Konrad Escher von der Linth (1767–1823) who was elected a member of the Grand Council in 1798. (W. E. Rappard, *loc. cit.*, p. 159).

[7] W. E. Rappard, *loc. cit.*, p. 198.

[8] W. O. Henderson, *Britain and Industrial Europe 1750–1870* (1954) second edition 1965), p. 201.

CHAPTER I

Fischer's Career as an Industrialist[1]

1. THE CRAFTSMAN

Johann Conrad Fischer was born in 1773 in Schaffhausen, a market town of some five thousand inhabitants. It was Protestant and German speaking. The picturesque little town lay on the right bank of the Rhine above the falls while the canton of Schaffhausen was a rural area to the north of the river, surrounded on three sides by German territories. This region formed part of the city state and the municipal authorities exercised sovereign rights over it.[2] In the eighteenth century Schaffhausen monopolised the shipping both above and below the Rhine Falls. The craft gilds had exclusive trading rights in the villages which were subject to the authority of the city magistrates.

Fischer's grandfather and father had been coppersmiths. As a journeyman Fischer's father had visited many European countries and had worked for a time in the royal gun foundry at Woolwich under his fellow townsman Andreas Schalch.[3] Fischer attended the local grammar school and at the age of fourteen entered his father's workshop. He continued his studies in mathematics and physics under two eminent scholars—Jezler and Hurter—and at the age of nineteen he left Schaffhausen to complete his training abroad. He was away from Switzerland for three years.[4] He began by working for six months as a coppersmith in Frankfurt am Main where he saw the coronation of the last Holy Roman Emperor. He moved to Saxony where he visited Freiberg in the Erzgebirge, long famous for its silver and lead mines. Fischer also worked in Chemnitz,[5] Berlin,[6] and Hamburg before leaving Germany. This visit to some of Germany's great centres of mining, commerce, and shipping was of great value to the young journeyman but it is going too far to assert that it was here that he obtained 'a thorough training in the arts of mining and working in metals'.[7]

In October 1793 Fischer went to Copenhagen where he stayed with his great-uncle Laurenz Spengler who had left Schaffhausen many years before as a journeyman carpenter and was now the art director at the royal palace.[8] Fischer learned some Danish and continued his studies in English and in physics. He made a favourable impression upon Spengler who wrote that his guest was an exceptionally able young man. 'That he has given complete satisfaction wherever he has worked is a remarkable achievement considering how limited have been his opportunities at home.'[9]

Accompanied by the journeyman Hans Jakob Wibert of Basel,[10] whom he had met in Berlin, Fischer now travelled in Denmark and Sweden. His visit to a Stockholm iron foundry was probably his first introduction to the art of working in iron since the forges of Schaffhausen were now derelict. In the spring of 1784 Fischer went to England where he worked for the London instrument maker Samuel Rhee.[11] He returned to Switzerland in 1795 as his father needed his assistance. Fischer now submitted a small model of a copper lion to the gild of smiths and became a master of his craft. He took over his father's copper works and at about the same time he was elected a member of the town council. Fischer soon opened a second workshop on the outskirts of Schaffhausen in which he made bells and fire fighting equipment. A testimonial from the local municipal authorities testified to his skill in this branch of working in metals.[12]

The year 1802 was a turning point in Fischer's career. In that year he set up a third workshop. This was a small smithy and steelworks in a mill called the *Kräutermühle* lying in the valley of the Durach stream which provided him with the power that he needed.[13] This valley was known as the Mühlental.[14] Eventually he had three small establishments in the Mühlental. They were the original smithy and steelworks (which were rebuilt after a fire in 1834), a plant on the Spitalwiese which was first a smithy (1810) and later a file manufactory; and a forge which was built in 1838. For a few years (1834–9) Fischer also operated a small forge some miles distant from his three other works. This was situated by the Paradise Convent (*Kloster Paradies*) on the river Rhine.[15] It was also in the year 1802 that Fischer travelled in France with his friend Hans Caspar Escher[16] and inspected the royal foundry in Strasbourg. Here he met Dubois, the master of the local mint. This visit appears to have been the starting point of Fischer's career as a steel manufacturer.[17] In the following year Fischer was appointed to the post of Director of Mines in the canton of Schaffhausen, a post which he held for fifty years.

2. THE INVENTOR

It has been seen that early in the nineteenth century Fischer added steelmaking to his existing trades of coppersmith, bell-founder, and manufacturer of fire pumps. His interest in iron and steel had been stimulated by visits to Stockholm (1794) and Strasbourg (1802). Many years later he told his friend Heinrich Zschokke[18]—who was planning the writing of a biography of Fischer—that he had started to make his own steel so as to become independent of an unsatisfactory supplier. Eventually he made a name for himself as a metallurgist. He broke the English monopoly of crucible cast steel and malleable cast iron and he successfully introduced these products onto the Continent. He also made a number of steel alloys and he invented steel castings independently of Jacob Mayer. His numerous discoveries were the result of applying to the practice of metallurgy a really thorough knowledge of physics and chemistry.

In 1800 crucible cast steel was a rare product and it could be obtained only from the Huntsman family and from a few other Sheffield steelmakers.[19] Before the Peace of Amiens[20] Britain and France had been at war for a decade and it had been difficult for Continental importers to secure cast steel for their customers. Continental ironmasters had a strong incentive to try to break the Sheffield monopoly. In France Sanche[21] and Clouet[22] claimed to have made crucible cast steel towards the end of the eighteenth century but there seems to be some doubt as to the success of their efforts.[23] Fischer succeeded in making crucible cast steel direct from bar iron—without using the intermediate process of cementation—early in the nineteenth century. In 1804 he showed samples of his steel at the Berne industrial exhibition, and in 1805 he had a pair of razors made from his steel by the cutler Kym of Berlingen. In his diary for 1814 Fischer stated that nine years previously—that is to say in 1805—he had made small quantities of cast steel. In 1808 an article in a German newspaper described his process[24] and mentioned that one of Fischer's main problems had been to secure suitable crucibles. Since German and Austrian crucibles could not stand the great heat to which they were subjected, Fischer made his own from kaolin found in the Reiath district by Lohn near Schaffhausen. When he saw some English crucibles in Tringham's shop in London in 1814[25] he was pleased to find that they were very similar to his own.[26] This experience of working with clay stood him in good stead when he invented a new kind of porous brick which he patented in Austria in 1827.[27]

Napoleon's Berlin and Milan decrees made it virtually impossible to secure English cast steel on the Continent. The firm of Huntsman for example received no order from the Continent for several years.[28] Several ironmasters—such as Poncelet of Liège, Friedrich Krupp of Essen, Andreas Küller of Wald (Solingen) and

J. C. Fischer of Schaffhausen—tried to solve the problem of how to make crucible cast steel of as good quality as that produced in Sheffield. In 1807 the French *Société d'encouragement pour l'industrie nationale* offered a prize for the production of high quality cast steel. Since Fischer could not comply with the conditions imposed upon foreign competitors he did not expect to secure an award but he did submit samples of his steel so as to secure an expert opinion upon it and to make it more widely known. Gillet-Laumont, a member of the French Mining Council, reported that Fischer's cast steel 'possède réellement les qualités d'un bon acier fondu, sans avoir les défauts'. A medal was awarded to Poncelet but the prize was held over.[29] Other contemporary references to Fischer as a successful manufacturer of crucible cast steel include Nemnich's recollections of his visit to Mühlental (1810),[30] Blumhof's description of the Fischer process (1821),[31] and an account of Fischer's technique in a German scientific journal (1821).[32] By the end of the Napoleonic wars Fischer was sufficiently well known for him to be visited by the Czar of Russia[33] and to be received by the King of Württemberg. The Czar suggested that Fischer might settle in Russia—an invitation which he declined —while the audience with the King of Württemberg was eventually followed by the establishment of a factory in Wangen im Allgäu for one of Fischer's sons.[34] Early evidence of the high quality of Fischer's steel comes from a letter written by a German silversmith named Peter Bruckmann recommending Fischer's steel since the quality of English steel had declined during the Napoleonic wars.[35]

The only description of the process from his own pen comes from a later period. In 1851 Fischer prepared for John Wilson a memorandum to supplement the description of his method of making cast steel which was printed in the catalogue of the Great Exhibition.[36] This account mentioned improvements—such as coke smelting and the hot blast—not used in the original process. Fischer claimed that his technique was better than Huntsman's since he saved money by placing more (though smaller) crucibles in his furnace; by charging his crucibles with wrought or scrap iron (instead of blister steel); and by using the hot blast instead of the cold blast.[37]

Soon after perfecting this process Fischer supplied customers in the Swiss and French Jura with steel from which files, springs, razors, knives, and gun barrels could be made. In 1806 he sent samples of his steel to the iron merchant Hans Martin Haffter of Weinfelden. Three years later he supplied the French clockmakers Japy Brothers of Beaucourt[38] and Badevel with springs for watches and by 1810 they had become his best customers. Fischer also sold his steel to firms in Seloncourt (County of Mont-bèliard) and La Chaux de Fonds (Neuchâtel).[39] Fischer was able to interest gunsmiths in his steel and two fowling pieces[40] and a pistol with barrels made of Fischer steel are preserved in the Town Museum of Schaffhausen.

In Fischer's obituary in a Schaffhausen newspaper it is stated that if Fischer had devoted himself entirely to the production of cast steel during the Napoleonic wars he could have made a fortune.[41] At this time, however, his energies were largely devoted to his public work, particularly to his duties as Director of Mines in the canton of Schaffhausen.

In 1814 when the war in Europe was drawing to a close Fischer visited England for the first time since 1794. His tour showed him the advances that British industry had made in the last twenty years. He realised that there would be severe competition from English steel manufacturers and, with some reluctance, he agreed to the suggestion of a Lyons merchant that he should adopt the questionable practice of stamping his steel 'B. Huntsman'. He tried to widen his markets abroad, particularly in Germany and in Austria, and for ten years or so he gave up his political activities so as to be able to devote more of his time to his business.[42]

At the same time Fischer was attempting to improve the quality of his steel by alloying it with other elements. Several metallurgists in England and on the Continent were trying to make steel alloys in the 1820s. In England Faraday and Stodart alloyed steel with aluminium and chromium.[43] In France the *Société d'encouragement pour l'industrie nationale* set up a commission to promote the production of steel alloys. Fischer succeeded in alloying steel with copper (1814),[44] silver (1817),[45] and chromium (1824).[46] Perreir, a cutler in Geneva, made a razor and several knives from Fischer's steel silver alloy.[47] In 1825 Fischer made a new kind of packfong. He claimed that his alloy of nickel, copper and zinc—originally produced in China—had a quite different composition from the packfong recently produced in Germany.[48]

Fischer went to Austria in 1824 to visit his son Georg who was studying at the Vienna Polytechnic.[49] Baron von Jacquin[50] showed him a collection of iron meteors which had fallen at Iglau in 1808. It was known that these specimens contained a small percentage of nickel. Fischer also saw the damascened Turkish swords displayed in the Venice arsenal and he concluded that they had been made from a steel nickel alloy. Fischer subsequently tried to imitate meteoric iron and damascened blades by alloying steel with nickel. He was successful[51] and he patented his new 'meteor steel' in Austria in 1825. The alloy was used to make files in Georg Fischer's manufactory at Hainfeld in Lower Austria. It has been observed that nickel-steel 'proved to be somewhat temperamental in tempering; it developed a mysterious embrittlement . . .'[52]

Fischer's journey to England in 1825 was undertaken to submit samples of his steel nickel alloy to the judgment of English experts. He brought with him percussion springs, razors, and small blocks of meteor steel. Faraday was impressed with the alloy while the gunsmith Joseph Egg declared that he 'never would have believed that both springs and razor blades could have been manufactured from the same steel, because the properties required in these two articles are opposite extremes and their combination in the same material is almost a paradox.'[53] After making a pair of razors from Fischer's steel Ebenezer Rhodes of Sheffield reported that the metal was 'of very fine quality, extremely hard, and admirably calculated to sustain a cutting edge'.[54] Before returning to Switzerland Fischer came to an arrangement with Martineau and Smith of London for the manufacture of his steel in England.[55]

At the same time that he was making steel alloys Fischer was also endeavouring to produce malleable cast iron. Such iron had been manufactured in England and in France in the eighteenth century and Réaumur had described a method of making it.[55a] Early in the nineteenth century it began to be made in England again by Samuel Lucas[56] and in France by Baradelle and Dédor. At this time the process of making malleable cast iron was kept secret in England. In 1814 Fischer visited a Birmingham factory where candle snuffers, stirrups, and other small articles were made from malleable cast iron.[57] On his return to Switzerland he tried to make such iron himself but without success.

On June 14, 1825 Fischer visited a 'malleable iron factory' in Birmingham. After talking to Mr. Cardwell, one of the partners, he wrote that he now had a clear idea of the nature of the process. 'The gaps in my knowledge have been filled and the doubts concerning my own experiments in this field have been removed.'[58] On the following day he looked over an ironworks in the Black Country 'where thousands of products are accurately moulded and successfully cast'. He continued his own experiments and on August 5, 1827—at his son's steel plant at Hainfeld in Austria—he succeeded in converting cast iron into malleable iron. He wrote in English in his note book: 'Entire success of the experiment for converting cast into malleable iron, for which important discovery I pay my humble thanksgivings to my Lord and preserver.'

Fischer showed some samples of his malleable cast iron to Archduke Johann of Austria in July 1827[60] and secured an Austrian patent for it on December 24, 1828.[61] In the following year the right to make this iron in Austria was assigned to Karl Wilhelm von Brévillier, for whom Berthold Fischer had erected a foundry at Neunkirchen.[62] When Brévillier's licence expired, Berthold Fischer made malleable cast iron himself at Traisen but it was not until after J. C. Fischer's death[63] that this iron was made at Mühlental by his grandson Georg Fischer II.

The next contribution that Fischer made to the advance of metallurgical science was his invention of a method of making castings from crucible steel in sand moulds. The development of the engineering industry had led to a demand for stronger machine parts than those cast in iron or made by the forging or rolling processes. The production of steel castings met this need. In 1824 F. H. W. Needham of London had patented a process for making steel castings but his experiments had not led to their production on a commercial scale.[64] An entry in his notebook for February 24, 1845 recorded Fischer's success in casting crucible steel. He soon showed samples of his cast steel products—such as horse shoes—to businessmen in Basel and to some of his English friends.[65] It has been claimed that the small tapered cast steel toothed wheel shown by Fischer at the Great Exhibition in London was 'the oldest authenticated example of a structural part cast from soft steel in a sand mould'.[66]

Fischer's process had been patented in Austria in 1845[67] and steel castings were manufactured there first by Ludwig von Brévillier and then by Georg Fischer at Hainfeld. But the output of these products in Austria was not very considerable. In Germany Jacob Mayer had, as early as 1841, discovered a method of making steel castings. He helped to found the Bochum Verein which became one of the great steelworks of the Ruhr.[68] At the end of his career Fischer was using a new steel alloy to make ball bearings for use in the axles of locomotive wheels and waggon wheels. He sold some of these ball bearings in England in the early 1850s.[69]

3. THE ENTREPRENEUR

The significance of Fischer's achievements as an entrepreneur lay in the reputation that he established for himself as a producer of high quality steel products. For nearly fifty years he made steel in his three little workshops at Mühlental but he probably never produced more than 25 tons in any one year. In the production of crucible cast steel, malleable cast iron, steel castings, and steel alloys he was a pioneer, yet some processes in his workshops were long carried out on traditional lines. Fischer relied upon the Durach stream for his power—inadequate though this sometimes proved to be—and he did not instal a steam engine. It was not until about 1825 that he began to use coke for smelting and this may have been due to the difficulty that he experienced in securing wood rather than to any conviction of the superiority of the coke process. The description of the steelworks at Mühlental given by Georg Moosmann suggests that by 1848 Fischer was using only coke in his furnaces.[70] Fischer never established a large undertaking in Switzerland and never sought to emulate his neighbour Neher whose iron smelting plant at Laufen earned him a fortune of a million francs.[71] Fischer left only 76,000 francs when he died though some of his capital had already been passed on to three of his sons in Austria. Fischer's failure to expand his Mühlental workshops and to make money out of cast steel— particularly at the time of the Continental System—may have been because he devoted so much of his time to his duties as Director of Mines and to his other public offices. Moreover Fischer did not have any incentive to expand his Swiss workshops for the benefit of his children. He had successfully established three of his sons in business in Austria and his eldest son Conrad—who might have inherited the Mühlental workshops—had been killed in an accident while still a young man.

Fischer made little attempt to secure control over the sources of the raw materials that he needed. No one had a better knowledge of the local bean iron ore deposits since he was the senior mining official in the canton.[72] He could have acquired an iron ore concession and he could have smelted his own ore. Fischer did use some local bean ore but for the most part he was content to buy iron bars from Neher or to import them from the Franche Comté. He also used some imported scrap iron and scrap steel. On the other hand he did make his own clay pots—from refractory clay found at Lohn near Schaffhausen—for the production of cast steel and he sold crucibles to other ironmasters. Fischer remained a craftsman all his life and his output was always small. But his products were of such high quality that they nearly always commanded a ready sale. Even in the early phase of the Swiss industrial revolution Fischer showed that a craftsman could successfully compete with industrialists who had much larger works than his own provided that his products were of good quality.

In the early nineteenth century the demand for good steel in Switzerland was a limited one. Fischer sold small quantities to

J. C. FISCHER'S STEELWORKS AT MÜHLENTAL IN THE EARLY NINETEENTH CENTURY
By courtesy of Georg Fischer A. G., Schaffhausen

HAMMERSMITH BRIDGE. DRAWN BY H. WINKLES
By courtesy of Hammersmith Public Library

local watchmakers, gunsmiths, and cutlers but some years elapsed before large machine building works—such as Escher and Wyss of Zürich—grew to such an extent that they could place substantial orders for steel files and spindles.[73] It became essential for Fischer to find new markets for his steel in the larger countries of Europe. He was a good linguist and throughout his life he travelled extensively, particularly in Austria, France, Germany, and England. His journals, note books, and business records contain many references to his efforts to extend his markets outside Switzerland. Sometimes he was able to sell his steel directly to foreign manufacturers such as Japy and sometimes he sold it to wholesalers (Haffter of Weinfelden, Ulrich of Zürich, Girerd and Dubreuil of Lyons). When orders from France declined after the Napoleonic wars Fischer found new customers in Germany and Austria.

After the Napoleonic wars the high import duties imposed by Britain, France, and Austria were a serious obstacle to the export of Swiss manufactures. During the severe trade slump of 1817 Fischer's steel output was only 5,500 lb. as compared with 9,500 lb. in 1816. The problems of Swiss exporters became even more acute in 1835 when the inclusion of Baden in the Zollverein brought German customs officials to the gates of Schaffhausen. Fischer adopted two methods to overcome these difficulties. First, he made arrangements whereby foreign manufacturers could exploit his inventions abroad under licence. Such contracts were signed with Japy in France, with Martineau and Smith in England, with Cockerill in Belgium, and with Brévillier in Austria. Secondly, he set up plants abroad either for other manufacturers or for his own sons. In France he erected steelworks at La Roche for Japy (1820)[74] while his son Berthold leased a forge for a few years at Montbéliard (1834-8). In Germany Fischer's son Wilhelm ran a steel plant at Wangen im Allgäu (Württemberg) for a short time. In England Fischer's plan to set up a steelworks (to be run by his son Conrad in association with Martineau and Smith) failed, while in Belgium his scheme to co-operate with John Cockerill of Seraing came to a tragic end when Conrad met with a fatal accident.

Fischer's greatest achievements as an entrepreneur outside Switzerland were in Austria where he successfully established three of his sons. Georg operated a steelworks and a spindle factory at Hainfeld; Berthold ran a similar plant at Traisen near Lilienfeld; and Wilhelm operated another at Salzburg. The records of various Austrian industrial exhibitions show that these establishments produced steel, spindles, and files of high quality.[75]

C

Fischer hoped to crown his business ventures in the Habsburg dominions by securing admission to the Austrian nobility but—despite his contacts with the Archduke Johann—his application was unsuccessful.

As an entrepreneur Fischer's career was full of contrasts. He had one foot in the age of the domestic system and the other in the modern world of great industries. His three workshops at Mühlental and his little forge on the Rhine by Kloster Paradies were quite small and he employed only a few skilled men. His output was on a very modest scale. His maximum production of steel in any one year was probably about 25 tons in 1839. Towards the end of his career his output had dropped to 9 tons.[76] He realised that for a Swiss manufacturer in the new industrial age the key to success lay in concentrating on the production of specialised goods and in exploiting the markets of the Continent by establishing new enterprises outside Switzerland. He made a name for himself as an inventor and as a founder of new plants abroad. Fischer was one of the first international entrepreneurs. His activities covered much of western Europe and he played his part in fostering the industrial expansion of Austria. Yet he would have been equally at home in the eighteenth century as in the modern Europe of the Common Market. Fischer enjoyed good health all his life. He died at the end of 1854 at the age of 81. In the last year of his life he made about 7 tons of steel. He wrote his biographical notes and he was in correspondence with the firm of Cockerill concerning the exploitation of his steel castings in Belgium. He was also still interested in promoting the sale of his ball bearings in England.

4. THE DIARIST

Fischer was a prolific writer and correspondent. Some of the journals which he kept on his travels—those concerning journeys in France and in Austria—have been lost[77] but the diaries dealing with England were published separately in his lifetime and were reprinted in a single volume in 1951.[78] To the complete edition of the diaries the editor added Fischer's biographical notes of 1854 and an extract from his notebook of 1827 containing an account of a meeting with the Archduke Johann of Austria. Fischer's accounts of London and the manufacturing districts of the North and Midlands are historical records of considerable value from the pen of an exceptionally well-informed foreigner who was one of the leading metallurgists of his day. Fischer learned English when he worked in London as a journeyman and he spoke the language fluently. His reputation as a metallurgist and his knack of getting letters of introduction from influential people opened many doors to him and he visited numerous steel-works and other industrial establishments to which foreign visitors were rarely admitted. A good many foreigners visited England in the first half of the nineteenth century and wrote accounts of their travels. Fischer was unique because he paid nine visits to this country between 1794 and 1851 and six of his journals dealing with his travels in England in the period 1814–51 have survived. His accounts of what he saw and heard throw a vivid light upon the changes that were taking place in London and the manufacturing districts of England at that time.[79]

Fischer kept a journal of his travels as a journeyman and a part of it was published many years after it had been written. This dealt with his visit (with Hans Jakob Wibert)[80] to Denmark and Sweden in 1794. In August and September 1814 Fischer was away from Switzerland for about seven weeks, most of the time being spent in England. His travelling companion in London on this occasion was Ringk von Wildenberg. The London banker Yeates Brown,[81] whom he had met by chance in Switzerland, had given him letters of introduction to James Watt junior and to other manufacturers in the provinces. Fischer's journal of this tour was shown to a number of his friends who persuaded him to publish it in 1815. In May 1825 Fischer visited Paris, London and the industrial districts of England. He returned to Switzerland at the end of July and published a full account of his travels. Fischer was back in England on business in the autumn of 1825 and again in 1826 and in 1827. Only fragments of his diaries of those years appeared in print in 1829. Fortunately the manuscript of Fischer's note book for 1827 has survived and although the daily entries are brief they add to our knowledge of his visit to England in that year. Eighteen years elapsed before Fischer returned to England. Now in his seventies he visited London and some of the industrial regions of the provinces in 1845, in 1846, and again in 1851 and the journals that he kept of these visits were published in his lifetime.

The journal which Fischer kept during his visit to England in 1814 is particularly interesting. He was visiting a country which was grappling boldly with the difficulties caused by the long wars and the Continental System. He was struck by the great rise in prices that had occurred since he had last been in England in 1794[82] and he appreciated the connection between high prices and currency inflation. But recent advances in science and technology, the increased use of steam power, the introduction of improved machinery, and the opening up of new markets overseas, were all signs of recovery. The fine houses of the merchants and manufacturers—their costly furnishings, plate, pictures, libraries and gardens—gave the Swiss visitor some impression of the fortunes that had been made during the war.

In the Midlands Fischer visited Boulton and Watt's famous engineering works at Soho,[83] the Level Ironworks near Dudley,[84] and the Wedgwood pottery works at Etruria (Hanley).[85] In the northern industrial districts of Lancashire and the West Riding Fischer saw Philips and Lee's huge cotton mill at Salford which was already lit by gas,[86] and he inspected Benjamin Gott's large woollen mills in Leeds,[87] the Huntsman steelworks at Attercliffe (Sheffield),[88] and the pioneer railway between Middleton colliery and Leeds on which coal waggons were drawn by a locomotive.[89] On the way back to London at the end of this tour the stage coach stopped at an inn at Bedford so that the horses could be changed. It is said that over a century later the representatives of the firm of Georg Fischer of Schaffhausen arrived at the same hotel when they came to Bedford to set up the Britannia Iron and Steel Works.[90]

Eleven years elapsed before Fischer returned to England. In the summer of 1825 he set off from Schaffhausen and travelled through France where he visited the steelworks that he had erected for Japy as well as the ironworks at Audincourt which had been built by Aaron Manby of Charenton (Paris).[91] When he reached London he thought that the capital was growing faster than ever. He marvelled at the new docks and streets and bridges. The building of some 40,000 houses in a single year he regarded as little short of a miracle. He was astonished at the way in which gas lighting had turned night into day in central London. Fischer visited the Royal Institution to meet Faraday and to attend one of Brande's lectures on chemistry. In Birmingham he saw a wire-drawing works and a factory in which Britannia metal[92] was made. In Manchester he met Johann Georg Bodmer (a Swiss engineer), Richard Roberts (the inventor of the self actor), W. Fairbairn (one of England's ablest millwrights), and the cotton spinners Philips and Lee. In Leeds he renewed his friendship with the Gott family and also visited Marshall's flax mills. In Sheffield he inspected steel plants and cutlery works and secured from the razor maker Ebenezer Rhodes a memorandum testifying to the excellence of his steel nickel alloy. On the coach to Birmingham he met the Sheffield steel manufacturer Sanderson. Back in London Fischer met the civil engineer George Rennie[93] and Mr. Daniel, the secretary of the Imperial Gas Light Company. Soon after returning to Schaffhausen[94] Fischer was back in London on business in the autumn of 1825 and he paid further visits to England in 1826 and 1827. Only parts of Fischer's diaries for those years were printed but his note book gives some additional information concerning his visit of 1827. The passages of the diaries for 1825-7 contain descriptions of Fischer's visits to the Woolwich arsenal and to the Thames tunnel.

Fischer did not visit England in the 1830s but when he was over 70 he again crossed the Channel on three occasions. In 1845 he brought with him samples of his steel products weighing a kilogram. And he hoped to persuade English investors to co-operate with Swiss and German capitalists in financing the building of a railway from Waldshut to Constance. In 1846 the main purpose of his journey was to sell his steel dies to the Royal Mint. Railway building had brought about great changes in England since Fischer's previous visits in the 1820s. He marvelled at the speed with which the necessary capital was being raised and the skill and determination with which various railway engineering problems were being overcome. But he saw the dangers that might lie ahead if speculation in railway shares were allowed to continue unchecked. In 1845 Fischer visited several of his old friends—Michael Faraday, John Sanderson, and John Gott—and he went over the Low Moor Ironworks near Bradford. In 1846 he visited various steelworks including the Butterley Ironworks near Alfreton in Derbyshire;[95] Cammell's steelworks in Sheffield; and Horsfall's ironworks in Liverpool. At the Butterley ironworks Fischer was told that the firm had its own coalmine from which it could secure coal very much cheaper than it would cost in France. In his journal for 1846 Fischer observed that although in general the cost of living in England was high a 4 lb wheaten loaf cost only 8d which was much cheaper than on the Continent.

The veteran metallurgist visited England for the last time in the summer of 1851 to see the Great Exhibition and to try to sell his new steel alloy ball bearings. Fischer's display cabinet at the Crystal Palace included an engraving of his smelting works. In the Austrian section Georg Fischer of Hainfeld showed a selection of files while Berthold Fischer of Traisen displayed an assortment of articles made from malleable cast iron. At the age of 78 Fischer was as active as ever. Apart from touring the exhibition several times he visited Faraday, Brande, and Cammell and kept his journal up to date. In Birmingham he was shocked to discover that the Soho engineering works was now lying derelict. In Sheffield he visited the cutlery workshops of Rodgers & Sons as well as the steelworks of Johnson, Cammell & Co. and of Turton & Sons.

The concluding paragraphs of Fischer's last diary were devoted to a brief discussion of the merits of Free Trade. He argued that the recent adoption of this policy by Britain had been due purely to motives of self-interest. He rejected the view that a policy which would benefit the workshop of the world would also meet the needs of the less developed industrial states on the Continent. Fischer considered that the Continental countries could not compete on equal terms with Britain and that they needed protective tariffs to safeguard the interests of their manufacturers.[96]

Throughout his life Fischer had been impressed by Britain's industrial and commercial progress. His journals contained many tributes to Britain's remarkable achievements as the leading industrial power in the world. On one occasion he observed that 'the English not only have the intelligence to use everything which, in the sphere of physics, chemistry, and applied mathematics, can be adapted to the perfecting of industrial processes but . . . they have the courage to invest very large sums of money in researches which are virtually indispensable to the achievement of new and useful results—particularly in manufacturing—and they have the foresight, the persistence, and the endurance to accomplish anything to which they have set their hands.'

Fischer however was blind neither to the evils of the industrial revolution nor to the less pleasing aspects of the English character. He commented from time to time upon the miserable condition of some of the workers—their ragged clothes, their wretched cottages, their addiction to strong liquor,[97] and their cruel sports. He warned his countrymen against employing English workers. He wrote: 'Not only do they cost a damned lot of money but they are often intoxicated. English workers who are efficient and well behaved can earn a very good living at home. It is not uncommon to come across English workers in foreign countries who are far from competent in all the branches of their trade. One can expect a high degree of skill only from a foreman but not from the average worker. The English worker abroad seldom fulfils the sanguine expectations of his employer because he is handling materials with which he may be unfamiliar and because he is working with different people than at home.'[98] Fischer criticised the cheap tricks of English advertisers. He deplored the fact that railways provided luxurious accommodation for first class passengers but only wooden seats for second class passengers. And he saw some of the dangers that beset a country in which the

behaviour of all sections of society appeared to be dominated by a
worship of the golden sovereign.

1 For J. C. Fischer see the obituary by J. J. Freuler (in the Fischer
archives); a biography by K. Schib in the *Schaffhauser Biographien*,
No. 1 (*Schaffhauser Beiträge* published by the Historical Association
of Schaffhausen, Vol. XXXIII, 1956, pp. 152–165); K. Schib and R.
Gnade, *Johann Conrad Fischer, 1773–1854* (1954); R. Gnade, *The
Metallurgist Johann Conrad Fischer . . . and his Relations with
Britain* (1947); Otto Vogel, 'Johann Conrad Fischer und die
englische Tempergiesserei' (*Stahl und Eisen*, Vol. XL, 1920, pp. 869–
72); B. Schudel, *Johann Conrad Fischer, ein Schweizer Pionier der
Stahlindustrie . . .* (1921); F. M. Feldhaus, 'Zwei technologische
Reisen nach England, 1814 und 1825' (*Geschichtsblätter für
Technik und Gewerbe*, Vol. V. 1918); Hans Boesch, 'Die Unterneh-
mungen von Johann Conrad Fischer' (*Neujahrsblatt* issued by the
Natural History Society of Schaffhausen, 1952); Wolfram Fischer,
'Drei Schweizer Pioniere der Industrie' (*Tradition*, 1958); H. Buess,
'A Swiss Manufacturer sees the Industrial Revolution in England'
(*British Journal of Industrial Medicine*, Vol. IX, 1962, pp. 47–51);
K. Schib, 'Giessereigeschichtliches aus dem Kanton Schaffhausen'
(*Beiträge zur Geschichte der schweizerischen Eisengiessereien*, published by the Eisenbibliothek, Schaffhausen, 1960); a volume issued
to celebrate the 150th anniversary of the founding of the firm of
Fischer entitled *Hundertfünfzig Jahre Georg Fischer Werke 1802–
1952* (1952); and an article by R. Gnade in the *Neue Deutsche Biographie*, Vol. IV.
2 For a map illustrating the growth of the city state of Schaffhausen
see H. Amman and K. Schib, *Historischer Atlas der Schweiz* (second
edition, 1958), p. 47. For the industrial development of Schaffhausen
see H. Pfister, 'Entwicklung der Industrie der Stadt Schaffhausen' in
the *Festschrift der Stadt Schaffhausen zur Bundesfeier, 1901* (Schaffhausen, 1901) and K. Schib, *Geschichte der Stadt Schaffhausen mit
Anhang aus der Entwicklung der Stahlwerke Georg Fischer* (1946).
3 Andreas Schalch (1692-1776) was only 24 years of age in 1716 when
he was appointed Master Founder of the new royal brass gun
foundry at Woolwich. He held this post for over fifty years. Schalch
is mentioned in Fischer's *Tagebuch* for 1827 (p. 424). Fischer stated
that Schalch secured his rapid promotion by correctly forecasting
an accident in the foundry which duly occurred when his warning
was ignored.
4 *Johann Conrad Fischer 1773–1854*: *Tagebücher* (edited by K. Schib,
1951, pp. 5–56: cited as Fischer's *Tagebuch*). The diary for 1794,
dealing mainly with a journey to Sweden was not published until
1845. The title was: *Tagebuch einer Reise von Coppenhagen nach
Stockholm im Frühjahr 1794* (1845).
5 In Chemnitz he worked for the coppersmith Müller. In Freiberg he
worked for a brother of his Chemnitz employer.

[6] In Berlin Fischer had hoped to secure employment with the copper-smith Jury but he was unable to do so. He worked for Sasse of Potsdam but was frequently able to visit Jury's workshops to see the four great copper horses that were being made for the Brandenburg Gate at this time.

[7] Hans Boesch, *op cit.*, p. 12.

[8] Laurenz Spengler died in 1807.

[9] Laurenz Spengler to Schmid, 1793 (letter in the Schaffhausen muni-capal archives; copy in the Fischer archives).

[10] Hans Jakob Wibert (1771–1861) was training to be a silk dyer. In 1845 when Fischer published his travel diary for 1794 he dedicated it to Wibert.

[11] Samuel Rhee's workshops were in Shoe Lane, Fleet Street. Fischer lodged at the Cross Keys Inn at Cheapside.

[12] From this testimonial it appears that Fischer was already a bell-founder in 1802. The first bell known to have been cast by Fischer —and still in existence—was made for the church at Schleitheim in 1804. Examples of Fischer's fire pumps are preserved in museums at Schaffhausen and at Stein am Rhein. Fischer supplied bells to the towns of Schlettenheim (1804), Barzheim (1806), Merishausen (1815 and 1817), Buck (1822) and Neunkirchen (1825).

[13] But on November 7, 1827 Fischer wrote in his notebook that short-age of water had held up his smelting since early August.

[14] The valley of the Durach was called the 'Mühlental' after a small mill (*Kräutermühle*).

[15] In 1918 the buildings and some of the lands of the Kloster Paradies (Paradise Convent) were purchased by the firm of Georg Fischer. The premises were reconstructed and now contain the Fischer archives and a library (*Eisenbibliothek*) which specialises in books on iron and steel.

[16] For Hans Caspar Escher see an essay by Charlotte Peter in *Schweizer Pioniere der Wirtschaft und Technik*, Vol. VI, 1956, pp. 9–30. The manuscript of the diary which Fischer kept during his journey in France with Escher was later destroyed by fire.

[17] See Fischer's letter to Heinrich Zschokke (written in 1847) in *Beiträge zur Geschichte der schweizerischen Eisengiessereien* (1960), p. 176.

[18] For Zschokke see K. Schib, 'Heinrich Zschokke als Biograph des Schaffhausener Industriellen J. C. Fischer' (*Festgabe Otto Mittler*, 1960, pp. 242–60). Dr. Schib reprints a fragment of the biography of Fischer that Zschokke planned to write but never completed.

[19] For Benjamin Huntsman see Samuel Smiles, *Industrial Biography* (1863) and T. S. Ashton, *Iron and Steel in the Industrial Revolution* (1924), pp. 54–6. Fischer stated that in 1814 only three English firms made cast steel (Fischer's *Tagebuch*, 1814, p. 77).

[20] A French mining engineer named de Bonnard visited various English ironworks at the time of the Peace of Amiens but he was

more interested in the coke smelting process and in puddling than in the production of crucible cast steel.

21 P. F. G. Le Play, 'Mémoire sur la fabrication et le commerce des fers à acier dans le nord de l'Europe' in the *Annales des Mines*, 4th series, Vol. IX, 1846, p. 140 and A. L. Dunham, *The Industrial Revolution in France* (1955), p. 133.

22 S. T. McCloy, *French Inventions of the Eighteenth Century* (1955), p. 76.

23 It was not until after the Napoleonic wars that James Jackson set up steelworks at Assailly near St. Etienne for the manufacture of crucible cast steel from Swedish iron. For the Jacksons of Assailly see W. F. Jackson, *James Jackson et ses fils . . .* (1893).

24 *Morgenblatt für gebildete Stände*, March 23, 1808 and Schib and Gnade, *op cit.*, pp. 40–41.

25 Tringham's shop was at 3 Cary Lane, Foster Lane, Cheapside, London.

26 Fischer's *Tagebuch*, 1814, p. 84.

27 For this (Austrian) patent for porous bricks see *Beschreibung der Erfindungen und Verbesserungen für welche in den k. k. österreichischen Staaten Patente erteilt wurden und deren Privilegiumsdauer nun erloschen ist* (Vienna, 1841), p. 17.

28 The firm of Huntsman received six orders from the Continent in 1810 but it is not known if they were executed. See F. Crouzet, *L'économie britannique et le blocus continental 1806–13* (2 vols., 1958), Vol. II, pp. 516–7. For Switzerland during the Continental System see B. de Cérenville, *Le système continental et la Suisse, 1803–11* (1906).

29 *Journal des Mines*, Vol. XXVI, No. 151, July 1809. In 1811 Gillet-Laumont, in a second report, stated that six firms had entered for another competition—Fischer did not enter on this occasion—and that the prize had been awarded to Poncelet of Liège. In the Ruhr Friedrich Krupp claimed that he had produced cast steel in 1811.

30 P. A. Nemnich, *Tagebuch einer der Kultur und Industrie gewidmeten Reise*, Vol. 8 (1811), p. 69 *et seq.*

31 J. G. L. Blumhof, *Versuch einer Encyklopädie der Eisenhüttenkunde* (1817), pp. 507-8.

32 *Annalen der Physik und Physikalischen Chemie* (edited by L. W. Gilbert), Vol. LXIX, 1821, pp. 257–63.

33 Fischer to James Watt (junior), March 6, 1815 (in the Boulton and Watt correspondence in the Birmingham Public Library).

34 See Pauly, *Beschreibung des Oberamts Wangen* (Stuttgart, 1841), p. 123. Wilhelm Fischer's career as an industrialist in Württemberg was a short one. He soon transferred his plant to Salzburg in Austria.

35 There is a copy of Peter Bruckmann's letter of December 13, 1816, in the Fischer archives at the Klostergut Paradies (*Allgemeine Werksgeschichte*, Mappe 1).

36 Fischer's memorandum of 1851 is printed in Schib and Gnade, *op cit.*, pp. 73–5. John Wilson had been the Principal of the Royal

Agricultural College. The description of the process given in Martineau and Smith's specification (Patent 5259 of 1825) was based upon information supplied by J. C. Fischer.

37 That J. C. Fischer had used the hot blast as early as the 1830s can be seen from Beck's drawing of Fischer's steelworks which dates from that period. In 1851 Fischer charged a shilling a pound for his steel nickel alloy, 5d a pound for his best cast steel, and 3d a pound for cast steel made from scrap iron.

38 Beaucourt is in the Department of Doubs.

39 By 1811 Fischer's steel was sufficiently well known for dishonest rivals to pretend that their ordinary cementation steel was Fischer crucible cast steel.

40 One of these fowling pieces was made by the German gunsmith Franz Ulrich of Oberndorf am Neckar. The other fowling piece and the pistol were made by Fischer's eldest son Conrad and were shown at the Bern industrial exhibition of 1824. Fischer's interest in firearms had been stimulated by his appointment as artillery inspector of the canton of Schaffhausen (1809) with the rank of lieutenant colonel (1815).

41 *Tage-Blatt für den Kanton Schaffhausen*, December 28, 1854.

42 But Fischer continued to serve as Director of Mines and as Lieutenant Colonel in the artillery. In 1831-5 he served as first President (mayor) of the town of Schaffhausen under a new constitution.

43 Stodart and Faraday, 'On the Alloys of Steel' in the *Philosophical Transactions of the Royal Society*, 1822, Part ii and Sir Robert Hadfield, *Faraday and his metallurgical Researches* (1932).

44 Fischer steel copper alloy or "yellow steel" consisted of three parts of steel and one part of copper (see his *Tagebuch*, 1814, p. 72). Fischer produced another steel copper alloy in 1847.

45 Fischer's steel silver alloy ('silverat' or 'silveretto') consisted of 500 parts of steel and one part of silver.

46 This alloy consisted of seventy parts of steel and one part of chromium.

47 See L. W. Gilbert's article on Fischer's experiments: 'Einige Versuche über Legierungen des Stahls mit Aluminium und Silber' in *Annalen der Physik und der Physikalischen Chemie*, Vol. LXIX, 1821, pp. 257-63.

48 Fischer's *Tagebuch*, 1825, pp. 214 and 239. The German type of packfong was called 'German silver'.

49 In his diary for 1825 (*Tagebuch*, p. 213) Fischer wrote that the laboratories of the Vienna Polytechnic were 'truly imperial' in size and in equipment.

50 Baron Joseph Franz Jacquin (1766-1839) was professor of Botany and Chemistry at the University of Vienna.

51 Fischer made his steel nickel alloy, or meteor steel, by melting a mixture of 12 kilograms of cast steel, 248 grams of 'meteor powder' (four parts of nickel and one part of silver) and 186 grams of kaolin. The alloy was polished with a mixture consisting of 20 parts of

vinegar and one part of nitric acid. Domenico Donazzi wrote in 1841: 'The subsequent addition of a one-hundredth part of nickel produces a fairly hard product which has a very fine lustre. With the help of acids a damascened effect can be secured. Such a steel has been marketed by Fischer of Schaffhausen under the name of "meteor steel". The iron united with the nickel to produce a pure alloy which does not rust when exposed to the air' (*Guida for gli Orefici, Argentieri, Chincaglieri ed altri Artefici di Metallurgia per prepare la Leghe Metalliche da usare nei diversi Lavori . . .* (Bologna, 1841).

52 W. Alexander and A. Street, *Metals in the Service of Man* (Pelican Book, 1944), p. 116.

53 Fischer's *Tagebuch*, 1825, p. 230.

54 Fischer's *Tagebuch*, 1825, pp. 325-6. John Cockerill in Belgium and Berzellius in Sweden were also trying to make a steel nickel alloy at this time.

55 See *Patents for Inventions. Abridgements of Specifications relating to the manufacture of Iron and Steel*, Part I 1620-1866 (1883), No. 5259, p. 48. The applicants were J. Martineau junior and H. W. Smith (October 6, 1825).

55a R.A.F. de Réaumur, *L'art de convertir le fer forgé en acier . . .* (1722). An English translation was published by the University of Chicago Press in 1956.

56 Ibid., No. 2767, p. 31.

57 Fischer's *Tagebuch*, 1814, pp. 108-9.

58 Fischer's *Tagebuch*, 1825, p. 248.

59 Fischer's *Tagebuch*, 1825, pp. 250-4.

60 Fischer's note book for 1827 in his *Tagebuch*, p. 762.

61 In his diary for 1851 (*Tagebuch*, p. 655) Fischer stated that he had secured an Austrian patent for his malleable cast iron in 1829. The date of the patent was December 24, 1828. The patent lasted for only two years. See R. Gnade's note in Fischer's *Tagebuch*, p. 809.

62 Berthold Fischer (1807-79) was J. C. Fischer's fifth son. For K. W. von Brévillier's works at Neunkirchen (Lower Austria), founded in 1823, see Johann Slokar, *Geschichte der österreichischen Industrie und ihrer Förderung unter Kaiser Franz I.* (1914), p. 490. The number of workers employed by Brévillier rose from 150 in the 1830s to 300 in the 1840s. Brévillier was awarded gold medals at the Austrian industrial exhibitions of 1835 and 1839.

63 For a description—written a few years after J. C. Fischer's death—of Fischer's malleable cast iron process see Carl Schmidt, 'Die Fabrication von hämmer- und schweissbarem Gusseisen bei Georg Fischer von Schaffhausen' in the *Polytechnisches Journal*, fourth series, Vol. VII, 1860, p. 236. The article has been reprinted by Karl Schib in 'Geisereigeschichtliches aus dem Kanton Schaffhausen' in H. Boesch and K. Schib, *Beiträge zur Geschichte der schweizerischen Eisengiessereien* (Schaffhausen, 1960), p. 185.

[64] *Patents for Inventions. Abridgements of Specifications relating to the manufacture of Iron and Steel, 1620–1866* (1883), No. 5003, p. 45 and L. Beck, *Geschichte des Eisens*, Vol. IV (1889), pp. 279, 280 and 325.

[65] Samples of Fischer's steel castings were also shown at the Berne industrial exhibition of 1848. Fischer wrote in his note book for 1845: 'Very important. First class cast steel made by direct fusion from poor scrap iron and then cast in a mould on February 24' (Hans Boesch, *Die Unternehmungen von J. C. Fischer* (1951), p. 35).

[66] R. Gnade, *The Metallurgist Johann Conrad Fischer . . . and his Relations with Britain* (1947), p. 43.

[67] Another Austrian patent for a steel copper alloy was secured by J. C. Fischer in 1847.

[68] The first account of Jacob Mayer's invention of steel castings appeared in the *Gemeinnütziges Wochenbatt des Gewerbe–Vereins zu Köln*, January 1, 1842. This was three years before Fischer's invention. See also W. Bertram, *Jacob Mayer der Erfinder des Stahlformgusses* (1938); Eugen Reinert, 'Jacob Mayer, Erfinder des Stahlformgusses und Begründer des Bochumer Vereins, 1813–75' (*Schwäbische Lebensbilder*, Vol. II, 1941, pp. 340–50); and A. Heuvers, 'Jacob Mayer, der Erfinder des Stahlformgusses' (*Giesserei*, January 8, 1953).

[69] Fischer's *Tagebuch*, p. 710 and his biographical notes of 1854 (*Tagebuch*, pp. 792–5).

[70] See H. Boesch, *Die Unternehmungen von J. C. Fischer* (1951), p. 35.

[71] Johann Georg Neher (Fischer spells the name Näher) operated an iron mine at Gonzen, a blast furnace at Plons, forges at Thorenberg near Lucerne and iron works at Laufen (Rhine Falls) near Schaffhausen. See Karl Schib's biography of Neher in 'Schaffhauser Biographen des 18en und 19en Jahrhunders' in *Schaffhauser Beiträge zur vaterländischen Geschichte*, 1956, pp. 231–7 and W. E. Rappard, *La révolution industrielle et les origines de la protection légale du travail en Suisse* (1914), p. 217. The diary of Neher's son Bernhard is in the *Eisenbibliothek* (Klostergut Paradies, Schaffhausen). For Neher's iron ore mine see *Das Eisenbergwerk am Gonzen . . .* (Winterthur, 1944).

[72] Fischer himself had discovered new iron ore deposits in the Reiath district near Lohe by Schaffhausen. For mining in the canton of Schaffhausen see Robert Lang, 'Der Bergbau im Kanton Schaffhausen' in the *Zeitschrift für schweizerische Statistik*, 1903. For the medieval origins of iron ore mining in the canton of Schaffhausen see W. U. Guyan, *Bild und Wesen einer mittelalterlichen Eisenindustrie im Kanton Schaffhausen* (Basel, 1946) and 'Die Eisenöfen im Hochtal bei Bargen' in *Zeitschrift für schweizerische Archäologie und Kunstgeschichte*, 1957, pp. 159-174.

[73] By 1834, however, the firm of Escher and Wyss had become a very important customer. The payments of this firm to Fischer in that

year amounted to 3,902 francs. See H. Boesch, *Die Unternehmungen von J. C. Fischer* (1951), p. 65.

74 In his introduction to the collected edition of Fischer's diaries (p. xvi) Karl Schib states that Fischer established two plants for Japy, one at Badevel and one at La Roche (Voujaucourt). It seems clear however that the La Roche plant was the only one erected by Fischer for Japy.

75 Georg Fischer, for example, was awarded a bronze medal at the Vienna industrial exhibition of 1835 and a silver medal at the Vienna exhibition of 1845. For the establishment of the Hainfield steel works see J. Slokar, *Geschichte der österreichischen Industrie und ihrer Förderung unter Kaiser Franz I.* (1914). For Fischer's conversations with the Archduke Johann of Austria in 1827 and 1840 see his *Tagebuch*, pp. 749–65 (taken from the *Schreibkalender in the* Fischer archives) and Reiner Puschnig, 'Ein Tag im Hause Erzherzog Johanns' (*Zeitschrift des Historischen Vereins für Steiermark*, Vol. L, 1959, pp. 71–91).

76

Fischer Steel Output in lb.

1810–17		1839–40		1847–54	
1810	3,000	1839	53,000	1847	24,784
1811	4,000	1840	39,000	1848	12,225
1816	9,500			1849	17,334
1817	5,550			1850	19,330
				1851	22,150
				1852	17,218
				1853	13,168
				1854	14,786

These statistics are taken from H. Boesch, *Die Unternehmungen J. C. Fischer* (1951), pp. 19, 20, 50, 51.

77 Two fragments of Fischer's journals concerning Austria survive. They are:

(i) Fischer's record in his notebook (*Schreibkalender*) for 1827 of his conversations with the Archduke Johann. This was first printed by A. Schlosser in *Roseggers Heimgarten*, Vol. 28, June 1914 and it was also included by K. Schib in the complete edition of Fischer's diaries, pp. 749–765.

(ii) Fischer's account of his visit to the Archduke Johann on June 25, 1840 printed by Reiner Puschnig in the *Zeitschrift des Historischen Vereins für Steiermark*, Vol. 50, 1959, pp. 72–91.

78 *Johann Conrad Fischer 1773–1854: Tagebücher* (edited by K. Schib, 1951).

79 Two other Swiss industrialists visited England just after the Napoleonic wars. J. G. Bodmer of Zürich, an engineer who worked in Bolton for many years, kept a journal in 1816–17 and another in 1840. See Helen and Paul Schoch-Bodmer, 'Johann Georg Bodmer und sein Tagebuch von 1816–17' in the *Vierteljahrsschrift der Naturforschenden Gesellschaft*, Zürich, 1936, pp. 86–110 and articles in the *Transactions of the Newcomen Society*, Vol. VI, 1925–5, pp. 86–

110 and the *Journal of the Royal Society,* Vol. CI, No. 4905, August 7, 1953, p. 68 *et seq.* The journal kept by Hans Caspar Escher during his visit to Britain in 1814 appeared under the title 'Briefe aus England' in the *Zürcherische Beiträge zur wissenschaftlichen und geselligen Unterhaltung,* 1815–16, Vol I, Heft 2, pp. 100–117; Heft 3. pp. 103–119; Vol. II, Heft 4, pp. 91–122; Heft 5, pp. 110–112; Vol. III (supplementary articles), Heft 7, pp. 84–98; and Heft 8, pp. 113–121.

[80] In July 1845 Fischer—then on his way to England—met Wibert in Basel. He wrote in his diary: 'How sorry I was that he could not again join me on my journey to England as he had done fifty years ago' (Fischer's *Tagebuch,* 1845, p. 473).

[81] The offices of the banking firm of Brown and Siordet were at 66 Lombard Street. Yeates Brown's home was in Manchester Square, London.

[82] Hans Caspar Escher, who was also in England in 1814, declared that a thaler went further in Switzerland than a louis d'or in London. See his 'Briefe aus England' in the *Zürcherische Beiträge zur wissenschaftlichen und geselligen Unterhaltung,* Vol. II, 1815, Letter 4, p. 109. See also the last paragraph of Letter 3, p. 109.

[83] The sons of the two founders of the firm were managing the Soho works at the time of Fischer's visit. There is no truth in Hans Boesch's statement (*op cit.,* p. 21) that Fischer met the elder James Watt.

[84] For these ironworks see T. M. Hoskinson's paper in the *Transactions of the Newcomen Society,* Vol. XXVIII, 1951–2 and 1952–3.

[85] Josiah Wedgwood, the founder of the firm, had died in 1795. Fischer met his son.

[86] The factory had been erected in 1799–1800 and was one of the first iron-framed buildings in England. See an article in the *Architectural Review,* April 1950, pp. 231–46. George A. Lee (1761–1826) was described by Fischer as 'one of the most remarkable men in England' and by Robert Owen as 'one of the most scientific men of his day'. See obituary notices of Lee in the *Manchester Guardian,* August 12, 1826 and the *Gentleman's Magazine,* new series, Vol. XCVI, ii, July–December 1826, pp. 281–2 and A. E. Musson and E. Robinson, 'Science and Industry in the late Eighteenth Century' (*Economic History Review,* second series, Vol. XIII, December 1960, pp. 229–30). For William Murdock—Boulton and Watt's foreman and inventor of coal gas lighting—see the lives by S. Timmins (1864) and B. Taylor (1952) and A. Murdock, *Light without Wick* (1892). Fischer met Murdock in Birmingham in 1814.

[87] For Benjamin Gott see W. B. Crump (ed.), *The Leeds Woollen Industry 1780–1820* (1931).

[88] Benjamin Huntsman had died in 1776. The business was carried on by his sons.

[89] This locomotive, constructed under Trevithick's patent, was designed by Matthew Murray and John Blenkinsop. It was the first

locomotive to be fitted with flanged wheels to run on rails and it had a fifth wheel fitted with cogs to supply the drive. See W. G. Rimmer, 'Middleton Colliery near Leeds 1770–1830' (*Yorkshire Bulletin of Economic and Social Research*, Vol. III, 1955, pp. 41–57).

90 A. Stamm, *Georg Fischer. Werksentwicklung von der Kupfer-schmiede zum Grossbetrieb* . . . (typescript in the Fischer archives), p. 7.

91 Fischer's *Tagebuch*, 1825, pp. 201–2.

92 Britannia metal was 90 per cent. or more tin, 4 to 9 per cent. silver, and 3 per cent. copper.

93 Rennie encouraged Fischer to submit samples of his steel nickel alloy to the Royal Mint.

94 Fischer described this visit to England in an address to the Swiss Natural History Society: See *Verhandlungen der allgemeinen schweizerischen Gesellschaft für die gesammten Naturwissenschaften in ihrer elften Jahresversammlung zu Solothurn . . . 1825* (Solothurn, 1825), pp. 52–6.

95 A picture of the foundry at the Butterley ironworks in 1844 is re-produced by Chaloner and Musson, *Industry and Technology* (1963), Fig. 71.

96 Fischer expressed the same point of view in articles in the *Tage-Blatt für den Kanton Schaffhausen*, No. 88, April 15, 1852 and No. 89, April 16, 1852 (copies in the Fischer archives).

97 'It is drink that makes this city (London) poor and wretched and this applies to all classes of society' (Fischer's *Tagebuch*, 1851, p. 660).

98 Fischer's *Tagebuch*, 1827, pp. 455–6.

CHAPTER II

Fischer's Visits to London

1. METALWORKERS AND ENGINEERS

(i) *London as a Centre of Engineering*[1]

In the early nineteenth century London was one of the greatest centres of woodworking, metalworking and engineering in Britain. The raw materials—wood, iron and coal—were not to be found close at hand but skilled and unskilled workers were available and the London market was so big that a variety of light consumer industries in which wood and metals were used had developed in and around the capital. Several of these industries were associated with the river. The erection of bridges, the construction of the Rotherhithe-Wapping tunnel, the construction of the West India and the East India docks,[2] and the expansion of the shipbuilding and marine engineering industries brought building contractors and machine builders to the banks of the Thames. The coming of railways; the erection of waterworks and gas generating plants; and the construction of new streets, public buildings, shops and private dwellings also brought building contractors and civil engineers to the metropolis. Nationalised establishments such as the arsenal at Woolwich, the dockyard at Chatham, the new mint on Tower Hill and the post office all gave employment to a variety of skilled craftsmen.[3]

Men like Bramah, Maudslay, the Rennies[4], the Brunels,[5] Martineau, Philip Taylor, Jacob Perkins—and Roberts, Clement, Nasmyth, and Whitworth who were trained in London—helped to give the metropolis its reputation as a centre of engineering. The industry was organised both in large modern plants and in small workshops. The craftsmen included a variety of specialists such as watchmakers,[6] cutlers, locksmiths, gunsmiths, engravers, assayers, goldsmiths, silversmiths, opticians, and makers of precision tools and scientific instruments.[7] These mechanics did not make mass produced goods but manufactured high quality products for restricted markets.

(ii) *1794. Samuel Rhee*[8]

Little is known of Fischer's first visit to London in 1794. His journal for that year described only his travels on the Continent

The Transept of the Crystal Palace from the South Entrance

ROYAL MINT

GAS LIGHT COMPANY, WESTMINSTER

before he came to England. He simply stated that he was employed in the workshops of Samuel Rhee of Shoe Lane, Fleet Street. Rhee had been a pupil of the instrument maker Jesse Ramsden[9] and he had made a reputation for himself as a skilled mechanic. He had made a significant contribution towards solving the problem of mechanically dividing the graduated limbs of scientific instruments. He had improved Ramsden's circular dividing engine by using a screw with a continuous thread. Rhee had the reputation of being particularly skilful in the art of threading. In later journals Fischer mentioned that in 1794 he had lodged in Cheapside;[10] that he had made parts of textile machines such as metal cylinders for roller spinning; and that just before returning home he had bought samples of steel and various tools from Samuel Fenn of Newgate Street.[11] He recalled that in the 1790s the English had been extremely suspicious of foreigners and that any visitor to London who had been rash enough to appear in public dressed in an unusual manner would soon have had a mob at his heels.[12] Fischer declared that his first visit to London had given him the opportunity of comparing the mechanical arts in England with those on the Continent. 'I must admit', he wrote, 'that the comparison was entirely in England's favour. The English did not fear foreign competition in this or in other branches of industry. The system of granting patents, introduced into England at so early a date, protected and stimulated the industrial economy and probably helped to secure the production of manufactured goods which were practical, solid, and fully adapted to the purposes for which they were intended. But except for the steam engine—then hardly known on the Continent—I came across little that was actually novel in England. The manufactured goods which I saw were also made on the Continent but their quality was not so good as those produced in England.'[13]

(iii) *1814. Edward Stammers and Holtzapffel*

Fischer had two reasons for visiting England in 1814.[14] He wanted to see the progress that had been made in the metallurgical industries in the past twenty years[15] and he hoped to secure some orders for his cast steel. He had been told that only three English firms made such steel so he thought that there might be opportunities to sell his steel to cutlers, watchmakers, and gunsmiths. He called upon the cutler Edward Stammers[16] and admired his sharp, rustless silver-plated steel table knives. Stammers for his part was favourably impressed with the razors that the Swiss cutler Kym[17] had made from Fischer's steel. At first he doubted whether Fischer's steel would make good watch springs but eventually he agreed to use it for some springs ordered by the watchmaker Berola. Fischer also showed his rolled steel to Samuel Fenn whom he had met on his previous stay in London. Fenn agreed that steel of this type was not available in England and he praised its high quality. Fischer called upon Morris of Ludgate Hill whom he described as 'a famous gunsmith' but they discussed the merits of various types of gunpowder and not the merits of Fischer's steel. Fischer asked if he might test the gunpowder that Morris was selling so as to compare it with some powder which had been made in Berne.

The most distinguished London engineer visited by Fischer in 1814 was Holtzapffel, a German who had settled in England in 1787.[18] Fischer stated that Holtzapffel showed him a collection of turning lathes which were among the finest made in England at that time. Their prices ranged from 30 to 250 guineas.[19] In Holtzapffel's workshop Fischer saw a new tool for turning threads.

Fischer also called upon Peter Dollond,[20] the optician, with whom he discussed the advantages of substituting iron for copper in the making of mirrors. He visited the assayer James Tringham[21] and examined his crucibles for making cast steel. Fischer inspected two factories in which lead pencils were made and wrote that he was satisfied that the outstanding quality of the pencils was due to the use of really high grade graphite.[22]

(iv) 1825–7. Joseph Egg[23]

Fischer came to England in 1825 to show his steel nickel alloy to English experts and to try to establish his eldest son Conrad with an English firm.[24] Conrad, now aged 26, was a gunsmith who had been trained by Siber of Morges (Switzerland), Prélat and Le Page[25] of Paris, and Collier[26] and Egg of London. Conrad had helped his father in the Mühlental steelworks and had also made firearms in his own workshop on the outskirts of Schaffhausen—probably in the same premises that his father had once used for making church bells and fire pumps. Conrad's reputation as a skilled gunsmith was well established and he had been awarded a gold medal at the Berne industrial exhibition of 1824 for a five shooter fowling piece.

On reaching London in 1825 J. C. Fischer went to Joseph Egg's workshop in Piccadilly where Conrad had completed his training. Egg was the inventor of copper percussion caps and Fischer described him as a famous gunsmith who numbered members of the aristocracy among his customers.[27] Fischer showed him a steel nickel spring for firing a pistol and Egg was astonished that the same alloy could be used to make both springs and razors. Egg told Fischer how to apply for an English patent for his invention and Fischer later bought a book on English patent law.[28]

John Martineau[29]

On July 9, 1825 Fischer visited a large gasworks to inspect the plant but, as he explained in his diary, 'my conversation with one of the proprietors took a much more interesting turn than usual and it may perhaps in a few days decisively influence the future of my business and of my way of life'.[30] It is reasonable to assume that the works were those of the London Portable Gas Company and that the director with whom Fischer spoke was Henry William Smith.[31] A few days later on July 13 Fischer noted in his diary that he had discussed 'a particular piece of business' with the firm of Taylor and Martineau and on July 15 he stated that he had concluded 'a very important transaction concerning the transfer of my invention of a steel nickel alloy'.[32] This transaction was probably a preliminary understanding between J. C. Fischer, John Martineau, and Henry William Smith for the exploitation of Fischer's steel alloys in England. For Fischer it was the first step in the realisation of his plan to settle Conrad in England.

John Martineau was one of London's leading engineers in the 1820s. With his partner Philip Taylor[33] and his son John Martineau junior he ran a successful foundry and engineering works in the City Road. His standing may be judged by the fact that in 1824 he was the first witness to appear before the House of Commons committee which enquired into the laws prohibiting the emigration of skilled workers and the export of machinery.[34] The firm of Taylor and Martineau enjoyed an international reputation for the high quality of its products. In 1825 Taylor and Martineau put onto the market 'the now familiar small open-type factory engine having its cylinder, slide bars, and crankshaft-bearings on a horizontal cast iron bedplate of box girder section'.[35] Among other things the firm built steam engines, gas generating plants, and pumps.

Fischer saw a Taylor and Martineau steam engine at Brunel's sawmill at Battersea and a Taylor and Martineau gas generator at the Apothecaries Hall. He stated that the firm supplied steam engines to the Thames Tunnel Company and to the London Portable Gas Company.[36] Taylor and Martineau sold their engineering products abroad as well as at home. The Imperial Gas Light Company passed on to them enquiries from the Continent concerning gas generating plants. And in 1825 the French engineer Marc Séguin ordered from Taylor and Martineau an iron boiler and a three-cylinder steam engine. The partners may have designed the locomotive—built by Robert Stephenson—which ran on the first French railway from Lyons to St. Etienne.[37]

When Fischer visited the workshops of Taylor and Martineau in July 1825 he saw many machines being built including 18 steam engines, and several gas generators, gas cylinders, gas compressors, and pumps.[38] On another occasion he inspected the firm's laboratory where he saw an ice making machine and a new type of power loom.[39] He wrote: 'Quite apart from the financial gain, it must give the owners of so extensive an establishment great satisfaction to see such large and fine products leaving their plant. I love my fatherland and would not wish to be long away from it, yet the more I see of England the more I regret having spent the best years of my life in a country where a man's opportunities are so restricted.'[40]

Fischer left London on July 17th, 1825 soon after transacting his 'important piece of business' but he was back again in October of the same year. On October 6th Martineau and Smith applied for a patent 'to produce steel of improved quality and presenting the wavy appearance of Damascus swords'.[41] Shortly afterwards— in return for paying Fischer 'a respectable remuneration'—they secured the right to make his steel nickel alloy for 15 years.[42]

Fischer stated that his second journey to England in 1825 as well as his visits in the two following years were the 'result of the business contacts' which he had made in London.[43] In October 1825 he met Martineau and Taylor and discussed with them various methods of making steel.[44] Towards the end of 1826 Fischer and his son Georg[45] were in London to see Conrad who was testing his father's steel process in Martineau's foundry.[46] In January 1827 Fischer learned from Conrad that the experiments were making good progress[47] and on February 13 he sent to his associates in London a draft of a proposed new contract.[48]

In September and October 1827 Fischer was in London again. It has been seen that there are only brief references in his printed journal to this visit but there is a day to day summary of his movements in his note book for that year. On this occasion Fischer made some cast steel in Martineau's foundry by direct fusion from Russian pig iron[49] and he visited the Woolwich arsenal with Conrad.[50] After consulting the London banker Nathan Rothschild and his friend Benjamin Gott of Leeds, Fischer signed a new agreement. This was between John Martineau, Richard Carter Smith, Johann Conrad Fischer and Conrad Fischer. The signatories pledged themselves to establish 'certain furnaces and works' to make steel by the Fischer process.[51] In his notebook for 1827 Fischer wrote (in English) that October 27, 28, and 29 had been 'very pleasant days' for him. On the 28th he had received 'a considerable sum of money' as a result of his agreement with his London partners.[52] In the end, however, nothing came of Fischer's attempts to set Conrad up in business in England. The English partners soon ran into financial difficulties owing to unsuccessful speculations and in 1828 Conrad left London to seek his fortune in Belgium.[53] He worked with John Cockerill of Seraing (Liège) and his future seemed assured when he was accidentally killed while demonstrating a revolver.

Marc Isambard Brunel[54]

Another eminent London engineer whose acquaintance Fischer made in the 1820s was Marc Isambard Brunel who was the leading inventor of machines used in the woodworking industries. He was a Frenchman who had served for six years in the French navy before his royalist sympathies forced him to flee to the United States during the revolution. His reputation as an engineer and an inventor were soon firmly established.

Brunel came to England in 1800 and designed a complicated series of machines—constructed by Henry Maudslay—for executing the various processes of manufacturing pulley blocks in three sizes for the Royal Navy at Portsmouth dockyard. The 43 machines, driven by a 32 horse power engine, were ready in 1806 and they saved the Admiralty £17,000 a year. Several of these machines were in use for 150 years.[55] 'The project is of historic interest because it constituted one of the earliest examples of the use of machine tools for mass production.'[56] Brunel also invented various machines for sawing, cutting and bending timber and he set up his own saw mills at Battersea.

An introduction from John Martineau secured Fischer admittance to these works in July 1825. There he saw six circular saws, the diameter of the largest being 18 feet and that of the smallest 10 feet. Timber of the highest quality was being cut into pieces varying in thickness from $\frac{1}{4}$ inch to 1/13 inch for joiners, carpenters, and cabinet makers. Fischer wrote: 'Anyone who has inspected these saws and has realised that each of them is operated by only one man—whose output equals that of ten workers using conventional tools—will not be surprised to learn that Brunel has patented this invention and rarely allows visitors into his works. His system saves both time and money and it would be impossible to imagine articles made with greater precision and utility than those produced here.' Fischer saw what he described as 'a miracle in wood'—a faultless piece of mahogany (not even cut from the heart of the tree) which was 16 feet long and 5 feet broad. It had a uniform thickness of one foot and was quite ready for cutting.

In October 1825 Fischer called upon Brunel once more. This time he saw the world's first underwater tunnel under construction. In the previous February Brunel had started to build a road tunnel under the Thames between Rotherhithe and Wapping.[57] Already a shaft had been sunk and the digging of the tunnel itself had begun. To expedite the work Brunel had invented an ingenious device which became the prototype of later digging machines. This was a cast iron shield which reminded Fischer of the *testudo* of the Roman legionaries. The shield consisted of three tiers, one above the other, each tier being divided into twelve sections. The use of this structure enabled 36 miners—one in each section—to dig the tunnel simultaneously day and night at three different levels. As the work progressed the great iron shield was forced slowly forward a few inches at a time by a screw propellor. Behind the miners came workmen who constructed arches of quick setting Roman cement[58] to make the tunnel more secure. Fischer marvelled at the magnitude of the undertaking, the speed with which the work was being done, and the skill with which Brunel and his colleagues were solving the engineering problems involved in building the tunnel.[59]

In May 1827, despite the precautions which Brunel had taken, the tunnel caved in and flooding occurred. When Fischer saw it in September of that year Brunel told him: 'It has been no easy task to move between thirty and forty thousand cubic feet of water and mud. About a third of what had to be shifted was mud. And the hole in the bed of the river had to be plugged.'[60] This was done by filling it with Portland cement[61] and bags of clay. Fischer wrote that 'British will power coupled with Brunel's own genius and determination were such that no one was deterred by this misfortune. All the resources of the human spirit, all the knowledge of science, and all the aid that money could give were united to triumph over the effects of this disaster, even at the risk of life and limb.'[62] Shortly after Fischer's visit the building of the tunnel was resumed. But in January 1828 the workings were again flooded and this time the tunnel was bricked up for seven years. About £1,000 was raised by public subscription[63] but it was not until the government provided a loan that the work was resumed and then—despite two further floods—the tunnel was at last completed in the spring of 1843.[64] But it was not a financial success as a tunnel for pedestrians and it was eventually sold to a railway company.

Jacob Perkins[65]

In the early 1820s the claims of the American inventor Jacob Perkins concerning his steam engine and his steam gun had aroused much controversy and Fischer wished to see these inventions and to make his own judgment on their merits. As a young man Perkins had constructed a machine to cut and to head nails in one operation.[66] He had also invented a process of engraving bank notes on hardened steel plates[67] which made forgery much more difficult than before. His process had been adopted by the Second Bank of the United States.

Perkins came to England in 1819 and set up his workshops first at Austin Friars and then in Fleet Street. With his partners he engraved notes for a number of banks, though not for the Bank of England. He was soon acknowledged to be the leading exponent in England of the art of engraving on steel, but Perkins' patent did not protect him completely from competition. His son Angier March Perkins told Fischer that 'it had been a great mistake to patent only the process of taking impressions from plates of hardened steel. We should have made a lot of money if we had extended our patent to cover soft steel plates. Many copper engravers are now starting to use cast steel plates. Although these plates are only of soft steel it is possible to get from them a much greater number of sharp clear impressions than from copper plates.'[68] It was to some extent from the profits of the engraving business—but also from funds supplied by an unknown financial backer—that Perkins was able to defray the cost of establishing experimental engineering workshops first in Water Lane,[69] then in Regents Park (1824),[70] and finally in Gray's Inn Road (1827).[71] In these workshops he made many experiments involving the use of much higher steam pressures than those employed in other steam engines at that time.

In 1822 Perkins patented his first high pressure steam engine and put it on public display.[72] His reputation was such that in the same year he was asked to answer a questionnaire prepared by the Select Committee of the House of Commons which was considering the means of improving communications between England and Ireland. Perkins recommended installing high pressure boilers in steamship engines since they had already been successfully used in the United States.[73] By 1823 it was said that Perkins' fame had 'spread half over Europe.'[74]

Fischer thought highly of Perkins' ability[75] but several English engineers were suspicious of the American inventor's more extravagant claims. Robert Stephenson declared that 'Perkins knows nothing about the principle of steam engines' while Elijah Galloway stated that there had been so many exaggerations and misrepresentations about Perkins' steam engine 'that we cannot venture to give evidence to anything on the subject without seeing this alleged improvement in actual practice.'

In 1827 Perkins patented a new 'inverted single cylinder engine entirely different . . . from the horizontal machine of 1823.' It had a five-day test working a pump during the construction of St. Catherine's dock. Perkins stated that further work on the engine stopped because his 'monied partner failed and died and his creditors put the patent in Chancery.'[76] This was the first steam engine to be constructed on the 'uniflow' principle which was eventually successfully adopted in the twentieth century.[77]

In the 1820s Perkins invented a steam gun which caused as much controversy as his steam engine. This gun discharged bullets under a pressure of 1,500 lb. to the square inch. But the Ordnance Select Committee declined to recommend the expenditure of public money on further research while the French military authorities lost interest in the project when Perkins' mobile steam cannon—built by John Penn of Greenwich—failed to come up to expectations at its trials at Versailles in 1828. Among his other activities mention may be made of Perkins' discovery that air could be liquified and his system of mechanical refrigeration which he patented in 1834.[78]

When he arrived in London in June 1825 Fischer secured a copy of a description of Perkins' steam engine and steam gun. A letter of introduction from Faraday gained him admission to the inventor's workshops in Regents Park. Here he saw the steam engine and a model of a ship to be driven by the engine. He was shown the steam gun and was told that it would fire a thousand shots in a minute. Fischer also saw the hydraulic press and other apparatus with which Perkins was experimenting on the compression and liquifying of gases. Perkins impressed Fischer as a man destined to bestow many scientific discoveries on the world. 'The pursuit of far-reaching ideas interests him more than the dusty accumulation of worldy goods.'[79] On a second visit to the Regents Park workshops Fischer saw the steam engine in action and he stated that ' a few days ago several leading engineers examined the steam engine and could find no fault with it.'[80]

In December 1826 Fischer was shown round Perkins' engraving works in Fleet Street by Perkins' son and he gave a detailed description of the steel engraving process in his journal. In his diary for 1827 Fischer wrote at some length about Perkins.[81] He still regarded Perkins as one of the great inventors of his day and he paid a glowing tribute to Perkins for the way in which he had succeeded in improving his first high pressure steam engine. Fischer also referred his readers to articles in the *Register of the Arts and Sciences* on Perkins' engine and on the steam road carriages constructed by Goldsworthy Gurney in Regents Park and by Mosley in Southwark.

Thomson and Johnson[82]

In October 1827 Fischer had made some steel in Martineau's plant and wished to have it hammered. He took it to Messrs Thomson and Johnson's London Steelworks near Vauxhall Bridge. This plant produced a variety of cast steel products including coach springs made of German steel.[83] Fischer's description of these works was followed by a favourable comment on the skill shown by English industrialists in the application of heat to metal working, brickmaking and the manufacture of pottery. 'One must admire their talent for observation and for drawing conclusions from their observations when one sees the way in which they contrive ingenious devices and short cuts based upon a knowledge of physics and chemistry—two branches of science which will soon have to be considered as one.' It was at the London Steelworks that Fischer was approached by an artisan who asked him for a job on the Continent. Fischer declined to help him partly because he did not wish to offend the man's employers and partly because he thought that only the less efficient English workers wanted to emigrate.

(v) *1845–51*

Eighteen years passed after the failure of the plan to establish an English steel plant for Conrad before Fischer visited England again. In his three visits in 1845, 1846, and 1851 he renewed his old friendships with Faraday and Brande but he found that a number of his former acquaintances, such as Marc Isambard Brunel and Jacob Perkins, had now retired from business. In the provinces Fischer again inspected ironworks, steelworks, and engineering plants. But in London business affairs occupied a good deal of his time and he paid fewer visits to industrial establishments than before. He was engaged in selling steel dies and in finding customers for his steel ball bearings. He tried to patent his steel castings and he endeavoured to find financial backers for a proposed railway from Waldshut to Constance.

Fischer's enthusiasm for new inventions had not diminished with advancing years. Now it was photography and the atmospheric railway that claimed his attention. At first he regarded the atmospheric railway with suspicion but he changed his mind after seeing a model of such a railway displayed at the Polytechnical Institution in 1845. He was also impressed with the apparent success of the Dublin atmospheric railway and he now thought that this new type of railway might in some cases replace existing locomotives.[84] In October of the following year Fischer visited the terminus of the Croydon atmospheric railway and met its engineer Mr. Gregory.[85]

In 1851 Fischer once more arrived in England with a new steel product for sale. This time it was steel ball bearings for use in the axles of steam locomotives and railway waggons. At the Phoenix foundry in Southwark he saw how Dewrance's patent ball bearings were made and he met their inventor.[86] Later he secured an order for about a hundredweight of his own ball bearings.[87]

On this last visit to London Fischer paid many visits to the Great Exhibition at the Crystal Palace but he found time to call at the Millwall shipbuilding yard of Robinson and Russell[88] which had recently supplied a Swiss company with a river steamship called the *Stadt Schaffhausen*. On this occasion he did not see Mr. Baird—a representative of the firm whom he had previously met in Schaffhausen—but he was able to call on Mr. Baird on the last day of his stay in London.[89]

(vi) *The Gas Industry*[90]

Fischer showed considerable interest in the development of the gas industry.[91] In his journal for 1814 he expressed his admiration of the new gas lamps in Pall Mall and he inspected the gas generating plants which had been installed in their mills by Philips and Lee of Salford and by Benjamin Gott of Leeds. In Birmingham he met William Murdock, the inventor of gas lighting, and formed a high opinion of his scientific and technical abilities. He described Murdock as a benefactor of mankind.

Eleven years later Fischer observed in his diary that in central London the main thoroughfares, the shops and the houses were now lit by gas. He noted that grocers and butchers were particularly lavish in their display of gas lights.[92] By this time gas lighting had ceased to be a novelty in England and had become a well established public utility. In a report of January 1823 Sir William

Congreve had stated that there were four public companies in London which supplied gas to over 60,000 private and over 7,000 street lamps.[93] These companies produced gas from coal. In addition there were two companies in London which made gas from various types of oil. One of them had its works near Old Ford and operated seven miles of gas mains while the other—the London Portable Gas Company—supplied compressed gas in copper containers from its plant in Clerkenwall to premises which were not connected to gas mains. As there was some controversy concerning the relative merits of making gas by these two methods[94] Fischer decided to see for himself some of the plants in London for generating gas from coal and from oil.

Fischer discussed the problem with Mr. Hennel of the Apothecaries Hall where both types of gas generators were in use and gathered that the general opinion was that 'where coal is cheap, coal should be used, and where oil is cheap, oil should be used.'[95] At the Apothecaries Hall he saw an apparatus constructed by Taylor and Martineau for generating gas from fish oil. He praised the makers for the machine's 'simplicity and utility'. The apparatus, which cost £170, could make 80 cubic feet of gas out of a gallon of oil in an hour. The gas was stored in a gasometer with a capacity of between 900 and 1,000 cubic feet. From the gas supplied by such a gasometer 70 lights could burn for six or seven hours.[96]

Fischer also visited the works of the London Portable Gas Company where some 6,000 cubic feet of gas made from oil were sent to consumers in metal cylinders.[97] He thought that this method of supplying compressed gas to houses which were not connected to a gas main might be used on the Continent. But Mr. Daniel, the secretary of the Imperial Gas Light Company, with whom he discussed the matter argued that compressed gas did not give a very good light and that under pressure some of the gas was turned back into oil.[98] In 1825 Fischer inspected several gas generating plants in the provinces including the public gasworks at Leeds[99] and Sheffield and the private generating plants in Ormrod's engineering workshops, Philips and Lee's cotton mill and Lee's private house. It is clear from Fischer's address to the Swiss Natural History Society in 1825 that he had decided that the future lay with oil gas rather than with coal gas. He stated that oil gas was cheap, clean, and virtually odourless. It could be taken in containers to customers in areas which were without gas mains.[100]

2. PUBLIC INSTITUTIONS

(i) *Michael Faraday and the Royal Institution*

Although London had no university in the early years of the nineteenth century it was an important centre of higher education. There were facilities for training lawyers at the Inns of Court and doctors at the teaching hospitals. There were some excellent libraries such as those in the British Museum and the London Institution. The Royal Society, the Society of Arts and several scientific associations provided opportunities for the dissemination of scientific knowledge.[101] And the Royal Institution—founded by Count Rumford in 1800 to foster the application of scientific discoveries to industrial purposes—had a library, a laboratory, a reading room, a collection of minerals and geological specimens, and a lecture theatre. Courses of lectures were given there by eminent scientists. When Humphry Davy, the first Professor of Chemistry at the Royal Institution, retired in 1813 he was succeeded by William Thomas Brande while Michael Faraday became an assistant in the laboratory. For many years Brande and Faraday took the lead in chemical research and in the teaching of chemistry in London.

On his visit to London in June 1825 Fischer went to Albermarle Street to meet Faraday, whom he described as 'a highly skilled chemist and metallurgist.'[102] It was in this year that Faraday's scientific achievements were recognised by his election to a fellowship of the Royal Society. His greatest discoveries lay in the field of electricity and magnetism but Faraday was also responsible for pioneer researches in the production of alloys[103] and the liquification of gases.[104] 'From early manhood until his closing years, he made one discovery after another, some being of such importance that vast industrial enterprises have since arisen from them. Almost the entire electrical industry of today is founded on his discovery of the phenomenon of electro-magnetic induction.' Faraday held various public offices—a lectureship at the Woolwich military academy and a post at Trinity House—and he became 'a universal consultant' whose advice was sought by the government on such various problems as the sanitation of the River Thames, the acoustics of the new Houses of Parliament, and the treatment of the surfaces of the sculptures in the British Museum.[105]

When the two men met for the first time in 1825 Faraday conducted his guest round the laboratory of the Royal Institution while Fischer showed Faraday some samples of his alloys. It was through Faraday that Fischer was able to attend one of Brande's lectures at the Royal Institution, to secure admission to Woolwich arsenal, and to meet Mr. Hennel of the Apothecaries Hall and Jacob Perkins, the American inventor.[106] In November 1826 Fischer noted in his journal that he had discussed with Faraday the structure and properties of metals. Faraday had observed: 'I see well you are a practical man and the simple observations of such ones will do often more good to society than all our speculations.'[107] Fischer's note book (*Schreibkalender*) for 1827 contains a reference to a meeting between Fischer and Faraday on September 28 of that year.[108]

Nineteen years elapsed before Fischer saw Faraday again. On reaching England in July 1845 he learned that his 'worthy friend' was out of the country but Faraday was back at the Royal Institution before Fischer returned to Switzerland. They met on August 4. Fischer wrote in his journal that their conversation was mainly concerned with the electric telegraph. Fischer had frequently observed telegraph wires running parallel to railway tracks and he speculated upon possible further uses of this valuable new invention. Fischer showed Faraday a three ounce piece of platinum as well as a horse shoe, a gun cock, and a lock plate which he had cast in crucible steel. He made Faraday a present of one of his crucibles.[109]

In June 1851 Fischer was again cordially received by Faraday at the Royal Institution. The old friends enjoyed an hour's conversation 'on matters concerned with metallurgy and pyrotechnics' and on the exhibits that Fischer was showing at the Crystal Palace. This appears to have been their last meeting.[110] A few years later, when writing his biographical notes Fischer mentioned Faraday as a man whose name was honoured throughout the world of physics and chemistry.[111]

(ii) *W. T. Brande and the Royal Mint*

It has been seen that W. T. Brande[112] followed Humphry Davy as Professor of Chemistry at the Royal Institution. While his younger colleague Faraday was responsible for many scientific discoveries Brande's reputation rested upon his abilities as an administrator, a teacher, and a writer. He lectured at the Royal Institution; he served as secretary of the Royal Society; he was in charge of the Die Office of the Royal Mint; he was an editor of the *Quarterly Journal of Science;* and he wrote a standard text book on chemistry.[113]

At Faraday's invitation Fischer attended one of Brande's

lectures at the Royal Institution of June 10, 1825. He was impressed with Brande's wide knowledge, his lucidity as a lecturer, and his skill as a demonstrator. A month later Fischer met the engineer George Rennie[114] who suggested that he should submit some samples of his steel nickel alloy to the Royal Mint. Fischer took his advice and on the same day (July 11) he went to 'the new mint near the Tower'[115] where he met the officials Atkinson,[116] Parry, and Brande.[117]

They admired Fischer's damascened dagger blades and razor blades and Mr. Parry was given a piece of Fischer's steel nickel alloy to turn into dies. Fischer was shown round the mint. He examined six pairs of self-oiling presses, a drawing machine, and an engraving machine. Each press was tended by a small boy who inserted the blank pieces. The rest of the process—the stamping of the coins—was automatic and each machine produced 30,000 coins each day. The machines were all driven by steam engines. At the time of Fischer's visit coins were being minted for the East India Company.[118] On the following day Fischer met Brande at the Apothecaries Hall and they went together to the Royal Mint. Brande told Fischer that he had difficulty in securing reliable dies. That very morning eleven of them had been broken. He was satisfied if a die lasted for a couple of days. Fischer replied that he hoped that his steel nickel alloy would prove to be very satisfactory for dies. He does not appear to have sold any of his steel to the Royal Mint on this occasion.[119]

Twenty years elapsed before Fischer saw Brande again. When he was in London in July 1845 he called at the Royal Mint and showed Brande some samples of his steel dies for stamping coins.[120] This time he secured three orders for his steel within twelve months.[121] On January 1, 1846 Brande wrote to Fischer that he was 'well pleased' with these dies and that he would use them in future 'in preference to any which I have lately been able to procure.'[122] In October of that year Fischer came to London and was warmly welcomed by Brande. He secured further orders for dies and had a discussion with Brande about the physical structure of metals. Before leaving the mint he received a draft in payment of his steel which he promptly cashed at the Bank of England. He wrote in his journal: 'I have earned and spent a lot of money in my time, but no payment that I have ever received has pleased me as much as this one. It is cash which I have earned with the sweat of my brow, and I have got it from the English who normally take money from others!'[123] Fischer's last visit to the Royal Mint was in the summer of 1851. Once more he enjoyed a scientific discussion with Brande and once more he was shown round the mint. He wrote: 'What huge long bars of gold are stored here and minted into coins! It is incredible—or rather it is credible only if one grasps the fact that this little island rules the world more effectively than it was ever ruled by Napoleon or any earlier conqueror.'[124]

(iii) *The Apothecaries Hall*[125]

It has been seen that Fischer visited the Apothecaries Hall to examine different types of gas generators. A letter from Faraday introduced him to Mr. Hennel who showed the Swiss visitor round this important institution. The Apothecaries Company, which had received a royal charter in 1617, regulated the work of pharmaceutical chemists and endeavoured to promote the production of pure drugs. Its headquarters in Water Lane, Blackfriars, included a laboratory, a still house, a mortar room, a testing room, a drug-grinding mill, and a retail chemist's shop. In his diary for 1825 Fischer described the Apothecaries Hall as 'London's college of pharmacy' and he observed that it was a private institution which received no financial assistance from the government.

Fischer first examined Taylor and Martineau's gas generating plant and then he saw various pieces of apparatus for making chemicals and drugs on a large scale. He commented upon the great advantage which the public derived from an institution which aimed at maintaining high standards of purity in the chemicals used in the preparation of medicines. But Fischer added that nothing was being done to protect the public from the advertising campaigns of firms which offered cosmetics for sale. In his opinion the London advertisers of such products as 'aromatic creams' made even more excessive claims for their wares than their colleagues in Paris.

(iv) *Woolwich Arsenal*

Fischer had a considerable knowledge of firearms both as a metallurgist and as an officer in the Swiss artillery. On discovering how to make crucible cast steel and various alloys he appreciated the importance of gunsmiths as potential customers. His visits in 1814 to two gunsmiths—Morris in London and Pauli in Paris—show how interested he was in this branch of manufacture. Fischer's steel could be used to make gun barrels as well as parts of the firing mechanism of rifles. Moreover his eldest son Conrad was a trained gunsmith and Fischer's plan to establish a steelworks in England—in association with Smith and Martineau—may well have included the manufacture of steel components of firearms.

Fischer visited the gunsmith Joseph Egg several times when he was in London in the summer of 1825. On his second visit to London in the autumn of that year he went to the royal arsenal at Woolwich[126] where his father had once worked in the foundry. The name 'Royal Foundry' had been given in 1802[127] to a group of establishments which had developed from a small gun wharf attached to the Woolwich dockyard in Henry VIII's reign. The process of mechanising the work of the arsenal had made considerable progress since the days when Andreas Schalch of Schaffhausen had constructed the first boring machine. By the 1820s the arsenal had been supplied with steam engines, reverberatory furnaces and a circular saw.

Fischer inspected the arsenal's foundry where two bronze cannon were being cast.[128] He thought that the boring plant lacked some of the refinements that could be seen elsewhere but he declared that he had 'never seen better boring or turning.' He visited the workshops in which signal rockets were being made. Next he saw the building called the Repository which was a collection of all kinds of weapons and models. The guide, a veteran of the battle of Waterloo, showed Fischer various Congreve rockets,[129] Shrapnell grenades,[130] and a mechanical gunpowder mixer for blending different types of powder. More Congreve rockets were exhibited in the Rotunda. He saw a field workshop for saddlers and gunsmiths—'better suited for use in far off steppes or deserts than in our well populated regions.'[131] After this visit Fischer crossed Blackheath to Morden college in the dark—a hazardous undertaking in view of the depredations of footpads—and caught a coach to Canterbury.

Fischer inspected Woolwich arsenal again on September 26, 1827.[132] He was accompanied by his son Conrad who 'as a gunsmith and an artillery officer would benefit from the visit.' They saw an attempt to test the strength of a small blockhouse which was protected by a mesh of iron rods. Three 24 pounders fired at the iron curtain from a distance of 630 yards. Fischer was impressed both by the accuracy of the shooting and the protection afforded by the interlaced iron rods. Fischer and his son visited the model rooms, the foundry, and the boring workshop. They were particularly interested in two small cannon from Burma which fired balls weighing only three quarters of a pound. Fischer commented upon the technical knowledge and the skill of the craftsmen who had made these cannon.

THAMES TUNNEL
(This artist's impression appeared before the tunnel was completed.
It is inaccurate inasmuch as the slope of the tunnel did not permit a
through view as shown in the sketch)

LONDON BRIDGE CONSTRUCTED 1827-31

APOTHECARIES HALL

ROYAL ARSENAL AT WOOLWICH (THE MAIN GATE)
By courtesy of the British Museum

(v) *The Patent Office*[133]

It has been seen that Fischer desired to secure legal protection for his inventions in England. He regarded the English system of granting patents with mixed feelings. On the one hand he declared that nowhere else was an inventor's skill so handsomely rewarded as in England.[134] In 1814 James Watt junior told him that Richard Arkwright had made a fortune out of his water frame[135] and many years later Fischer heard of an English inventor who had just sold a patent for an annuity of £1,900.[136] On the other hand Fischer was critical of the complexities of the English patent law. After reading a summary of the patent regulations in 1825 he declared that both the Austrian and the French patent laws were superior to the English.[137] And in 1826 he wrote: 'It costs anything between £100 and £120 to take out a patent and even then many law suits may have to be fought to protect it. Surely it is better to keep a new process secret.'[138] In 1825 Fischer decided against patenting his cast steel process himself. Instead he gave Smith and Martineau permission to do so by an agreement dated October 21, 1825.[139]

Twenty years later, however, Fischer decided to try and take out two patents himself—one for his steel copper alloy and the other for his process of making steel castings. The first he described as 'an alloy, proper to be mixed or passed with pig iron, steel of every description, and also bar or forged of scrap iron' and the second as 'a new way of making horse shoes and also shoes for all other kinds of cattle.' In July 1845 he saw Mr. Poole, the secretary of the Patent Office, who gave him a pamphlet describing the patent regulations. Fischer paid a guinea each for two *caveats* concerning his inventions[140] but he later appears to have abandoned the idea of pursuing the matter any further. In 1851 Fischer once more called upon Mr. Poole.[141] This time he secured a *caveat* for his new steel copper alloy or 'Fischer metal' but in the end no patent seems to have been taken out.

(vi) *The British Museum*

In 1814 Fischer called on his compatriot Joseph Planta, the Principal Librarian at the British Museum.[142] Fischer found that the museum had been much improved since his last visit in 1794. Various useless objects had been removed and the exhibits were now arranged in a more systematic manner than before. He saw sculptures displayed in elegant galleries and wall paintings from Herculaneum with inscriptions in Greek, in Coptic, and in Egyptian hieroglyphics.[143] He also admired a fine cabinet con-

41

taining minerals arranged according to the classifications of Hauy and Werner.[144]

When he was next in London in 1825 Fischer visited two exhibitions—one illustrating ancient and modern Mexico (in Piccadilly Circus)[145] and one of Egyptian antiquities (in Leicester Square).[146] In the Egyptian exhibition Fischer saw a facsimile model of the tomb of Setis I, excavated by G. B. Belzoni,[147] and various relics of ancient Egypt, including a roll of papyrus. In 1826 accompanied by his sons Conrad and Berthold, he again visited the Mexican exhibition which also included objects from ancient Egypt and spoils from the recent Burma campaign.[148] Fischer was particularly interested in the state coach of the ruler of Burma which was on show.

3. THE GREAT EXHIBITION[149]

Fischer had not intended to send anything to the Great Exhibition held in London in 1851 but the municipal authorities of Schaffhausen asked him to display some of his cast steel products at the Crystal Palace so that the canton might be represented in the Swiss section. He agreed to do so and his display cabinet included two crucibles for making cast steel; samples of cast steel and a new steel-copper alloy;[150] two pairs of razors; and a gear wheel cast in a sand mould from scrap iron converted into steel by direct fusion. Fischer also showed a view of the interior of his foundry reproduced from an engraving by J. J. Beck. The jury awarded Fischer an honourable mention for his steel bars. Two of Fischer's sons showed samples of their steel products in the Austrian section. Georg Fischer of Hainfeld displayed cast steel files while Berthold Fischer of Traisen showed spindles as well as various cast iron products.[151] Fischer himself not only sent samples of his cast steel products to London but—although 78 years of age—he undertook the journey to England to see the exhibition for himself. He combined business with pleasure for he was interested in selling his new steel ball bearings to English manufacturers.

On his first evening in London Fischer went to Hyde Park to see the Crystal Palace from the outside. He was not impressed with the proportions of Paxton's glass building since the Crystal Palace was too low in relation to its length and there were so many trees in the vicinity that one could not secure a good view of the building as a whole. When Fischer saw the interior of the Crystal Palace on the following day he was astonished at the daring idea of showing the products of all the nations under one roof and at the speed and skill with which the idea had been translated into reality. 'No other country in the world' he declared 'could have brought together so wonderful a collection of the artistic and industrial products of the human race, from the most civilised to the most primitive peoples.'[152] The first objects to attract his attention were the fountain in the centre of the transept[153] and a waxwork display of Red Indians.

Fischer was naturally particularly interested in the metals, the alloys and the various products of the engineering industry. In the British section he inspected materials—such as plumbago[154] and cement—which might be used to make crucibles; briquettes made of compressed coal dust and tar; and various steels smelted direct from iron ore. He described the ironware and metal alloy products displayed by Stirling and Morris but was critical of the firm's 'patent toughened iron'[155] and copper-iron alloy. Nor was there anything original in the firm's 'Union metal'—six parts of cast iron and one of tin—which had been described long ago by Sven Rinmann.[156] Among the achievements of the British steel-makers and engineers he mentioned Sheffield steel and Lancashire textile machinery. He admired the series of machines employed in the cleaning, preparation, spinning, and weaving of cotton.[157] He also saw a block of pure English silver weighing $7\frac{1}{2}$ cwt., produced from argentiferous lead ore by Pattinson's process.[158] Fischer admired the powerful hydraulic press which had raised into position the tubes of the Britannia railway bridge over the Menai Strait.[159]

When Fischer visited the sections devoted to the British Empire he examined various types of Indian steel and described the famous damascened wootz made in Bombay. He remarked that this steel was very hard and was difficult to hammer. It did not have a good cutting edge. On the other hand he considered the tough Golconda steel from Hyderabad to be of excellent quality.[160] The Koh-i-nor diamond was a disappointment to Fischer who declared that he would not pay a penny to see it again. Among the Australian exhibits he saw a sample of copper ore from the recently opened Burra Burra mine[161]—70 per cent pure metal—and among the Canadian exhibits he admired a novel fire engine made by Messrs Perry of Montreal.[162] This appliance could throw a jet of water to a height of 180 feet and it was of interest to Fischer since at one time he had made many fire fighting appliances himself.

In the foreign sections Fischer often visited the Swiss and the Austrian exhibitions to which he and his sons had made their modest contributions. In the Swiss section 121 firms had taken part, their most important exhibits being textiles,[163] clocks,

43

watches and wood carvings.[164] Fischer also mentioned the pottery shown by Ziegler-Pellis of Schaffhausen. The Austrian display included a variety of metal products—such as files, scythes, sickles and spindles—as well as high quality glassware from Bohemia. In the Zollverein section Fischer admired the cast iron products of the Berlin Royal Foundry as well as some bronze lions from Bavaria. To illustrate recent advances in German engineering Fischer mentioned that Uhlhorn's coining press—which he had seen at work in Munich—had 'gained a victory' over Maudslay's press and had been admired both by Queen Victoria and the Duchess of Nemours.[165] In the French section Fischer praised the exhibits from the Sèvres porcelain works. In the Egyptian section he noticed a sword from Damascus but he had no opportunity of inspecting it closely.

In the course of an address to the Swiss Natural History Society at Glarus, delivered soon after his return from the Great Exhibition, Fischer summed up his impressions of industrial England. He said: 'I have just come back from England. In that country great things—I might say almost unbelievable things—have been achieved. English experience proves clearly what can be done by the co-operation of individuals who are imbued with the same spirit and who are working towards the same ends. More has been achieved by these means than were achieved in former times by the imperative orders of an autocratic ruler. This is obviously the more agreeable aspect of England's achievements. There is, however, another side of the picture. The situation of the actual producer of goods—the true worker, not the man behind the office desk—is not an enviable one even although he may appear to be getting high wages. Not one of many thousands of English factory workers owns even a scrap of land. They cannot enjoy all the varied beauties of nature (that we have). Even if they existed in England they would be hidden by the great clouds of smoke which pour out of thousands upon thousands of chimneys.'[166]

---

[1] For the London engineers in the early nineteenth century see Samuel Smiles, *Lives of the Engineers* (three volumes, 1861–3) and *Industrial Biography* (1863); R. Beamish, *Memoir of the Life of Sir Marc Isambard Brunel* (1862); J. Nasmyth, *An Autobiography* (edited by Samuel Smiles, 1883); C. B. Noble, *The Brunels, Father and Son* (1937); L. T. C. Rolt, *Isambard Kingdom Brunel* (1957); D. Lampe, *The Tunnel* (1963); H. W. Dickenson, 'Joseph Bramah and his Inventions' (*Transactions of the Newcomen Society*, Vol. XXII, 1941–2, pp. 169–186); H. Straub, *A History of Civil Engineer-*

ing (1952); and Charles Singer (and others), *A History of Techno-logy*, Vol. IV (1958).

2 In 1809 it was reported that 'of the great movements now going on, the most important are those of its port, consisting of a vast plan of docks and warehouses for the West India trade in the Isle of Dogs, another for general purposes, and an East India dock at Blackwell' (*England Delineated*, 1809, p. 218).

3 It was, however, difficult in the early nineteenth century for a skilled mechanic from the provinces to establish himself in London. William Fairbairn stated that when he first went to London 'a young man from the country had no chance whatever of success, in consequence of trade guilds and unions . . . Laws of a most arbitrary character were enforced, and the unions were governed by cliques of self-appointed officers, who never failed to take care of their own interests' (*Minutes of Proceedings of the Institution of Civil Engineers*, Vol. XXXIX, session 1874–5, Part I, p. 253).

4 John Rennie (1761–1821) and his sons John (1794–1874) and George (1791–1866).

5 Sir Marc Isambard Brunel (1769–1849) and his son Isambard King-dom Brunel (1806–59).

6 In the early nineteenth century 7,000 persons in Clerkenwell were engaged in various branches of watchmaking. See *The Picture of London for 1810*, p. 55.

7 A geography textbook 'for the use of young persons' stated: 'a variety of works in gold, silver, and jewellery; the engraving of prints; the making of optical and mathematical instruments are likewise principally or solely executed here, and some of them in greater perfection than in any other country' (*England Delineated*, 1809, p. 217).

8 For Samuel Rhee (or Rhé) see Fischer's *Tagebuch*, pp. 19, 467, 647, and 718; Maurice Daumas, *Les instruments scientifiques aux xviie et xviiie siècles* (1953), pp. 670–80 and C. Singer (and others), *A History of Technology*, Vol. IV (1958), p. 388.

9 Jesse Ramsden (1735–1800) improved various scientific instruments such as the sextant, the theodolite, and the barometer. According to the *General London Guide* for 1794 (p. 81) his workshop was at 199 Piccadilly.

10 Fischer lodged at the Cross Keys Inn, Wood Street; see his *Tage-buch*, 1851, p. 665.

11 Fischer's *Tagebuch*, 1846, pp. 577–8. The *Post Office Annual Directory* for 1814 and the *Triennial Directory of London, West-minster, Southwark . . . for the Years 1817, 1818, 1819* list Samuel Fenn as a watchmaker, clockmaker, and manufacturer of mechanical tools of 105 Newgate Street.

12 Fischer's *Tagebuch*, 1851, p. 680.

13 Fischer's *Tagebuch*, 1845, p. 467.

14 Fischer's *Tagebuch*, 1814, pp. 76–87.

15 Fischer's *Tagebuch*, 1814, p. 61.

[16] The London *Post Office Annual Directory* for 1814 listed Edward Stammers of 99 The Strand as a 'wholesale and retail cutler'.

[17] Kym was a Swiss cutler whose works were in Berlingen.

[18] The *Post Office Annual Directory* for 1814 listed Holtzapffel and Deyerlein as 'tool and engine manufacturers' of 10 Cockspur Street. Holtzapffel's son Charles (1806–47) followed in his father's profession and wrote a standard work on metal turning (1843).

[19] Fischer's *Tagebuch* 1814, p. 85.

[20] The firm of Peter and George Dollond, opticians of 59 St. Paul's Churchyard was listed in the *General London Guide* for 1794 (p. 80) and in the *Post Office Annual Directory* for 1814. The firm had been founded by John Dollond (1706–61), the inventor of the achromatic telescope. His son Peter (1730–1820) and his nephew George Higgins (or Dollond) (1774–1852) carried on the business.

[21] The *Post Office Annual Directory* for 1825 listed James Tringham of 3 Cary Street as an 'assayer of ores, metals etc'.

[22] They were Brookman and Langdon (not 'Brokman' as in Fischer's *Tagebuch,* p. 80) of Great Russell Street and J. Middleton & Co. Fischer gave Middleton's address as Shoe Lane, Fleet Street, while the address given in the *Post Office Annual Directory* for 1814 was Vine Street, Piccadilly. Fischer was mistaken in supposing that the graphite came from Cornwall. It came from Cumberland.

[23] Joseph Egg was described as a gunmaker and truss maker in the *Triennial Directory of London, Westminster, Southwark . . . for the Years 1817, 1818, 1819.* His address was given as the 'corner of Piccadilly, Haymarket'.

[24] Fischer visited London twice in 1825. For the first visit see his *Tagebuch,* pp. 213–36 and 343–66. For his second visit in the autumn of 1825 and for his visits in 1826 and 1827 see his *Tagebuch,* pp. 373–462. For the visit of 1827 see Fischer's note book for that year in the Fischer archives.

[25] Le Page was mentioned in Fischer's diary for 1814: see *Tagebuch,* pp. 69–70.

[26] Collier was the inventor of a five shooter.

[27] Fischer was present when the son of the Duke of Norfolk and a friend purchased a pair of guns from Egg for 50 guineas each; see *Tagebuch,* p. 351.

[28] For Fischer's visits to Egg see his *Tagebuch,* pp. 214, 228–30, 346 and 351.

[29] For Fischer and Martineau see Fischer's *Tagebuch,* pp. 233, 254, 356–62, 378, 402, 411, 455 and 780. Fischer gave the name of the firm as Taylor and Martineau junior. There are two entries concerning the firm in the *Post Office Annual Directory* for 1825: (i) Taylor and Martineau, engineers, near the Canal Bridge, City Road, (ii) Philip Taylor and John Martineau, engineers and chemists, 72 White Cross Street, City Road.

[30] Fischer's *Tagebuch,* pp. 347–8.

31 Fischer's *Tagebuch*, pp. 358-9. Here Fischer wrote about his friend 'Mr. Smith, one of the directors of the establishments for portable oil gas' (i.e. the London Portable Gas Company), The firm of Henry and H. W. Smith of 5 Laurence Poutney Hill was listed in the *Post Office Annual Directory* for 1818 and the *Triennial Directory of London, Westminster, Southwark . . . for the Years 1817, 1818, 1819.* Henry William Smith was a director of the London Dock Company.

32 Fischer's *Tagebuch*, p. 356 and p. 360.

33 Philip Taylor was also a partner in a large ironworks and steelworks in Warwickshire.

34 *First Report of the Select Committee on Artisans and Machinery (Parliamentary Papers*, 1824, Vol. V, p. 5).

35 Charles Singer (and others), *A History of Technology*, Vol. IV (1958) p. 197.

36 For the London Portable Gas Company see Fischer's *Tagebuch*, pp. 233, 354, 359, 362, and 411. The address of the firm's works was 1 Little Sutton Street, Clerkenwell and that of the offices was 7 Basinghall Street: see *Robson's London Commercial Directory . . . for 1826-7.*

37 See articles by F. Achard and L. Seguin in the *Transactions of the Newcomen Society*, Vol. III.

38 See Fischer's address to the Swiss Natural History Society in 1825: *Verhandlungen der allgemeinen schweizerischen Gesellschaft für die gesammten Naturwissenschaften . . . 1825* (Solothurn, 1825).

39 Fischer's *Tagebuch*, p. 361 and p. 411.

40 *Ibid.*, p. 361.

41 *Patents for Inventions. Abridgments of Specifications relating to the manufacture of Iron and Steel*, Part 1 1620-1866 (1883), No. 5259, p. 48. The applicants were John Martineau junior and Henry William Smith.

42 The agreements of October 21st and 22nd, 1825 are in the Fischer archives. Both were signed by Henry William Smith, John Martineau junior and Johann Conrad Fischer. The first concerned Fischer's process 'of making British or any other description of iron into steel by a new and simplified process' while the second was concerned with Fischer's steel silver alloy (silveret).

43 Fischer's *Tagebuch*, p. 373 (introduction to the fragments of the journals for 1825-7).

44 Fischer's *Tagebuch*, p. 378 (October 30, 1825).

45 Fischer's *Tagebuch*, p. 396 (November 30, 1826).

46 Fischer's *Tagebuch*, p. 402 (December 5, 1826).

47 Fischer's note book (*Schreibkalender*), January 12, 1827 (in the Fischer archives): see also Schib and Gnade, *Johann Conrad Fischer* (1954), p. 121.

48 Fischer's note book for 1827. There are references in this note book to several letters written by Fischer to H. W. Smith.

49 Fischer's *Tagebuch*, Oct 12, 1827, p. 455.

[50] Fischer's *Tagebuch*, September 26, 1827, p. 421.

[51] A comparison between the agreements of October 1825 and that of October 1827 shows that in the new contract Richard Carter Smith replaced Henry William Smith and Conrad Fischer now became a full partner. The elder Fischer secured £300 under the new agreement while Conrad was under an obligation to live in England and to devote all his time to the manufacture of steel by his father's process.

[52] Fischer's note book for 1827 (in the Fischer archives). It may be added that in September 1827 J. C. Fischer gave Martineau an opportunity of manufacturing under licence his new porous bricks in return for one third of the profits. Nothing appears to have come of this offer. Fischer had patented his brick making process in Austria in August 1827.

[53] Schib and Gnade, *op cit.*, p. 121. For Fischer's attempts to establish Conrad in England see also H. Boesch, *Die Unternehmungen von J. C. Fischer* (1952), pp. 56–9.

[54] For Fischer's contacts with Marc Isambard Brunel see his *Tagebuch*, pp. 362–5, 417–20, and 784. For Marc Isambard Brunel (1769–1849) see R. Beamish, *Memoir of the Life of Marc Isambard Brunel* (second edition, 1862); Samuel Smiles, *Industrial Biography* (1863), pp. 215–222; Celia Brunel Noble, *The Brunels, Father and Son* (1938); D. Lampe, *The Tunnel* (1963); and an article in the *Dictionary of National Biography*, Vol. VII (1886), pp. 144–7.

[55] A. Rees, *The Cyclopaedia. A Universal Dictionary of Arts, Sciences and Literature* (1819); article on 'Machinery for manufacturing Ships' Blocks' and Andrew Ure, *A Dictionary of Arts, Manufactures and Mines* (second edition, 1840), pp. 145–9. Rees's encyclopaedia was published between 1802 and 1819 but each volume is dated 1819. Samuel Smiles wrote that these machines 'constitute one of the most ingenious and complete collections of tools ever invented for making articles in wood, being capable of performing the most practical operations of carpentry with the utmost accuracy and finish' (*Industrial Biography*, 1863, p. 222).

[56] C. Singer (and others), *A History of Technology*, Vol. IV (1958), p. 427.

[57] For a contemporary account of the beginning of the construction of the Thames tunnel see H. Law, *A Memoir of the several Operations and the Construction of the Thames Tunnel* (1857).

[58] Roman cement—patented by James Parker in 1796—was made from septaria (or 'noddles') which were found on the coasts of Kent and Essex wherever the London clay bordered on the sea shore. See A. P. Thurston, 'Parker's "Roman" Cement' in the *Transactions of the Newcomen Society*, Vol. XIX, 1938–9 pp. 193–206.

[59] Fischer stated in his diary (*Tagebuch*, p. 417) that he inspected the Thames tunnel again in 1826 but he gave no details of this visit.

60 Fischer's *Tagebuch*, 1825–7, p. 418.

61 Portland cement had been patented by Joseph Aspdin in 1824.

62 Fischer's *Tagebuch*, 1825–7, p. 419.

63 The *Sunday Times* of February 24th, 1828 reported that 'upwards of £1,000 has been subscribed as voluntary contributions for completing the Thames tunnel. Earl Spencer sent £100'.

64 Brunel's son, Isambard Kingdom Brunel (1806–59), assisted his father in the construction of the Rotherhithe-Wapping tunnel and became the resident engineer of the project.

65 For Jacob Perkins (1766–1849) see the *Minutes of Proceedings of the Institution of Civil Engineers*, Vol. XXV (1865–6) pp. 516–9; G. and Dorothy Bathe, *Jacob Perkins* (Historical Society of Pennsylvania, 1943); G. and Dorothy Bathe, 'The Contribution of Jacob Perkins to Science and Engineering' (*Transactions of the Newcomen Society*, Vol. XXIV (1943–4 and 1944–5). For Fischer's meetings with Perkins see Fischer's *Tagebuch*, pp. 225–8, 346–8, 362, 402–10, 433–8, 450, and 517–8.

66 J. C. Dyer introduced Perkins' nail-making machine into England where it was used successfully in the Britannia Patent Nail Factory (Birmingham).

67 The firm set up by Perkins changed its title as the partners changed, e.g. Perkins, Fairman & Heath; Perkins & Heath; Perkins Bacon & Co.; Perkins, Bacon & Petch. In 1840 the firm printed the penny black and the twopenny blue stamps. A description of Perkins' engraving process is given in W. Graham, *The One Pound Note in the History of Banking in Great Britain* (1911), p. 321.

68 Fischer's *Tagebuch*, p. 406.

69 Water Lane ran from Fleet Street to Friar's Dock.

70 Perkins' address in the *Post Office Annual Directory* for 1825 was 'near the Diorama, Regents Park'. These premises were taken over in about 1827 by Goldsworthy Gurney, a well known pioneer constructor of steam carriages which ran on the public highway.

71 Fischer's *Tagebuch*, p. 434.

72 Jacob Perkins, *An Account of the Concentrating Steam Engine* (London, 1824).

73 *Fifth Report of the Select Committee on the Roads from London to Holyhead (Steam Boats, etc.)* (*Parliamentary Papers*, 1822, Vol. VI): see answers of Jacob Perkins respecting steam engines, pp. 237–8. Perkins recommended the use of 'high pressure engines built on Oliver Evans' plans'. A somewhat similar recommendation was made to the Committee by Alexander Galloway (p. 189). See also G. Bathe and Dorothy Bathe, *op cit.*, p. 94.

74 Joshua Field to Michael Longridge, May 6th, 1823, quoted by G. Bathe and Dorothy Bathe, *op. cit.*, p. 99.

75 Fischer's *Tagebuch*, p. 433.

76 G. Bathe and Dorothy Bathe, op cit., p. 138. Angier March Perkins

stated in his memoirs that his father's 'steam engine business did not succeed and (we) were obliged to give it up' (*ibid.*, p. 120).

77 See G. Bathe and Dorothy Bathe, op cit., pp. 99, 105, 120 & 121. For the subsequent history of the uniflow steam engine see J. Stumpf, *Una-flow steam engine* (1912), T. B. Perry, 'The uniflow steam engine' (*Proceedings of the Institution of Mechanical Engineers*, 1920, p. 731) and H. W. Dickinson, *A Short History of the Steam Engine* (new edition with introduction by A. E. Musson, 1963) pp. 153–6.

78 See T. C. Crawhill, 'The Genesis of Mechanical Refrigeration' in *Engineering*, August 10th, 1934 and E. C. Smith, 'Some Pioneers of Refrigeration' in the *Transactions of the Newcomen Society*, Vol. XXIII, 1942–3, pp. 99–107.

79 Fischer's *Tagebuch*, pp. 228.

80 *Ibid.*, p. 346.

81 There are also references to Perkins in Fischer's note book (*Schreib-kalender*) for 1827 (in the Fischer archives). Fischer visited Perkins on September 28th and September 29th of that year. Fischer stated that the alloy used by Perkins for his pistons was composed of 20 parts of copper to 4½ parts of tin.

82 For Thomson and Johnson see Fischer's *Tagebuch*, pp. 455–8. In Fischer's note book for 1827 there are references to earlier visits to the London Steelworks on September 21 and September 24. The address of the London Steelworks was given as Thames Bank, Chelsea in *Robson's London Commercial Directory . . . for 1826–7*.

83 Fischer's *Tagebuch*, p. 456.

84 Fischer's *Tagebuch*, pp. 493–4 and 504–6. Fischer was accompanied by his nephew August Winz when he went to the Polytechnical Institution on July 25th, 1845 to see a model of the atmospheric railway made by Samuda and Clegg. Fischer was greatly impressed by the collection of models exhibited at the Polytechnical Institution.

85 For the Croydon atmospheric railway see Fischer's *Tagebuch*, p. 562 and p. 571 and an article in the *Railway Magazine*, Vol. LXXII, January—June 1933, pp. 407–14. The line ran from the Dartmouth Arms at Forest Hill to West Croydon from October 27th, 1845 to May 4th 1847. There was an extension from Forest Hill to New Cross, 3 miles from London Bridge Station.

86 Fischer's *Tagebuch*, p. 684.

87 Fischer's *Tagebuch*, p. 792 and p. 795 (Fischer's biographical notes).

88 This yard for building iron ships had originally been set up in 1838 by William Fairbairn and Andrew Murray.

89 Fischer's *Tagebuch*, p. 673 and p. 730. The firm of Robinson and Russell was, at this time, involved in a dispute with the Swiss company concerning the steamship. The Swiss claimed that the vessel had been constructed in a faulty manner. Im Thurn, one of Fischer's friends, acted as arbitrator in the dispute and he awarded the Swiss firm £96 19s.

90 For the English gas industry in the early nineteenth century see S. Timmins, *William Murdock* (1864); A. Murdock, *Light without Wick* (1892); B. Taylor, William Murdock (1952); F. C. Accum, *Description of the Process of Manufacturing Coal Gas . . .* (1815); *Report from the Select Committee on Gas Establishments* (Parliamentary Papers, 1823, Vol. V); William Matthews, *An Historical Sketch of the Origin and Progress of Gas Lighting . . .* (1827 and 1832); William Matthews, *A Compendium of Gas Lighting . . .* (1832); an article on 'Gas Light' in Andrew Ure, *Dictionary of Arts . . .* (edition of 1840); Dean Chandler and A. Douglas Lacey, *Lighting by Gas. An Outline of its History* (Gas Council, 1949); and Stewart, *Town Gas . . .* (Science Museum, 1949).

91 Fischer's *Tagebuch*, p. 85. At this time London already had over 26 miles of gas mains.

92 Fischer's *Tagebuch*, p. 210.

93 They were the London Gas Light and Coke Company; the City of London Gas Light Company; the South London Gas Light and Coke Company; and the Imperial Gas Light and Coke Company. These firms operated eight gas plants in 1823. For the Gas Light and Coke Company see W. Thornley, *An Account of the Progress of the (Gas, Light and Coke) Company from its Incorporation . . . to the Present Time* (1912) and S. Everard, *History of the Gas Light and Coke Company* (1949).

94 Michael Faraday and Sir William Congreve, for example were among the supporters of gas made from oil.

95 Fischer's *Tagebuch*, p. 215.

96 Fischer's *Tagebuch*, pp. 231–5. Portable oil gas was used at the Royal Institution (1828–34) and at Covent Garden Theatre. These installations were found to be unsatisfactory and eventually the use of gas made from oil was largely confined to lighting railway carriages, steamships, and buoys at sea.

97 Fischer's *Tagebuch*, pp. 358–60.

98 Fischer's *Tagebuch*, p. 354. Andrew Ure stated that 'when the oil gas is compressed by a force of from 15 to 20 atmospheres as was the practice of the Portable Gas Company, about one fifth of the volume of the gas became liquified into an oily, very volatile fluid . . . .' (*Dictionary of Arts*, second edition, 1840, p. 547).

99 The Leeds plant was one which made oil gas: see Fischer's *Tagebuch*, p. 259.

100 *Verhandlungen der allgemeinen schweizerischen Gesellschaft für die gesammten Naturwissenschaften . . . 1825* (Solothurn, 1825), p. 56.

101 See D. McKie, 'Scientific Societies at the end of the Eighteenth Century' (*The Philosophical Magazine*, 150th Anniversary Number, 1948, pp. 133–143); D. Hudson and K. W. Luckhurst, *The Royal Society of Arts 1754–1954* (1954); and Sir Henry Lyons, *The Royal Society* (1944).

102 Michael Faraday (1791–1867) was later appointed Fullerian Professor of Chemistry at the Royal Institution (1833–61). For Fischer's

51

visits to Faraday see Fischer's *Tagebuch*, 1825 (summer), pp. 209, 211, 215, and 225; 1825 (October), p. 375; 1826, p. 395; 1845, pp. 490 and 542; 1846, p. 571; and 1851, pp. 650, 653, and 676. See also Fischer's *Tagebuch*, p. 784 (biographical notes).

[103] Stodart and Faraday, 'On the Alloys of Steel' in the *Philosophical Transactions of the Royal Society* (London, 1822, Part 2) and Sir Robert Hadfield, *Faraday and his Metallurgical Researches* . . . (1932).

[104] Faraday liquified chlorine in 1823.

[105] C. R. Fay, *Round about Industrial Britain 1830–60* (1952), ch 9.

[106] Fischer's *Tagebuch*, pp. 213–5.

[107] Fischer's *Tagebuch*, p. 396: in English in the original.

[108] Fischer's note book (*Schreibkalender*) for 1827 (September 28) in the Fischer archives.

[109] Fischer's *Tagebuch*, 1845, p. 543.

[110] *Ibid.*, 1851, pp. 653–4.

[111] *Ibid.*, p. 748.

[112] For William Thomas Brande (1788–1866) see *Haydn's Universal Biography* (edited by J. B. Payne, 1870). For Fischer and Brande see Fischer's *Tagebuch*, 1825, pp. 214, 218, 228, 349, 353–4; 1845, pp. 494 and 497; 1846, p. 553 (letter from Brande to Fischer), and pp. 562, 567, 574-6; and 1851, pp. 675-7.

[113] W. T. Brande, *Manual of Chemistry* (six edition, 1813–48).

[114] Fischer wrote, 'Mr. Rennie' in his diary for 1825 (*Tagebuch*, p. 349 and p. 353). Since this Rennie had been in charge of the Die Office of the Royal Mint (*Tagebuch*, p. 353) it is clear that Fischer met George Rennie (1791–1866). The Rennie mentioned on p. 357 of the *Tagebuch* as the architect of London Bridge was John Rennie (father of George Rennie) who had died in 1821. For John Rennie's career see C.T.G. Boucher, *John Rennie 1761–1821* (1963). and an article in the *Transactions of the Newcomen Society*, Vol. xxxiv, 1961-2, pp. 1–13. In his journal for 1846 (*Tagebuch*, p. 573) Fischer stated that he had met the builder of London Bridge twenty years previously but this was a mistake.

[115] Fischer's *Tagebuch*, 1825, p. 349.

[116] Henry W. Atkinson was Provost of the Moneyers at the Royal Mint.

[117] W. T. Brande's official title at the Royal Mint was 'Clerk of the Irons and Superintendent of Machinery'.

[118] Fischer's *Tagebuch*, 1825, pp. 349–50.

[119] Fischer's *Tagebuch*, 1825, pp. 353-4.

[120] Fischer's *Tagebuch*, 1845, p. 494 and p. 497. Fischer also showed Brande a copy of a letter written by Herr Haindl of the Munich mint to M. Barrie of the Paris mint concerning the quality of Fischer's steel dies.

[121] Fischer's *Tagebuch*, 1846, p. 563.

[122] Fischer's *Tagebuch*, 1846, p. 553.

[123] Fischer's *Tagebuch*, 1846, p. 577.

[124] Fischer's *Tagebuch*, 1851, p. 677.

125 For a description of the Apothecaries Hall at this time see an article in the *Quarterly Journal of Science, Literature, and the Arts*, Vol. XVI, January 1824, pp. 193–202. For Fischer's visit to the Apothecaries Hall see his *Tagebuch*, 1825, pp. 230–6.

126 For Fischer's visit to Woolwich arsenal on October 22nd, 1825 see his *Tagebuch*, pp. 383–95. For the royal arsenal see O.F.G. Hogg, *The Royal Arsenal* (two volumes, 1963) and 'The Development of Engineering at the Royal Arsenal' (*Transactions of the Newcomen Society*, Vol. XXXII, 1959-60. pp. 29–42).

127 *Gentleman's Magazine*, July 27th, 1805.

128 The metal used was an alloy of 100 parts of copper and 11 parts of tin. The cannon were 'carronades' (named after the Carron foundry where they were first made in 1779). Fischer referred to them by the popular name 'Miller's cannon' but they had been invented by General Robert Melville and not—as was sometimes supposed—by Patrick Miller.

129 The Congreve rocket had been invented by Sir William Congreve (the second baronet) in 1806 and was first used in the Napoleonic wars and the Anglo-American war of 1812. Congreve (1772–1828) succeeded his father as Comptroller of the Royal Laboratory at Woolwich in 1814.

130 The Shrapnell shell which burst into a number of fragments had been invented by Henry Shrapnell (1761–1842) of the Royal Artillery at the end of the eighteenth century.

131 Fischer's *Tagebuch*, p. 393.

132 For Fischer's visit to Woolwich in September 1827 see his *Tagebuch*, pp. 421–33 and his notebook (*Schreibkalender*) for that year. The commandant of the arsenal at this time was Major General G. Bulteel Smith.

133 See H. Harding, *Patent Office Centenary. A Story of 100 Years in the Life and Work of the Patent Office* (1953).

134 Fischer's *Tagebuch*, p. 666.

135 *Ibid.*, p. 718.

136 *Ibid.*, p. 666.

137 *Ibid.*, p. 344.

138 *Ibid.*, p. 605.

139 *Patents for Inventions. Abridgments of Specifications relating to the manufacture of Iron and Steel*, Part I 1620–1866. (1883), No. 5259, p. 48.

140 Fischer's *Tagebuch*, pp. 497–504 (July 24th, 1845). 'A *caveat* was a request by an inventor for notification of any applications for patents which were filed and he then had seven days in which to lodge an objection to the grant of the patent' (Information kindly supplied by Mr. A. Green of the Patent Office).

141 Fischer's *Tagebuch*, p. 710 and Fischer's biographical notes of 1854 (*Tagebuch*, pp. 792–5).

142 Joseph Planta (1744–1827) of Süs settled in London with his father. He became a member of the Royal Society (1774) and was the Prin-

cipal Librarian of the British Museum between 1799 and 1827. He was the author of a *History of the Helvetic Confederacy* (two volumes, 1800) which was based on Johannes von Muller's history. For Joseph Planta see the *Gentleman's Magazine*, Vol. XLV, pp. 397–8. For Fischer's visit to the British Museum in 1814 see his *Tagebuch*, p. 79.

143 See Daremberg and Saglio, *Dictionnaire des antiquités grecques et romaines,* (1877–1919) Vol. VII, p. 583.

144 René Just Hauy (1743–1822) was in charge of the *cabinet des mines* in Paris. For his life see *La grande Encyclopédie*, Vol. 19, p. 939. A. G. Werner (1749 or 1750–1817) was a German mineralogist and geologist. For his life see the *Allgemeine Deutsche Biographie*, Vol. 42, pp. 33–39.

145 Fischer's *Tagebuch*, p. 217.

146 Fischer's *Tagebuch*, pp. 219–225.

147 Giovanni Baptista Belzoni (1778–1823) of Padua—described as 'actor, engineer and traveller'—settled in London in 1803. He undertook important excavations in Egypt. For his life see the *Dictionary of National Biography*, Vol. IV 205–6.

148 Fischer's *Tagebuch*, pp. 396–401.

149 See Fischer's *Tagebuch*, 1851, pp. 631–709. For the Great Exhibition see the *Great Exhibition of the Works of Industry of all Nations. Official . . . Catalogue* (3 volumes and a supplementary volume, 1851, Vol. III *Foreign States*, p. 1269 No. 47 J. C. Fischer); *The Illustrated Exhibitor* (1851); C. Babbage, *The Exposition of 1851;* R. Hunt, *Handbook for the Official Catalogue* (2 vols. 1851); *Lectures on the Results of the Great Exhibition of 1851 delivered before the Society of Arts* (1852); Robert Wunderlich, *Der Beobachter und Berichtstatter in London, seiner Umgebung und seinem Kristallpalaste . . .* (Winterthur, 1851); Yvonne ffrench, *The Great Exhibition: 1851* (1950) C. R. Fay *Palace of Industry* 1851 (1951).

150 Eight parts of scrap iron and three parts of copper: Fischer's *Tagebuch*, 1851, p. 676.

151 Berthold Fischer, like his father, was awarded an honourable mention for his steel bars.

152 Fischer's *Tagebuch*, pp. 652–3.

153 Fischer considered that the fountain could be used as 'the world's largest and finest candelabria'.

154 The plumbago came from the Borrowdale mine in Cumberland.

155 '(Stirling and Morris's) so-called patent toughened iron is made from puddled iron. While this is still in a fluid state in the furnace, scraps of wrought iron are added. But these pieces of wrought iron do not unite completely with the puddled iron. Only an Englishman with a mania for patents could claim that this was a first class product' (Fischer's *Tagebuch*, p. 697).

156 S. Rinman, *Versuch einer Geschichte des Eisens . . .* (German translation by J. G. Georgi, Berlin, 1785).

157 This series of machines—awarded a Council medal—was made by Hibbert, Platt and Sons.

158 Fischer described the process in his *Tagebuch* for 1851 (p. 696). For another account of the Pattinson process see *The Illustrated Exhibitor* (1851), p. 409. H. L. Pattinson was awarded a prize medal for his 'process for treating lead ores, and separating silver from lead'.

159 Constructed by Robert Stephenson and William Fairbairn.

160 Fischer's *Tagebuch*, p. 688.

161 The Burra Burra copper deposits had been discovered in 1845. They were 'at one time the greatest centre of mining activity' in Australia. See the *Oxford Survey of the British Empire*, Vol. V. Australia (1914), p. 308.

162 An article on this fire engine appeared in *The Illustrated Exhibitor* (1851), p. 136.

163 Fischer observed with regret that Escher Wyss of Zürich had not submitted any cotton goods or textile machinery.

164 Two prize medals were awarded to Swiss firms at the exhibition— Neuhaus and Blösch of Bienne and Mathey and Sons of Le Locle— while Fischer secured an honourable mention. See S. J. Jeans, *Steel, History, Manufacture, Properties, and Uses* (1880), p. 317. For the Swiss exhibits at the Crystal Palace in 1851 see an article in the *Leokalender* (St. Gallen, 1951) entitled 'Schweiz. Landesausstellung in London 1851' (pp. 57–59). The report of the Jury on Fischer's display was as follows: '. . . Mr. Fischer has added to his exhibition a drawing representing the interior of his establishment, from which it appears that the smelting furnaces are very small and may be conveyed from one place to another without any other expense than that incurred by the removal of the bellows. Mr. Fischer states that he manufactures cast steel by a peculiar method; but the drawing, the only document the Jury are enabled to refer to, does not indicate any difference between his method of melting and those already known, except in the small scale on which the operation is carried on'.

165 Fischer had been given this information by Ludwig Kachel of the Baden mint when he visited Carlsruhe on his way to London to see the Exhibition (see his *Tagebuch*, pp. 636–7). Uhlhorn's coining press was awarded a Council medal.

166 Quoted by K. Schib and R. Gnade, *Johann Conrad Fischer 1773– 1854* (1954), pp. 133–4.

CHAPTER III

Fischer in the Manufacturing Districts

INTRODUCTION

It has been seen that Fischer kept a detailed record of his journeys to England. He regularly visited London, the industrial Midlands, and the manufacturing districts of Lancashire and the West Riding. Few foreigners acquired a more intimate knowledge of the English industrial regions than Fischer and his accounts of the factories and plants that he saw in the days when Britain was the workshop of the world are of considerable interest to the economic historian.

Fischer wrote about ironworks, engineering plants, textile factories, communications and public utilities. Much research has been undertaken concerning the leading inventors and entrepreneurs who were active during the period of the Industrial Revolution but less is known of their successors. The careers of such pioneers as Josiah Wedgwood, John Wilkinson, Benjamin Huntsman, Matthew Boulton, and James Watt have often been described but we are less well informed about the later history of the firms that they founded. Fischer's diaries contain numerous accounts of firms at a time when they were run by those who followed the pioneers of the Industrial Revolution. He referred also to the activities of men like George A. Lee, Richard Roberts, and J. G. Bodmer who enjoyed a high reputation in their own day but whose achievements have seldom been discussed in modern works on the economic history of the early nineteenth century.

In one respect Fischer's journals may lead historians to modify their views about the English industrialists in the early nineteenth century. It is sometimes imagined that the typical manufacturer of that period was a tough individual who spared neither himself nor those who worked for him in his ruthless efforts to maintain a high output of cheap goods. He was supposed to lack any semblance of culture and to have a single-minded devotion to the task of making as much money as possible. Many later writers have echoed the views of the correspondent to the *Manchester Observer* who wrote in 1818 that the local manufacturers were 'without education or address, except what they have acquired

56

BENJAMIN GOTT'S PARK MILL, LEEDS

Source: W. H. Chaloner and A. E. Musson, *A Visual History of Modern Britain—Industry and Technology*. (Vista Books, 1963)

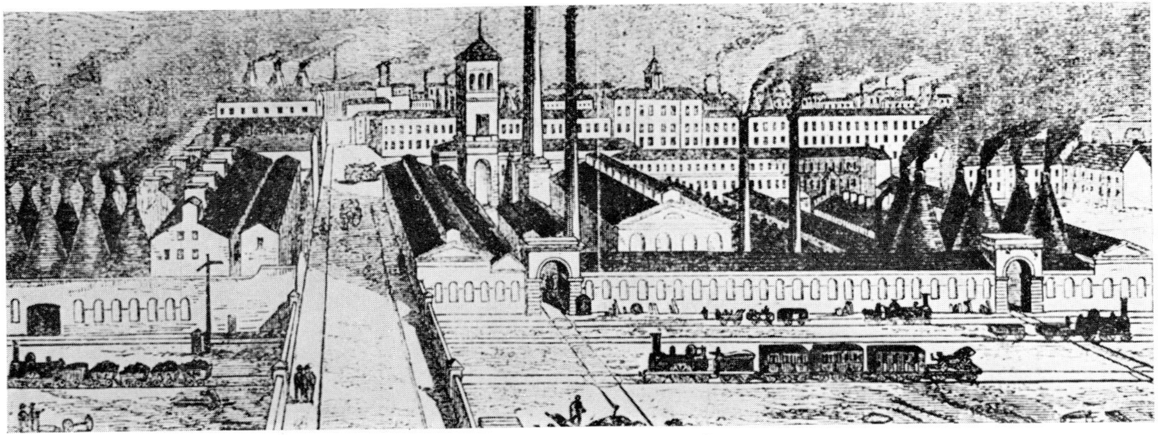

CAMMELL'S CYCLOPS STEELWORKS, SHEFFIELD
By courtesy of W. H. Chaloner and A. E. Musson

by their intercourse with the little world of merchants in the Exchange.' The reader of Fischer's diaries finds himself in quite a different world. The industrialists Fischer learned to know—men like the younger Watt, Murdock, Philips, Lee, Benjamin Gott, Sanderson, Charles Cammell and many others—were not merely successful businessmen. They were often men of considerable scientific attainments. They read widely. Their homes contained well stocked libraries, good furniture, and fine paintings. They travelled on the Continent for business and pleasure. They were patrons of learning and the arts. They had a sense of responsibility towards their workers and towards the communities in which they lived. The greedy manufacturers who were attacked by Dickens, Carlyle, and Engels undoubtedly existed but they were not the only representatives of their class. Many of those who showed Fischer over their factories and entertained him in their homes were men who not only ran great firms, but also devoted themselves to public affairs and appreciated the finer things of life.

1. THE TEXTILE MANUFACTURERS

(i) *Philips and Lee of Salford*[1]

When Fischer first visited Manchester and Salford in 1814 he came to two adjacent industrial towns which had a population of about 110,000. At that time there were over 40 cotton mills in the Manchester district employing some 13,000 operatives and the town was also the commercial centre of the Lancashire cotton industry. When the Swiss traveller Hans Caspar Escher visited the town in that year he counted over 60 spinning mills in a walk that lasted only fifteen minutes. He wrote that in a single street in Manchester there were more cotton spindles than in the whole of Switzerland. Escher found the Manchester manufacturers 'secretive and suspicious' but that was not Fischer's experience. Fischer had a letter of introduction to George A. Lee from Boulton and Watt. Lee, described by Robert Owen as 'a very superior and scientific person', was a partner in the firm of Philips and Lee, cotton spinners of Chapel Street, Salford. The firm employed over 900 operatives and was one of the largest in the district.[2] Its seven storey mill, erected in 1799–1801, had probably been designed by Boulton and Watt. It was one of the earliest fireproof iron framed buildings in the country[3] and one of the first to be heated by steam and lit by gas. The gas lighting equipment, installed by its inventor Murdock in 1805, cut the cost of lighting the factory from £2,000 to £600 a year. Fischer

57

did not inspect the mill on this occasion but in his journal he summarised an article written by Murdock describing its gas generating plant.[4] Fischer was entertained by Lee and his sister Harriet, the novelist.[5] In his diary he described his host as 'one of the most remarkable men in England.' Lee subsequently visited Fischer at Schaffhausen[6] and when Fischer published the journal of his tour in England in 1814 he sent Lee a copy.[7]

When Fischer visited Manchester in 1825 he again dined with George A. Lee. Before dinner he inspected the apparatus for generating gas from oil which Lee used to light his house. This was the last occasion on which the two men met for Lee died in the following year. Lee's partner Philips,[8] who had lived in Switzerland for nearly a year, showed Fischer over the Salford cotton mill. Fischer was particularly interested in the gas generating plant and in the hoist which conveyed goods from one floor of the factory to another. Fischer visited Philips at his home ('The Dales') and admired his host's greenhouse. The conversation after dinner included a discussion of labour problems in England and in Switzerland. Fischer wrote in his journal that many Swiss artisans would envy the English worker his high wages—twenty four shillings a week for unskilled men and up to £3 a week for skilled men. But he added that the cost of living was higher in England than in Switzerland.

(ii) *Benjamin Gott of Leeds*[9]

Whenever he went to Leeds Fischer visited Benjamin Gott who had been a pioneer in transforming the manufacture of woollen cloth from a domestic to a factory industry. It had been largely owing to his initiative that the firm of which he was a partner had erected Park Mill at Bean Ing near Kirkstall Abbey in 1792. This was one of the most up to date cloth factories in the country. The power was supplied by a 40 h.p. Boulton and Watt rotative engine —one of the first to be erected in a Yorkshire mill[10]—and gas lighting and steam heating had been introduced early in the nineteenth century. When Fischer first met Gott in 1814 the firm had successfully surmounted the perils of the Napoleonic wars and the Luddite riots and was a flourishing concern. By this time Benjamin Gott controlled three factories[11] and was described as 'the greatest cloth manufacturer in England.'[12]

Fischer first visited Leeds early in September 1814.[13] On his arrival he inspected the three and a half mile coal railway which ran across Hunslet moor from Middleton colliery to Leeds.[14] He wrote in his journal: 'The steam engine is on a waggon which in size and shape is similar to that of a wine cart with a single vat. This waggon—like those attached to it—has four low iron wheels. There is also a fifth toothed-wheel in front, which is in the middle of the left two wheels before and behind. This toothed wheel grips the cogs and is moved by the two smaller front wheels.' Fischer rode on the locomotive and became alarmed lest the boiler should explode. He was duly impressed with a locomotive that could haul 23 waggons each filled with half a ton of coal. Fischer hoped to meet Matthew Murray,[15] the designer and constructor of this locomotive, and—armed with a letter of introduction from George A. Lee—he called upon Benjamin Gott in the hope of discovering where Murray was to be found.

His quest was unsuccessful but his meeting with Gott proved to be the beginning of a long friendship. Gott's eldest sons—John and Benjamin—showed the Swiss visitor over Park Mill. Fischer was astonished at the size of the factory[16] and at the extensive use of the most modern installations such as carding machinery, a steam engine, a hydraulic press, and a gas generating plant. He subsequently wrote to Gott that this 'extensive manufactory . . . most likely has not its mate in the Kingdom. Indeed it is not a trifle to execute on so large a scale an idea, for which mankind must be beholden to you, on account of the great benefits resulting from it, and that you did it in spite of the prejudices and the ridicule of the public which is always in opposition with the introduction of novelties, be they ever so well founded in sound reasoning or the most decisive experiments.'[17]

In the autumn of 1816 'young Mr. Gott of Leeds' stayed with the Fischers at Schaffhausen[18] and in the autumn of 1824 Gott's two eldest daughters and one of his sons visited Fischer. In the summer of 1825 Fischer was in Leeds once more.[19] On June 27 accompanied by Henry Gott,[20] he visited an exhibition of contemporary paintings and also looked over the recently established Philosophical Hall with its museum and scientific laboratory.[21] He again inspected Park Mill and was astonished at the changes that had taken place in the past eleven years. Two six storey extensions had been built. In each case the framework consisted of cast iron pillars and girders. The larger building had taken three months to erect, the latter only six weeks. A new 80 horse power steam engine had been installed.

Fischer stayed a night at Benjamin Gott's mansion Armley House—which had been rebuilt from Sir Robert Smirke's designs —and he was impressed by its costly furnishings, paintings and books. On the following day (June 28) Fischer visited Gott's Armley Mill which was one of the largest factories in England to be operated by water power. Three great iron wheels generated as much energy as a steam engine of 120 horse power. The wheels worked either singly or together so that if a mechanical defect put one of them out of action the other two could keep the factory machinery working.

On leaving these works Fischer told Benjamin Gott that he was interested in mechanical flax spinning. Pointing to William Marshall's works, which were only half a mile away, Gott told Fischer: 'This establishment is likely to prosper most in our country. It is the best flax mill I know of.' A letter of introduction from Gott enabled Fischer to inspect Marshall's flax mill, although foreign visitors were not normally admitted. Marshall himself conducted Fischer through his works. Fischer was particularly impressed with the heckling and fibre-sorting machines. Marshall told him that flax spinning in England was not so far advanced as cotton spinning but he hoped to make many improvements in the next two years.[23]

Detailed information concerning Fischer's contacts with the Gott family between the visit of 1825 and the one which he paid to Leeds twenty years later is lacking. It is known, however, that in the autumn of 1827 Fischer lunched with Benjamin Gott and discussed with him—and with Gott's solicitor—the terms of a new agreement that he was negotiating with Smith and Martineau.[24] There is also a reference in his journal to a conversation with 'young Mr. Gott' at this time.[25] They discussed the changes in manners and customs that had occurred in the north of England in the last thirty years. Gott agreed with Fischer that prize fighting and cock fighting had both declined and observed that the former sport was now largely confined to the lower classes while the latter was still patronised by the aristocracy. Fischer also enquired about the extent of the coal deposits in the Midlands and Gott showed him a geological map of the region.[26]

When Benjamin Gott died in 1840 the business was carried on by his sons John and William. It was John Gott who welcomed Fischer to Leeds in July 1845.[27] Fischer spent a day inspecting the Low Moor Ironworks on the Bradford–Huddersfield road, under the guidance of Mr. Dawson, one of the partners of the firm.[28] But he returned to Leeds in the evening to dine at Armley House. When the ladies had retired he endeavoured to interest John Gott in the projected railway line from Schaffhausen to Constance.[29] On the following day John Gott took Fischer for a walk in Leeds and Fischer observed in his journal that the trade of the city appeared to be booming and that both the woollen and the linen mills were busy.[30]

2. A VISIT TO ETRURIA

On his way to Manchester from Birmingham in 1814 Fischer broke his journey at Newcastle-under-Lyme where he spent the night. On the following morning he walked three miles to Etruria to see the famous pottery works established there by Josiah Wedgwood.[31] He had already visited the Wedgwood showrooms in London and had admired the many fine pieces of chinaware on show there. When he came upon a network of iron tramways and rows of workers cottages he knew that he was approaching his goal.

The founder of the firm had died in 1795 and the business was now carried on by his son Josiah Wedgwood junior. Fischer was shown round the works and in his diary he described in some detail the various aspects of the manufacture of chinaware from the preparation of the raw material—clay and ground flints—to the baking, glazing, and colouring processes. Fischer observed that Wedgwood had been able to mechanise some operations which were still performed by hand on the Continent. He described how the speed at which the potters wheels (driven by steam power) revolved could be regulated by the workmen. He observed that sand was used for bedding the chinaware in kilns to reduce the danger of distortion in the firing process. He gave an account of the way in which china plates were made by preparing a clay 'bat' on a revolving wheel and then shaping it on a plaster jig. In the studios and decorating workshops Fischer examined the method of making transfers from engraved copper plates. He claimed that this process had been invented some 35 years previously by his fellow townsman Johann Adam Spengler, the director of porcelain workshops at Zürich.[32]

Fischer noted the efficiency of the transport system inside the works. Raw materials and chinaware were conveyed from one department to another in small manually propelled waggons runing on rails. Each waggon and its load weighed nearly twelve hundredweight. Fischer also commented upon 'the clever apportioning of the work' in Wedgwood's plant. After visiting the factory Fischer was entertained to lunch by Wedgwood. When he told his host that he would like to buy a porcelain tea service Wedgwood advised him to get one in Paris on his way home. The French, said Wedgwood, could secure better raw materials than their English rivals and their products were 'fine and better' than his own. Wedgwood added that he was thinking of giving up the manufacture of porcelain altogether. Fischer however purchased a dinner service and a tea service to take back to Schaffhausen, and this is said to have led to an increase in Wedgwood's sales in Switzerland.[33] Fischer concluded his account of his visit to Etruria as follows: 'I took leave of this man whose father, an ordinary Staffordshire potter, founded an earthenware factory which made articles of such high quality that they were exported to all parts of the world. His son is now doing everything possible to enhance the already established reputation of the firm.'

3. THE MANCHESTER ENGINEERS[34]

When Fischer visited Manchester and Salford in 1825[35] various engineering firms already enjoyed a high reputation there. Among the most important were Peel, Williams & Co. (Phoenix and Soho foundries); Radford & Waddington; Galloway, Bowman & Glasgow; T. and J. Sherratt; Sharp, Hill & Co.; Richard Ormrod (St. George's foundry); Hewes and Wren (Dale Street works); and Fairbairn and Lillie.[36] Fischer called upon some of his compatriots who were living in Manchester at this time. One was Johann Georg Bodmer[37]—one of the leading engineers of his day—who had recently settled in England. At this time he was employed by Sharp, Hill & Co. and was lodging in Oxford Road where he had gathered around him a group of young men from Switzerland who were completing their training in the textile and engineering industries. One of them was Albert Escher[38]—a son of Fischer's old friend Hans Caspar Escher—who was then working in William Fairbairn's engineering workshops.

(i) Sharp, Hill & Co.

Bodmer introduced Fischer to Hill, a partner in the firm of Sharp, Hill & Co., manufacturers of textile machinery. Fischer was shown over the works by Richard Roberts, the inventor of the self-acting mule.[39] He was impressed by the large output of the firm and by the high quality of its products. Sharp, Hill & Co. turned out 80 powerlooms a week. They were used for weaving cotton cloth but could also be adapted to the manufacture of carpets. In these works Fischer admired a machine for making weavers' reeds which Roberts had invented.

(ii) Richard Ormrod

Fischer was taken by Albert Escher to Richard Ormrod's engineering works—the St. George's Foundry—in Minshull

Street. He saw how hydraulic power was used to raise a bridge whenever a barge passed beneath it. The bridge, 38 feet in length, spanned the Rochdale Canal to link two parts of Ormrod's works. From his own observations and from the firm's catalogue Fischer saw that a great variety of products were made including textile and milling machinery, steam engines, boilers, stoves, wheels, coupling boxes, weighing machines for bleachers and paper makers, rails for collieries, ornamental railings, gas generating plants, and steam heating plants. Ormrod showed Fischer his collection of wooden patterns[40] and declared: 'I challenge the whole world to show me anything as good as this. These patterns have cost me £10,000 and, as you can see, I keep them in a completely fireproof building.'[41] Ormrod had his labour troubles. He told his visitor that it was difficult to secure good workers and Fischer observed in his journal that there were good opportunities for employment in England for artisans from the Continent.

(iii) *William Fairbairn*

Fischer's Swiss friends also introduced him to William Fairbairn,[42] who had been to Zürich in the previous autumn to erect mill gearing and water machinery at Hans Casper Escher's cotton spinning mill. Fairbairn was now training Albert Escher as an engineer. Fischer formed the opinion that Fairbairn was one of the most skilful millwrights in England. He observed that English millwrights now worked largely with iron whereas millwrights on the Continent still worked largely with wood. In a brief account of Fairbairn and Lillie's engineering workshops he stated that he had been particularly interested in the wiredrawing machines and in a portable circular saw. At this time Fairbairn was employing between sixty and seventy men.[43] Fairbairn's works later grew to be one of the most important engineering plants in Manchester and their owner became 'one of the most influential and successful mechanical engineers.'[44] The only other reference to Fairbairn in Fischer's journals occurs many years later. In his account of his last visit to Manchester in 1851 Fischer referred to Fairbairn as an old friend who was now the owner of large workshops for the constructions of steamships and steam engines. When Fischer called at the Polygon in Ardwick Fairbairn was away from Manchester at a meeting of the British Association and Fischer was entertained by his son.[45]

(iv) *Thomas C. Hewes*[46]

In 1825 when visiting Benjamin Gott at Leeds Fischer met the Manchester engineer Thomas C. Hewes who was erecting a suspension bridge over the River Aire at Armley Mill. Hewes has been described as 'a man of science' who had 'eminent talents in the various branches of the mechanical art.'[47]

4. THE STEELMAKERS AND CUTLERS OF SHEFFIELD[48]

(i) *The Huntsman Family*

Fischer often included Sheffield in his itinerary when visiting the manufacturing districts of England. In 1814 he wished to see some of the famous works in which the best cast steel in the world was made by the crucible process.[49] The Continent had been short of cast steel during the Napoleonic wars and many attempts had been made to discover the secret of the crucible process. Fischer himself had made small quantities of cast steel of high quality by this method. In 1814 he first visited Rotherham where he saw the works of Walker and Booth, who claimed to make cement steel and cast steel on a larger scale than any other firm.[50] 'Here there were 12 coke fired furnaces and the steel when melted was teemed into octagonal iron moulds. Fischer . . . compared the Sheffield workers' skill in pouring smooth castings unfavourably with that of his own Swiss workmen.'[51]

Next Fischer called at the home of the Huntsman family at Attercliffe which was situated next to the building in which they did their smelting. So shabby was the house that Fischer wondered whether he had found the right place. He met two members of the family and purchased some samples of their cast steel. 'What interested Fischer most was to discover that his own cast steel had the same general properties as Huntsman's.'[52] When Huntsman learned that Fischer came from Switzerland he produced an old letter which his father had once received from a Swiss manufacturer. This had been an enquiry concerning the possibility of securing the services of two craftsmen from Attercliffe but the elder Huntsman had turned down the request. Huntsman remarked that he knew of 'a certain Mr. Fischer' who had made good crucible cast steel but Fischer did not volunteer the information that he was the inventor whom Huntsman had in mind. It was after this visit to the Huntsman works that Fischer wrote: 'Now I have achieved everything that I had set out as the aim of my journey.'

A note in his diary for 1827 shows that Fischer was in Sheffield in October of that year and that he met a member of the Huntsman family by chance in a steel plant. Huntsman told Fischer that if he came to Attercliffe he could see some cast steel that would cut glass. In August 1845 Fischer visited the Huntsman foundry on the River Don which was operated by water power. He did not meet any member of the family on this occasion. In the following year he again went to the foundry and this time he met a member of the Huntsman family whom he had not seen for twenty years. He showed Huntsman the painting by Beck of his works at Mühlental. On his last visit to England Fischer called at this plant again in the summer of 1851.[53]

(ii) Sanderson Brothers[54]

Fischer's first contact with Sanderson Brothers, a firm famous for its cast steel,[55] was in 1825 when he met John Sanderson, one of the partners, on the coach from Sheffield to Birmingham.[56] They spent a morning together and Fischer stated that this 'very respectable gentleman' was one of three brothers—Thomas, James, and John—who operated the largest steel plant in England. The firm, founded in 1776, had a substantial export trade with North and South America. Sanderson was surprised to discover that Fischer had a detailed knowledge of English methods of making crucible cast steel and he was favourably impressed with the pair of razors that Ebenezer Rhodes of Sheffield had made from Fischer steel-nickel alloy. This alloy would naturally be of interest to John Sanderson since it was in Sanderson Brothers' West Street plant that Michael Faraday had recently (1820–22) carried out his experiments in the production of a steel-nickel alloy.[57]

In October 1827 Fischer visited Sanderson Brothers' foundry in West Street where Swedish 'Hoop L' iron[58] was being turned into cast steel. In his journal for 1845 Fischer stated that Sanderson Brothers had 36 blast furnaces and 6 cementation furnaces and were still one of the largest producers of cast steel in Sheffield. He visited their works and saw how the cast steel was made. When Fischer told Sanderson how much coke he used at Mühlental to make a hundredweight of steel Sanderson exclaimed: 'You beat us!' In 1846 Fischer visited Sanderson Brothers' forging, tilting, and rolling mills at Attercliffe. On Fischer's last visit to Sheffield in 1851 he had a two hour conversation with Sanderson at his home. Sanderson promised to send Fischer a sketch of a small cupola furnace suitable for smelting the bean iron ore found in Switzerland.[59]

(iii) Charles Cammell[60]

Charles Cammell was another Sheffield steelmaker with whom Fischer was acquainted. His industrial career had begun in 1837 when he joined with two brothers Thomas and Henry Johnson to set up a firm of steel and file manufacturers in Furnival Street. He has been described as 'extremely industrious, hard working, plodding, and pushing.' In 1846, when Fischer first met Cammell, the firm had just moved to Savile Street East (Brightside) near the station of the Sheffield and Rotherham Railway. Fischer was impressed by the size of the Cyclops Works which were one of the largest in Sheffield. It had 20 blast furnaces—all tapped three times a day—and four large cementation furnaces, each with a capacity of over 200 hundredweights. The firm made many steel products, the most important being files and axle springs. Although Fischer marvelled at the scale of Cammell's operations he saw little that was novel from a technical point of view. And when he learned that the firm had patented a process for using iron shavings to make cast steel he expressed his doubts concerning the likelihood of the process being a success.

In 1851 Fischer met Cammell several times in London and the two industrialists exchanged prints of their steelworks.[61] Fischer considered Cammell to be 'the greatest steel manufacturer in England' since his plant turned out 50 tons of steel a week. Fischer went to Sheffield and was shown over the Cyclops works by Johnson, one of Cammell's partners.[62] Fischer observed that, in view of the expansion of the business, the partners were generally to be found in their offices rather than in the plant. Responsibility for work done on the shop floor now devolved upon the foremen and much depended upon their efficiency. At this time the firm had full order books and was turning out large quantities of axle springs for the railways. Improved methods of manufacture coupled with a fall in the cost of coal and coke—a fall of nearly 30 per cent in the last four years—had enabled Cammell to cut the price of steel (for making springs) to $2\frac{1}{2}$d a pound.

(iv) *Thomas Turton & Sons*[63]

Fischer first visited the Sheffield steelmakers Thomas Turton & Sons in August 1845. They made cementation steel, crucible cast steel, welded steel, and axle springs for locomotives and railway carriages. He formed a high opinion of the efficiency of the plant and remarked that there was a rather greater economy in the use of coke than in Sanderson's works. In the following year Fischer visited the firm again and described a machine which tested the strength of steel springs. In 1851 Fischer inspected both the foundry (Park and Spring Works) and the newly opened rolling mills (Sheaf Works) of Turton & Sons and observed in his journal that their axle springs were of better quality than those made by Cammell.

(v) *Three Sheffield Cutlers*

Sheffield had been famous for its cutlery long before it became the main British centre for the production of cast steel. In the nineteenth century Sheffield cutlers enjoyed a world wide reputation. Fischer called on cutlers and file makers in the city on several occasions to secure expert opinions on the merits of his own steel and alloys. In 1814 he visited Bramall's file manufactory at the 'White House'[64] and purchased a number of samples of steel as well as a set of turning tools. He asked the proprietor if he could see how files were manufactured and added that in Switzerland it was generally supposed that Sheffield files were now being made by machinery. Bramall replied that this was not so and he allowed Fischer to look over his workshops where files, made from cement steel and cast steel, were being made by hand. Fischer made various other purchases in Sheffield at this time. They included files, knives, scissors, razors, and a circular saw. He thought that Sheffield hand saws were no better than those made in Switzerland by David Mathis. On the other hand circular saws were unknown in Switzerland at that time.[65]

In 1825 chance led Fischer to the workshops of Ebenezer Rhodes, one of the leading cutlers in Sheffield. He had been Master Cutler in 1817 and had written both a pamphlet on razors and a pioneer work on the scenery of the Peak district. Fischer asked Rhodes to make a pair of razors from his own steel. When Fischer collected the razors Rhodes said that he would like to know a little more about the steel from which they had been made. Fischer replied: 'I should be glad to have a few lines from you containing your opinion about it.' Rhodes thereupon wrote a short memorandum in which he praised the quality of Fischer's steel.[66]

On his visit to Sheffield in 1846 Fischer called upon the old established firm of Joseph Rodgers and Sons[67] whom he described as 'the most famous razor makers' in the country. The firm was a family concern which had moved to its Norfolk Street premises in the 1780s and had been master cutlers to the royal family since 1821. Its trade mark was known all over the world. Fischer had brought with him two new razors made from his own steel on which he desired an opinion from a Sheffield cutler. Joseph Rodgers and Sons ground and polished the razors for him and gave him an excellent testimonial concerning the quality of the steel from which they were made. In 1851 Fischer once more asked the firm for an opinion of his razors. This time they were made from his steel nickel alloy and again the firm expressed the view that Fischer's steel was of really high quality.

5. THE IRONMASTERS AND ENGINEERS OF THE MIDLANDS[68]

(i) *The Soho Foundry*

On his first tour in the Midlands in 1814[69] Fischer—armed with an introduction from the London banker Yeates Brown—visited James Watt junior and Matthew Robinson Boulton, whose engineering works, situated just outside Birmingham, had played an important part in the industrial revolution in England. In the last quarter of the eighteenth century the firm of Boulton and Watt had been the most important in the country for the production of steam engines.[70] By 1814 Matthew Boulton had died, the elder James Watt had retired and the firm was being run by their sons. William Murdock, the greatest of their employees, was still an active member of the firm. The partners had two establishments—the manufactory and the foundry. The Soho Manufactory had been set up by the elder Boulton and by his partner Fothergill in 1762-5 to make 'Birmingham toys' and it subsequently turned out many metal products[71] including coining machines. The Soho foundry, opened in 1796, included an engineering plant for the construction of machine parts and the assembling of steam engines.

As soon as he reached Birmingham at the end of August 1814 Fischer called upon James Watt junior and was invited to dine at Heathfield Hall on the following day. Watt showed his guest over the Soho manufactory where they were joined by Matthew Robinson Boulton. After inspecting large quantities of machine parts Fischer saw some of the finished steam engines and went on to look over the wire drawing workshop and the smithy. At dinner he showed his hosts a sample of his steel copper alloy and was introduced to William Murdock,[72] the inventor of gas lighting, whom he described as 'a very experienced metallurgist.'

On the following day Watt took Fischer to the Soho foundry which was situated on the Birmingham and Wolverhampton canal. On the way they passed a number of 'pleasant cottages for the workers.' Although visitors were seldom admitted,[73] Fischer was allowed to inspect these famous engineering works and in his journal he described in some detail the blast furnace, the foundry, the pattern shop, the cylinder casting pit, and the gas generating plant.[74] Watt told Fischer that he had his doubts, concerning the suitability of English iron ore for making steel.[75] He gave Fischer some samples of these ores for future testing. On his return to Schaffhausen Fischer sent Watt samples of steel made from the English ores which were in his opinion 'as fit as any other iron for being converted into a very good sort of cast steel provided the composition of the flux be calculated according to its nature and properties.'[76] Fischer did not meet Watt on his next visit to the Midlands in 1825. A quarter of a century later he went to Soho again but by this time both Watt and Matthew Robinson Boulton were dead and their once flourishing engineering works lay empty and deserted.

(ii) *The Level Ironworks near Dudley*

On August 29, 1814 Fischer spent the day with James Watt junior in the Black Country. They rode on horseback from Birmingham to Dudley through a dismal smoky hive of industry containing some 500 plants and factories. Between Bilston and Wednesbury they passed the famous Bradley ironworks which were one of the largest in the district since they employed some 5,000 workers. They had been founded by the great ironmaster John Wilkinson in the middle of the eighteenth century[77] and were now being run by Samuel Fereday.[78] Fischer did not visit these ironworks and it may be assumed that the brief account of them which he gave in his diary for 1814 was based upon information supplied by James Watt junior. Some letters preserved in the Boulton and Watt correspondence suggest that Watt had visited Bradley and had dined with Fereday's family.

In the afternoon Fischer and Watt were shown over the Earl of Dudley's Level Ironworks by Benjamin Gibbon. At this plant, situated three miles from Dudley, Fischer saw three blast furnaces each 42 feet high and each making from 70 to 100 tons of iron. They were blown by a nine foot cylinder worked by a powerful steam engine. Fischer also inspected three refining furnaces and a puddling furnace. He described the iron making process in his diary and commented upon the high quality and the low cost of Staffordshire iron.[79] Only eight years later the effects of the Level Ironworks came under the auctioneer's hammer. On their way home Watt and Fischer called upon Joseph Priestley junior.[80] The final stage of the return journey to Birmingham was made on roads illuminated by the glare from some 150 chimneys.

(iii) *The Ironworks near Wednesbury*

In his journal for 1825 Fischer described his visits to several engineering workshops in Birmingham[81] but only a few names were mentioned—Cardwell, a partner in a firm which made malleable cast iron; George Attwood[82] who owned the only cast steel plant in the city,[83] and Henry Adcock,[84] the proprietor of one of the oldest jewellery businesses in Birmingham. Fischer commented upon the low price of Adcock's gold-plated jewellery.

On June 15 Fischer visited a 'large iron foundry on the canal' near Wednesbury where malleable cast iron was made. Over a hundred men were employed at his plant. Fischer saw two cupola furnaces at work which had an hourly output of twelve hundred-weight of grey Staffordshire pig iron. The principal ironwares cast in the foundry were kitchen utensils, ornaments and nails. After passing through the annealing furnaces, the utensils were ready for turning, boring, filing, and tinning.[85] Fischer was particularly interested in the way in which nails were made at this plant. Some years previously he had asked Murdock about the manufacture of nails in England 'by mechanical means' and James Watt (junior) had given him some samples of such nails.[86] Now he was able to see for himself how nails could be cast.

Fischer's last visit to Birmingham was in the summer of 1851.[87] He saw Ralph Heaton's engineering workshops where copper coins were being minted for the Republic of Chile and commented that 'there is not a corner of the earth that does not make use of England's arts and industries. Chile sends her precious metals to England and gets copper coins in exchange.'

6. A VISIT TO LIVERPOOL[88]

Fischer had often been to Manchester but it was not until the autumn of 1846 that he paid a brief visit to Liverpool. He walked from the Adelphi Hotel to the River Mersey and was impressed by the straight wide streets, the imposing shops, and the countless warehouses in which cotton, timber, iron, and many other products were stored. His first impression was that Liverpool, even more than London, was a port to which came ships from all over the world. Fischer went to an eating house by the river and had roast beef, potatoes, vegetables, bread, and ale. The cost of the meal was ninepence and Fischer declared that he would have paid nearly five times as much in his London hotel. And the beer was the best that he had ever tasted in England.

On the following day Fischer found himself in a street where there were a number of iron foundries and workshops in which chains and anchors were made. The gate of one smithy—that of Betteley and Roberts—was open and in spite of the usual notice: 'No admittance except on Business' Fischer asked if he could look round. He was allowed to do so. Mr. Bettely showed him a chain in process of construction. When finished it would be 300 yards long and would weigh 240 cwt. Fischer was impressed by the fact that the making of the links of the chain had, to some extent, been mechanised.

Fischer then visited the Horsfall Iron and Steel Works. He first inspected the steel plant which was very similar to others that he had seen elsewhere. The workshops in which large machine parts were being made were of greater interest to Fischer. He saw a sixty hundredweight shaft under construction. This was to be part of a steam engine to drive a warship. He wrote in his journal: 'I was astonished to see how the heaviest pieces of iron, such as shafts weighing several hundredweights, were being repaired or improved. The forging was being done as beautifully and as accurately as if they had been little rods.'

There followed one of the many tributes to Britain as the workshop of the world that are to be found in Fischer's diaries. He wrote: 'The more I come to England and the better I get to know the English the more I am convinced that it is not the size of a country's population which makes its people great, wealthy, powerful, and therefore—as we are accustomed to judge worldly affairs—happy. On the contrary these things are achieved by moral strength, by a diffusion of knowledge and by the existence of free institutions, limited only by the laws. It is extraordinary how English influence and English power make themselves felt everywhere although the size of the island's population is only quite a small proportion of that of Europe, let alone the world as a whole.'[89]

---

[1] Fischer's *Tagebuch,* pp. 128–144, 261, 277–8, and 282–91. In his note book (*Schreibkalender*) for 1827 Fischer stated that Archduke Johann of Austria 'was personally acquainted with my friend Mr. Lee of Manchester'. There is a reference to Lee's meeting with Archduke Johann in the *Minutes of Evidence of the Select Committee on the State of Children employed in the Manufactories of the United Kingdom,* 1816, p. 345. For George A. Lee (1761–1826) see the *Gentleman's Magazine,* Vol. XCVI (New Series. Vol. 19). July–December 1826, Part ii, pp. 281–2 and the *Manchester Guardian,* August 12, 1826.

[2] Philips and Lee employed 937 operatives in 1816 (Lee's evidence before the *Select Committee on the State of Children employed in*

the Manufactories of the United Kingdom, 1816, p. 339). The only larger cotton firms in the area at that time were Adam and George Murray (1,215 operatives) and McConnel and Kennedy (1,020 operatives).

3 See T. C. Bannister, 'The first iron-framed Buildings' (*Architectural Review*, Vol. CVIII, April 1950, pp. 231–46) and H. R. Johnston and A. W. Skempton, 'William Strutt's Cotton Mills, 1793–1812' (*Transactions of the Newcomen Society*, Vol. XXX, 1956, pp. 149–56).

4 Murdock had written a paper on gas lighting for the Royal Society which was read by Sir Joseph Banks, the President of the Society, on February 25, 1808. The account of gas lighting incorporated by Fischer in his journal was translated from 'a small treatise' by Murdock which George A. Lee sent to Fischer in 1816. Fischer refers to this pamphlet in his letters to Benjamin Gott, Murdock (both February 20, 1816) and George A. Lee (June 16, 1817). Hans Caspar Escher, who visited Manchester in 1814, wrote in his diary (October 4): 'The spinning mills now work until 8 p.m. with (gas) light and it is impossible to describe the magnificent appearance of a single side of a mill when 256 windows are all alight, as if the most brilliant sunshine were streaming through them.'

5 In a letter to George A. Lee (June 16, 1817) Fischer wrote: 'I have taken the liberty to translate into German some of those fine novels she modestly calls but "Canterbury Tales"'. Some of Harriet Lee's 'Canterbury Tales' were written in collaboration with her sister Sophia.

6 In March 1815 Fischer wrote to James Watt junior that 'Mr. Lee of Manchester is expected within a few days here'. On February 20, 1816, Fischer wrote to Murdock: 'Mr. Lee of Manchester, who did me the honour of visiting me at Schaffhausen since I left England had the goodness to send me a few weeks ago your most interesting treatise on gas light'.

7 Fischer to George A. Lee, June 6, 1817 (in the Fischer archives), a letter introducing the ironmaster J. G. Neher (Fischer spells the name Näher) of Laufen (Rhine Falls) to Lee.

8 This was Nathaniel Philips whose address was given as The Dales, Pilkington in Pigot's *Manchester Directory* for 1832 (p. 214).

9 Benjamin Gott (1762–1840) became a junior partner in the firm of Wormald, Fontaine and Gott in 1785 and five years later the partnership was controlled by Benjamin Gott and Harry Wormald. The partnership ended in 1817 after which the Gott family ran the business. For Benjamin Gott see W. B. Crump (ed), *The Leeds Woollen Industry 1780–1820* (1931) and articles by H. Heaton, in the *Journal of Economic and Business History*, Vol. II, No. 1, the *Economic History Review*, Vol. III, 1931, pp. 45–60 and the Thoresby Society, Vol. 32, 1931. For the correspondence between Benjamin Gott and Sir Thomas Lawrence see *Country Life*, Vol. 117, Part 2, pp. 1372–3 (1955).

BOULTON & WATT'S SOHO MANUFACTORY, BIRMINGHAM
Source: W. K. V. Gale, *Soho Foundry* (1946)
By courtesy of W. & T. Avery

VIEW OF ETRURIA (STOKE-ON-TRENT)
Source: Alison Kelly, *The Story of Wedgwood* (1962)
By courtesy of Josiah Wedgwood & Sons Ltd.

THE WEDGWOOD SHOWROOMS IN LONDON
Source: Alison Kelly, *The Story of Wedgwood* (1962)
By courtesy of Josiah Wedgwood & Sons Ltd.

10 For a list of Boulton and Watt engines erected in Yorkshire between 1784 and 1796 see R. Offer in W. B. Crump, *op cit.*, pp. 191–2.

11 The three factories were
  (i) Park Mill which was managed by Joseph Cresswell,
  (ii) Birley Mill where blankets were made,
  (iii) Armley Water Mill.
All were situated in the valley of the River Aire. For Park Mill in 1816 see Cresswell's evidence before the *Select Committee on the State of Children employed in the Manufactories of the United Kingdom* (1816), pp. 129–131. There is a brief description of Gott's factories in 1817 in the diary of the Swiss engineer J. G. Bodmer. See Helen and Paul Schoch-Bodmer, 'Ein Tagebuch von Johann Georg Bodmer (1786–1864) aus den Jahren 1816–17 . . .' (*Vierteljahrsschrift der Naturforschenden Gesellschaft in Zürich*, Vol. LXXXI, 1936, p. 21).

12 Fischer's *Tagebuch*, p. 133. The economist J. R. McCulloch later described Gott as 'one of the most extensive and best informed manufacturers in the Empire' (*Dictionary of Commerce*, edition of 1846, p. 1368).

13 Fischer's *Tagebuch*, pp. 145–158.

14 For this railway see W. G. Rimmer, 'Middleton Colliery near Leeds, 1770–1830' in the *Yorkshire Bulletin of Economic and Social Research*, Vol. III, 1955, pp. 41–57 and C. F. Dendy Marshall, *A History of British Railways down to the Year 1830* (1938), pp. 37–8. Authority to construct the original waggon-way was secured by Act of Parliament in 1758. The locomotive was introduced in 1812. Other descriptions of the Middleton colliery railway include those by Oeynhausen and Dechen in the *Archiv für Bergbau und Hüttenwesen*, Vol. XIX, 1829 (summarised in the *Transactions of the Newcomen Society*, Vol. XXIX, 1953–4 and 1954–5, pp. 1–12) and by Marc Seguin in the *Transactions of the Newcomen Society*, Vol. VII, 1926–7, pp. 64–5.

15 Matthew Murray (1765–1826) was a partner in the engineering firm of Fenton, Murray and Ward which had been established at Holbeck near Leeds in 1795. See Samuel Smiles, *Industrial Biography* (1863), pp. 259–64; G. F. Tyas, 'Matthew Murray, a Centenary Appreciation' (*Transactions of the Newcomen Society*, Vol. VI, 1925–6, pp. 111–143); Kilburn Scott (ed), *Matthew Murray, Pioneer Engineer* (1928), and L. T. C. Rolt, *Great Engineers* (1962).

16 The records of Park Mill show that 761 operatives were employed there in September 1813 (W. B. Crump, *op. cit.*, p. 307).

17 J. C. Fischer to Benjamin Gott, February 20, 1816.

18 Fischer to George A. Lee, June 16, 1817: 'I was highly pleased with that young gentleman and know not whether I should more admire his learning and parts or his modesty. I only regretted his parting so soon'.

19 Fischer's *Tagebuch*, pp. 292–311.

G

[20] Henry Gott was Benjamin Gott's fourth son who died in 1826 at the age of 22.

[21] The Leeds Philosophical Hall had been built in 1819 by the Leeds Philosophical and Literary Society. Benjamin Gott was one of the founders of this society.

[22] For Sir Robert Smirke see the *Dictionary of National Biography*, Vol. LII, p. 407.

[23] For Marshall's mechanical flax spinning mill see W. G. Rimmer. *Marshalls of Leeds . . . 1788–1886* (1960). Fischer refers to Marshall simply as 'Mr. M' in his diary. For this visit see Fischer's *Tagebuch*, 1825, pp. 305–10.

[24] See Fischer's note book (*Schreibkalender*) for 1827 in the Fischer archives.

[25] This might be either John Gott or William Gott.

[26] Fischer's *Tagebuch*, pp. 445–8.

[27] Fischer's *Tagebuch*, pp. 510–27.

[28] The Low Moor Ironworks (Messrs. Hird, Dawson and Hardy) had been established in 1788 on the Royds Hall and Wibsey estate. The first two furnaces had been blown in 1791. The firm (a partnership of three families) had both coal and iron ore on its own property. It was stated in *The Irish Industrial Exhibition of 1853* (Dublin, 1854) that 'Low Moor iron is perhaps the best in Great Britain for making wrought iron, such as that for boiler plate and railway axles for which purpose it is in great request' (p. 63). The Mr. Dawson who showed Fischer round the works was Christopher Holdsworth Dawson, son of Joseph Dawson, one of the original partners. A few years later the firm was awarded a medal at the Great Exhibition of 1851 for the high quality of its iron. For these ironworks see W. Cudworth, *Round about Bradford* (1876), pp. 54–67; *Fortunes made in Business* (by various authors), Vol. I, pp. 89–128; and a brochure issued by the company entitled: *A Record of the Origin and Progress of Low Moor Ironworks from 1791 to 1906* (1906).

[29] The Gotts had been concerned with railway developments in Yorkshire. John Gott had been the first chairman of the Leeds, Dewsbury and Manchester Railway Company.

[30] Fischer did not visit Leeds when he came to England in 1851. In that year John Gott was one of the commissioners responsible for the organisation of the Great Exhibition at the Crystal Palace. An obituary of John Gott stated that 'it was not less due to his sound sense of manufacturing and mercantile pursuits that he was appointed one of the Royal Commissioners for the Great Exhibition of 1851' (quoted by C. R. Fay, *Palace of Industry 1851* (1951), p. 39). For John Gott (1791–1867) see *Memoirs of Eminent Men of Leeds* by a Leeds Man (C. S. Spence) (Leeds, 1868), pp. 73–4.

[31] Fischer's *Tagebuch*, p. 86 and pp. 116–127. For the Wedgwoods see S. Shaw, *A History of the Staffordshire Potteries . . .* (Hanley, 1829); L. Jewitt, *The Wedgwoods . . .* (1865); Eliza Meteyard, *The Life*

of *Josiah Wedgwood* (2 Vols., 1865–6); Eliza Meteyard, *A Group of Englishmen, 1795–1815* (1871); Samuel Smiles, *Josiah Wedgwood* (1894); A. H. Church, *Josiah Wedgwood, Master Potter* (1894); K. E. Farrer (ed), *Wedgwood's Letters* (3 vols., 1903–6); E. Hubbard, *Josiah Wedgwood and Sarah* (1906); Josiah C. Wedgwood, *A History of the Wedgwood Family* (1908); Josiah C. Wedgwood, *Staffordshire Pottery and its History* (1913); Julia Wedgwood, *Personal Life of Josiah Wedgwood* (revised by C. H. Herford, 1915); W. Burton, *Josiah Wedgwood and his Pottery* (1922); Ralph M. Moore, 'The Wedgwoods. Ten Generations of Potters' (*Journal of Economic and Business History*, Vol. IV, No. 2, February 1932); E. J. D. Warrillow, *History of Etruria . . .* (1952); Alison Kelly, *The Story of Wedgwood* (1962). Josiah Wedgwood (junior) in evidence before the *Select Committee on the State of Children employed in the Manufactories of the United Kingdom* (1816) stated that he employed 387 persons in his works (p. 60). The younger Josiah Wedgwood was born in 1769 and died in 1843. See also W. Mankowitz, *Wedgwood* (1953).

[32] According to Alison Kelly, *op. cit.*, p. 47 Fischer gave the date of Spengler's invention as 1761. Fischer actually wrote in his *Tagebuch* (p. 122) that Spengler's process was discovered 'about 35 years ago' (i.e. about 1779). Sadler and Green, however, had used this process in the middle of the eighteenth century, some years before the date of Spengler's invention.

[33] See an article in the *Emmenthaler Blatt*, May 29, 1959 (copy in the Fischer archives).

[34] See A. E. Musson and E. Robinson, 'Science and Industry in the late Eighteenth Century' (*Economic History Review*, second series, Vol. XIII, No. 2, 1960, pp. 222–244), 'The early Growth of Steam Power' (*ibid.*, Vol. XI, 1958–9, pp. 418–39), and 'The Origins of Engineering in Lancashire' (*Journal of Economic History*, June 1960, pp. 209–33); A. E. Musson 'An early Engineering Firm. Peel, Williams & Co., of Manchester' (*Business History*, Vol. III, No. 1, pp. 8–18) and W. H. Chaloner, 'John Galloway (1804–94), Engineer of Manchester and his "Reminiscences"' (*Transactions of the Lancashire and Cheshire Antiquarian Society*, Vol. LXIV, 1954, pp. 93–116).

[35] Fischer's *Tagebuch*, pp. 261–89.

[36] Of the firms mentioned Fairbairn and Lillie was the smallest. It later grew to be one of the largest engineering works in the district.

[37] Bodmer's residence in England was interrupted by a visit to the Continent between 1829 and 1833. For J. G. Bodmer see a memoir in the *Minutes of Proceedings of the Institution of Civil Engineers*, Vol. XXVIII, 1868–9, pp. 573–602; an article by K. Karmarsch in the *Allgemeine Deutsche Biographie*, Vol. III, pp. 18–19; a biographical sketch in the *Quarterly Review of Machine Tools and Workshop Practice*, 1895; T. Midgley and L. Hamer, *John George*

Bodmer . . . 1786–1864. Exhibition illustrating his work whilst in Bolton, 1828–43 (Chadwick Museum, Bolton, 1928); H. T. Walker, *John George Bodmer . . .* (MS in possession of the Institution of Civil Engineers); B. Buxbaum, *Johann Georg Bodmer* (Beiträge zur Geschichte der Technik und Industrie, XII, 1922, pp. 128–135); D. Brownlie, 'John George Bodmer' (*Transactions of the Newcomen Society*, Vol. VI, 1925–6, pp. 86–110); H. W. Dickinson, 'Diary of John George Bodmer, 1816–17' (*ibid.*, Vol. X, 1929–30, pp. 102–114); Helen and Paul Schoch-Bodmer, 'Ein Tagebuch von Johann Georg Bodmer . . .' (supplement to the *Vierteljahrsschrift der Naturforschenden Gesellschaft in Zürich*, 1936). Among Bodmer's many inventions the cast toothed wheel and the mechanical chain-grate stoker deserve special mention.

38 Albert Escher (1807–45), then aged 17, was the eldest son of Hans Caspar Escher (1775–1859), partner in the firm of Escher, Wyss & Co., cotton spinners and builders of machinery. It was on a journey that J. C. Fischer and Hans Caspar Escher had made in France together in 1802 that Fischer's attention had first been directed to steel making. For Hans Caspar Escher see F. H. Hoigné, *Gründung und Entwicklung der Spinnerei und Maschinenfabrik Escher, Wyss & Cie, 1805–1859* (Zürich, 1916); Charlotte Peter's essay in the *Schweizer Pioniere der Wirtschaft und Technik,* Vol VI, 1956, pp. 9–30; and a volume issued to mark the 150th anniversary of the firm entitled *150 Jahre Escher Wyss 1805–1955.* For Hans Caspar Escher's diary of a journey to England and Scotland in 1814 see his articles in the *Zürcherische Beiträge zur wissenschaftlichen und geselligen Unterhaltung, 1815.*

39 For Richard Roberts (1789–1864) see Samuel Smiles, *Industrial Biography* (1863), pp. 265–72; H. W. Dickinson, 'Richard Roberts, his life and inventions' (*Transactions of the Newcomen Society*, Vol. XXV, 1945–7, pp. 123–7); and an article in the *Dictionary of National Biography*, Vol. XLVIII, p. 393. Roberts went to Alsace in 1826 to supervise the establishment of André Koechlin's new engineering workshops at Mulhouse. In 1828 he went into partnership with Sharp Brothers. Edward Baines junior described Roberts as 'an extremely ingenious machine maker'. The first patent for the self actor was taken out in 1825 but it was not entirely successful. The second patent was taken out in 1830 and within four years the patentees had made over 500 self actors.

40 In 1808 the value of the patterns for wheels assembled by Peel, Williams & Co., of Manchester, had been estimated at £4,000 so that the value which Richard Ormrod placed upon his collection may not have been an unreasonable one.

41 Fischer's *Tagebuch*, p. 272.

42 For William Fairbairn (1769–1874) see W. Pole (editor), *The Life of William Fairbairn* (1877); Samuel Smiles, *Industrial Biography* (1863), ch 16; and articles in the *Dictionary of National Biography*, Vol. XVIII, pp. 123–5 and the *Minutes of Proceedings of the In-*

stitution of Civil Engineers, Vol. XXXIV, 1874-5, Part 1, pp. 251–64. One of Fairbairn's most important inventions was the rivetting machine.

[43] See Fairbairn's evidence in the *Fifth Report from the Select Committee on Artisans and Machinery* (*Parliamentary Papers,* 1824, Vol. V).

[44] Samuel Smiles, *op cit.,* p. 300.

[45] Fischer's *Tagebuch,* pp. 717–8. Fischer stated that he had visited Manchester in 1827 but no record of this visit has survived. Indeed it may be doubted whether Fischer was in Manchester in that year. His note book (*Schreibkalender*) for 1827 (in the Fischer archives) records visits to Sheffield and Leeds but not to Manchester.

[46] Thomas C. Hewes (1768–1832) was a partner in the firm of Hewes and Wren of Dale Street works, Manchester, which at that time was one of the largest engineering plants in England. For his evidence before the *Select Committee on Artisans and Machinery* see the *Fourth Report,* pp. 340–50.

[47] *Manchester Guardian,* February 11, 1832.

[48] For the early history of steel in England see Charles Sanderson, 'The Manufacture of Steel' (*Journal of the Society of Arts,* 1855, p. 258); W. T. Jeans, *Creators of the Age of Steel* (1884); T. S. Ashton, *Iron and Steel in the Industrial Revolution* (1924); M. W. Flinn and A. Birch, 'The English Steel Industry before 1856 with special Reference to the Development of the Yorkshire Steel Industry' (*Yorkshire Bulletin of Economic and Social Research,* Vol. VI, No. 2, July 1954); and A. Birch, *The Economic History of the British Iron and Steel Industry 1784–1879* (University of Manchester Ph.D. dissertation, 1953). For the cutlery industry see G. I. H. Lloyd, *The Cutlery Trades* (1913). Fischer's friend Hans Casper Escher, who was in England in 1814, had no hesitation in asserting that 'English steel and metal goods are superior to anything that the Swiss can produce'.

[49] For Fischer's visit to Sheffield in September 1814 see his *Tagebuch,* pp. 158–177. Fischer did not give Huntsman's name in full but simply wrote 'H . . n' of 'A'. At this time the firm was run by James and Francis, the two surviving sons of the elder Huntsman who had died in 1776. Le Play, writing in 1846, stated that Huntsman steel was the best in the world. 'The buyer of this article, who pays a higher price for it than other sorts, is not acting merely in the blind spirit of routine, but pays a logical and well deserved homage to all the material and moral qualities of which the true Huntsman mark has been the guarantee for a century' (*Annales des Mines,* 4th series, Vol. IX, p. 266 and Samuel Smiles, *Industrial Biography* (1863), p. 111). For the firm of Huntsman see *A brief History of the Firm of B. Huntsman Ltd., 1742–1930* (1930).

[50] In his journal for 1814 (pp. 158–9) Fischer gave only the initials of the town ('R' for Rotherham) and of the partners of the firm

('W and B' for Walker and Booth) but the names were given in full in a letter to Yeates Brown (October 15, 1814) and in the diary for 1846 (p. 594). The Walker family had made iron and steel since the 1740s. According to Samuel Smiles (*Industrial Biography* (1863), ch. 6) Samuel Walker stole the secret of Huntsman's invention of crucible cast steel. For the history of the firm see John Guest, *Relics and Records of Men and Manufacturers of Rotherham* (1866), pp. 389-91; H. G. Baker, Samuel Walker and his Partners: *the Kimberworth Ironfounders of 1745-1782* (1945) and A. H. John (ed), *Minutes relating to Messrs. Samuel Walker and Co., Rotherham, Ironfounders and Steel Refiners, 1741-1829 and Messrs. Walker, Parker and Co., Lead Manufacturers, 1788-1893* (Council for the Preservation of Business Archives, (1951).

51 M. W. Flinn and Alan Birch, 'The English Steel Industry before 1856 with special Reference to the Development of the Yorkshire Steel Industry' (*Yorkshire Bulletin of Economic and Social Research*, Vol. VI, No. 2, July 1954, p. 171).

52 M. W. Flinn and Alan Birch, *op cit.*, p. 171.

53 For Fischer's visits to the Huntsman family see his *Tagebuch*, p. 441, pp. 533-8, pp. 592-3, p. 605, and p. 726 and his notebook (*Schreibkalender*) for 1827 (Friday, October 5). It may be added that the famous French engineer and sociologist Le Play gave a detailed description of the Sheffield steel industry in the *Annales des Mines*, 1843, p. 583 *et seq.* He wrote that the Sheffield district made more steel than all the rest of Europe put together. In Sheffield 'all the conditions of prosperity were brought together in the highest degree'. Le Play described the Huntsman steelworks which, at the time of his visit, were run by a grandson of the first Benjamin Huntsman.

54 For Fischer and Sanderson Brothers see his *Tagebuch*, pp. 336-7, 440, 442, 528-38, 605-13, and 726-7. The firm was listed at 132 West Street in *White's Gazetteer and Directory of Sheffield* (1852). For a brief history of the firm see T. W. Willis, '150 Years of Progress—Sanderson's 1776-1926' in *The House of Saben*, Vol. II, No. 12, 1926, pp. 24-36.

55 Samuel Smiles, *Industrial Biography* (1863), p. 113.

56 Fischer's accounts of his meetings with members of the firm of Sanderson Brothers are confused. His journal for 1825 refers to a meeting between himself and 'John Sanders' on the Sheffield-Birmingham coach (p. 336) but his journal for 1845 says that he met a 'Mr. Sanderson' on that occasion (p. 538). The journal for 1827 refers to 'Sanderson' on one page (p. 440) but to 'Sanders'—whose works were in West Street—on the next (pp. 441-2). Fischer's note book (*Schreibkalender*) for 1827 refers to 'Sanderson' twice—on Friday, October 5 and on Monday, October 8. The travel journal for 1851 states that 'Charles Sanderson' then owned the West Street foundry. The references to 'Sanders' on p. 336 and on p. 441 of the *Tagebuch* are obviously mistakes for 'Sanderson'.

It is not always clear to which member of the firm Fischer refers. His main contact with the firm was probably John Sanderson (1777-1852). For the closing of the West Street works in 1952 see the article on 'Sanderson break last Link with West Street' in *The House of Saben*, new series, Vol. II, No. 4, pp. 5—8 and a brief note in *The British Steelmaker*, March 1953, p. 125.

[57] See Sir Robert Hadfield, *Faraday and his Metallurgical Researches* . . . (1932).

[58] According to Andrew Ure, *A Dictionary of Arts* . . . (1840), p. 708 'all the best English cast steel is made from Hoop L iron from Dannamora in Sweden'. In the middle of the nineteenth century Sheffield produced about 18,000 tons of steel a year from 120 cementation furnaces and 100 cast steel melting furnaces.

[59] Although Fischer refers to 'Charles Sanderson' it is not certain whether it was old Mr. John or young Mr. Charles whom he visited in his home. The description Fischer gives of a man who had been a semi-invalid for some years would fit John Sanderson (who died in the following year) much better than Charles Sanderson. It may be added that Charles Sanderson (1803–73) was the second son of John Sanderson. He had a considerable knowledge of metallurgy and several patents concerning the making of steel are attributed to him.

[60] For Fischer and Cammell see Fischer's *Tagebuch*, pp. 589-92, 684-92, 705, and 723-8. For an account of Cammell's career see *Cammell Laird & Co. Ltd.: Steelmakers, Engineers, Repairers* (Sheffield and Birkenhead, 1919); a memoir in the *Minutes of Proceedings of the Institution of Civil Engineers*, Vol. LVI, 1878-9, pp. 288-9; J. H. Stainton, *The Making of Sheffield, 1865-1914* (1924), p. 249; W. Odom, *Hallamshire Worthies* (1926), pp. 164-5 and an obituary in *Newspaper Cuttings relating to Sheffield* (Sheffield Reference Library), Vol. 13, p. 113. For the main products made by the firm see *Drawings of Patent Buffers, Railway Springs, Ordnance Forgings in Cast Steel manufactured by Charles Cammell & Co. Ltd. Cyclops Steel and Iron Works* (Sheffield, 1864). Charles Cammell was born in Hull in 1810 and died in London in 1879.

[61] On seeing the print of Fischer's works Cammell said: 'That's where I would like to live. I won't stay in London. The bustle is too great—and nothing but wear and tear'.

[62] At this time the firm had three partners—Cammell, Johnson, and a German named Gosse (Cammell's brother-in-law). For social conditions in Sheffield in 1850 see S. Pollard, *A History of Labour in Sheffield* (1959), pp. 3-49.

[63] See Fischer's *Tagebuch*, p. 531, pp. 533-4, pp. 608-10, p. 724 and pp. 728-9. In the diaries for 1845 and 1846 the name is given as 'Messrs. T . . . & S . . .' For the firm of Thomas Turton & Sons see J. H. Stainton, *The Making of Sheffield, 1865-1914* (1924) and an obituary of T. B. Turton in *Newspaper Cuttings relating to Sheffield* (Sheffield Reference Library), Vol. 13, p. 46. The Park

and Spring Works (Russell Street) were at Bow Spring while the Sheaf Works were on the River Don. Both plants were listed in *White's Gazetteer and Directory of Sheffield for 1852*.

[64] Fischer wrote 'Bramale' instead of 'Bramall' when he first mentioned the firm. It is not clear to which Bramall he refers. The 'White House' branch of the family consisted of Thomas Bramall, the founder of the firm in the eighteenth century, his sons (i) Samuel who was born in about 1750, and (ii) Daniel who was born in about 1765, and also Samuel's son (Samuel junior who was born in about 1780). Another branch of the family was that of James Bramall who, with his partner Spear, operated a file manufactory in Gibraltar Street, Sheffield. It may be mentioned that White House lane in which the 'White House' cutlery works were situated was later named Bramall Lane. I am indebted for this information to Mr. John Bebbington, the City Librarian of Sheffield.

[65] Fischer's *Tagebuch*, 1814, pp. 170–2. The workshops of David Mathis were at Ober Oenz in the canton of Bern.

[66] For Fischer's visits to Ebenezer Rhodes (1762–1839) see his *Tagebuch*, pp. 321, 325, 328, 337 and 343. *Wardle and Bentham's Commercial Directory for 1814–15* lists the firm of Rhodes, Champion & Son of Wicker while the *Sheffield Directory* for 1825 lists Ebenezer Rhodes & Co. of 10 The Wicker. For Ebenezer Rhodes see John Holland, 'Memoir of Ebenezer Rhodes' (*The Reliquary*, January 1863, pp. 121–134). Rhodes was the author of *Peak Scenery*—the first volume appearing in 1817—and of a brochure entitled *Essay on the Manufacture, Choice, and Management of a Razor* (1809). Rhodes extended his activities to the engraving of steel plates in 1826 and went bankrupt in the following year.

[67] For Joseph Rodgers & Sons see Fischer's *Tagebuch*, pp. 588, 595, 607, 725 and 730. The address of the firm was 6 Norfolk Street (*Wardle and Bentham's Commercial Directory for 1814–15*). There are brief references to the history of the firm in two souvenir brochures—(i) *Joseph Rodgers & Sons, Ltd. Under five Sovereigns* (1918); (ii) *Joseph Rodgers & Sons, Ltd. A Royal Record: the brief History of a famous Sheffield House* (1930).

[68] For the industrial history of the Midlands see W. H. B. Court, *The Rise of the Midland Industries 1600–1838* (1938) and G. C. Allen, *The Industrial Development of Birmingham and the Black Country 1860–1927* (1929).

[69] Fischer's *Tagebuch*, pp. 89–107.

[70] For Boulton and Watt see the article on Watt in the *Encyclopaedia Britannica*, seventh edition, 1842, Vol. xxi, pp. 815–20; J. P. Muirhead, *The Origin and Progress of the Mechanical Inventions of James Watt* (three volumes, 1854); Samuel Smiles, *The Lives of Boulton and Watt* (first edition 1865, second edition 1866); J. P. Muirhead, *Correspondence of the late James Watt . . .* (1846); J. P. Muirhead, *Life of James Watt and Selections from his Correspondence* (1859); T. E. Pemberton, 'James Watt of Soho and

Heathfield' in *Annals of Industry and Genius* (Birmingham, 1905); H. W. Dickinson and Rhys Jenkins, *James Watt and the Steam Engine* (1927); Erich Roll, *An early Experiment in Industrial Organization* (1930); S. Timmins, 'James Watt' in the *Transactions of the Birmingham and Midland Institute*, Vol. III for 1872 (printed 1873); S. Timmins, 'Matthew Boulton' in the *Transactions of the Birmingham and Midland Institute*, Vol. II (archeological section, 1871); H. W. Dickinson, *Matthew Boulton* (1937); A. E. Musson and E. Robinson, 'The early Growth of Steam Power' in the *Economic History Review*, second series, Vol. XI, No. 3, April 1959, pp. 418–39.

71 Boulton and Fothergill made 'steel jewellery' (i.e. buckles, watch chains, buttons etc.) and 'Sheffield plate' (i.e. copperware covered with a thin layer of silver). For Boulton and Fothergill see E. Robinson, 'Eighteenth Century Commerce and Fashion: Matthew Boulton's Marketing Techniques' in the *Economic History Review*, second series, Vol. XVI, No. 1, August 1963, pp. 39–60.

72 For William Murdock see S. Timmins, *William Murdock* (1864); A. Murdock, *Light without Wick* (1892); and B. Taylor, *William Murdock* (1952). Fischer wrote to Murdock on February 20, 1816: 'Though the time was so very short during which I had the advantage of your society and profit of your conversation, yet it was long enough to establish and consolidate with me that high esteem I always think myself owing to men, who not only excel in talents and skill, but also who are so happy as to become benefactors of mankind in the application of them'.

73 Joshua Field wrote in 1821: 'The Soho works are never shown, no person can obtain leave or an order to see them, but without professing to show them, they can be seen'. For Field's visit to Soho see J. W. Hall, 'Joshua Field's Diary of Tour in 1821 through the Midlands' (*Transactions of the Newcomen Society*, Vol. VI, 1925–6, pp. 6–12).

74 For the Soho foundry see W. K. V. Gale, *Soho Foundry* (1946) and 'Soho Foundry—Some Facts and Fancies' (*Transactions of the Newcomen Society*, Vol. xxxiv, 1961–2, pp. 73–87). A letter from J. C. Fischer to James Watt junior of March 5, 1815 thanking Watt for the civilities shown to him on his visit to Soho in the previous year is in the Boulton and Watt collection in the Birmingham Public Library.

75 Fischer's *Tagebuch*, 1814, p. 184.

76 Fischer to James Watt junior, March 6, 1815 (in the Boulton and Watt collection in the Birmingham Public Library).

77 For John Wilkinson see W. H. Chaloner, *People and Industries* (1963), pp. 21–30. For an account of the Bradley ironworks in 1815 see the extract from Thomas Butler's journal in Alan Birch, 'The Midlands Iron Industry during the Napoleonic Wars' (*Edgar Allan News*, August—September 1952).

78 Samuel Fereday (1758–1839) began as a coal heaver. At one time

he and his partners controlled a dozen blast furnaces. It was said that he issued over two million trade tokens. He went bankrupt in 1816 partly because he failed to obtain a French import licence to send 200 miles of water pipes to Paris. After failing to get his bankruptcy certificate in 1821 he went to France where, according to an English newspaper, he 'projected a manufacture of plate iron in Paris which has been taken up warmly by the French' (Information kindly supplied by Mr. R. P. Fereday). Fischer spelt the name 'Ferryday' (*Tagebuch*, 1814, p. 101).

[79] For another account of these ironworks (written a year later) see Alan Birch, *op cit*. See also T. M. Hoskinson, 'The Earl of Dudley's Level New Furnaces' in the *Transactions of the Newcomen Society*, Vol. XXVII, 1951, 1952 and 1952–3. The rolling mill, puddling furnaces, castings, floor plates, and other effects of these ironworks were sold by auction by Mr. Moreton on November 18, 1822. A broadsheet advertisement of the sale is preserved in the Dudley Public Library.

[80] Joseph Priestley (junior) was one of the sons of Dr. Joseph Priestley (1733–1804), the famous scientist and republican, who had emigrated to the United States (1794) where he had died. Joseph Priestley (junior) came to England in 1812 and was living near Birmingham at the time of Fischer's visit in 1814. He was engaged in business—probably the iron trade—near Dudley.

[81] For Fischer's visit to Birmingham in 1825 see his *Tagebuch*, pp. 237–257 (June 1825) and pp. 335–341 (July 1825).

[82] Matthias Attwood, an ironmaster and steel manufacturer, went into partnership with Isaac Spooner in 1791 to establish the 'Birmingham Bank' (Spooner, Attwood & Co.). The Attwood to whom Fischer referred was George (the eldest son of Matthias) who ran the bank and the steelworks. His brother Thomas (1783–1856) was Member of Parliament for Birmingham and a leading Chartist. Charles, another brother, was a partner in the Weardale Iron and Coal Company and founder of the Northern Political Union.

[83] The Adelphi Steel Works, which were situated in Broad Street.

[84] Fischer stated that he met a 'Mr. Alcock' of Summer Hill. There is no record of any Birmingham jeweller of that name. But the name of Henry Adcock—described as a 'jeweller and gilt toymaker and button and bead manufacturer'—appears in R. Wrightson, *Triennial Directory of Birmingham*, 1825, p. 2. Adcock's address was Summer Hill Terrace and he also had an office in London at 28 Kirby Street, Hatton Garden, London.

[85] Fischer stated that these ironworks were situated on a branch of the Birmingham and Wolverhampton Canal. They may have been those owned by the Lea Brook Furnace Company. Mr. J. F. Ede, author of a *History of Wednesbury* (1962) suggests that the works described by Fischer may have been in West Bromwich which was well known as an important centre for the production of iron hollow ware.

86 Fischer to Murdock, February 20, 1816. Fischer stated that nail making 'without anvil and hammer' was being introduced into Austria and Switzerland. In a letter to George A. Lee (June 16, 1817) Fischer stated that his neighbour J. G. Neher of Laufen (Rhine Falls) was making nails by mechanical means. See also J. C. Fischer's letter to G. M. Stierlin, February 22, 1816, reprinted by Karl Schib in *Nachrichten aus der Eisenbibliothek der Georg Fischer Aktiengesellschaft*, December 1957, No. 12, pp. 47–48. For mechanical nailmaking in England see Louis Rackebrandt, *Abhandlung und Beschreibung der englischen Nagelmaschine* (Quedlinburg and Leipzig, 1839).

87 Fischer's *Tagebuch*, pp. 709–717.

88 For Fischer's visit to Liverpool see his *Tagebuch*, pp. 596–604. The firm of Betteley and Roberts which Fischer visited had two addresses at this time: East Side, Union Dock and 58 Waterloo Road.

89 Fischer's *Tagebuch*, pp. 603-4.

CHAPTER IV

The Rise of the Firm of Georg Fischer[1]

1. GEORG FISCHER II AND HIS FITTINGS

When Johann Conrad Fischer died the steel industry was on the eve of a new era. Almost exactly a year after Fischer's death Henry Bessemer took out a patent for his converter. This invention—and the later Siemens-Martin open-hearth furnace and the Gilchrist Thomas process—revolutionised the steel industry.[2] Instead of being a semi-precious metal—an expensive raw material used in small quantities by cutlers, watchmakers, gunsmiths and mints—steel came to be made in large quantities and to replace iron for many purposes. The new inventions enabled those who made steel to meet the heavy demands for this product in the second half of the nineteenth century. As the industrialisation of Europe gathered momentum more machines were needed. As more and more railways and tramways were built more iron and steel was needed for the rails and the locomotives. The introduction of more steamship services stimulated the demand for steel plates and for marine engines. As living standards rose more towns had their waterworks, gasworks, and electrical undertakings so that orders flowed to firms able to supply pipes, wire, and 'fittings'. As the armies and navies of the world grew so the armament manufacturers used more and more steel. It was because they were able to adapt themselves to the needs of the new age of steel that J. C. Fischer's grandson and great-grandson were able to transform a tiny workshop into a large modern steel and engineering plant.

J. C. Fischer left his works at Mühlental—the foundry, the smithy and the file manufactory—to his son Georg Fischer (1804–88) who is known as Georg Fischer I to distinguish him from his son Georg Fischer II (1834–87) and grandson Georg Fischer III (1864–1925). Georg Fischer I had been living at Hainfeld in Austria for thirty years. Here his father had purchased a file factory in 1826. These works had been burned down in 1827 but J. C. Fischer had lost no time in rebuilding them. The new plant soon produced crucible cast steel ingots of high quality (by the process invented by J. C. Fischer early in the century) as well as a variety of steel products such as hammers, rollers, saws, and files.

In 1833 Georg Fischer I became the owner of these works and he also established a new spindle factory at Traisen which he later transferred to his brother Berthold. Eventually George Fischer I added steel castings—invented by his father in 1845—to the other steel products which he made at Hainfeld.

By 1854 Georg Fischer I had been living for so long in Austria that he was not prepared to return to Switzerland to run the tiny plant which he had inherited from his father. He sent his son Georg Fischer II to manage the Mühlental works in the autumn of 1856. Georg Fischer II, then only 22 years of age, was no stranger to Schaffhausen since (owing to the early death of his mother) he had been brought up in the home of his grandparents. J. C. Fischer and Dr. Eduard Fischer had supervised his early practical training in the Mühlental plant. In 1850 Georg Fischer II had returned to Austria to study—as his father had done—at the Vienna Polytechnic. He had then been put in charge of his father's plant at Hainfeld where 150 workers were employed. The date of his move to Schaffhausen may have been connected with a desire to avoid military service in Austria.[3] It was no easy matter for the young man to revive his grandfather's business. He seems to have received little financial help from his father and he found it difficult to recruit skilled labour and to recapture lost markets.

Output was resumed at Mühlental at a time when many Swiss industries were expanding. The recent abolition of internal customs dues coupled with the building of a railway network stimulated trade between the various Swiss cantons. In 1857 Schaffhausen was linked by rail with Zürich and the drawbacks of an isolated location on the frontier were overcome. Georg Fischer II was now able to market his products more easily than had been possible in his grandfather's day. On the other hand the railways and the relatively low Swiss import duties enabled foreign —particularly German—steel firms to send more of their products to Switzerland than before. Consequently Georg Fischer II, like many other Swiss makers of steel goods, tended to concentrate his output on specialised and high quality products.

At first steel files were by far the most important product made at the Mühlental works. But Georg Fischer's display at the Berne industrial exhibition of 1857 showed that the firm was making a fairly wide range of other steel products as well. The report on the exhibition praised the high quality of his files, cast steel ingots, and machine parts. There was no mention of malleable cast iron products in this report but it was stated that Georg Fischer II was extending the Mühlental plant and would soon be doubling the number of workers employed from 40 to 80. This proved to be a somewhat optimistic forecast since Georg Fischer II's labour force actually only rose from 42 to 67 between 1863 and 1871.

In 1859[4] Georg Fischer II began to manufacture malleable cast iron products in the Mühlental plant[5] and in 1861 he notified the local commercial registry that the firm should now be described as one which produced 'malleable cast iron, cast steel and files.' The Georg Fischer works were the first to make malleable cast iron in Switzerland.[6]

Georg Fischer II used the process invented by his grandfather in August 1827 and patented in Austria in the following year. Malleable cast iron had been produced in Austria first by Wilhelm von Brévillier (1829–43) and then by Berthold Fischer of Traisen. In 1860 a description of the malleable cast iron process, as practiced by Georg Fischer II at Mühlental, appeared in the *Polytechnisches Journal*. The author stated that 'really first class malleable cast iron' was being made at Mühlental. About 20 tons of this iron was produced in a year, the average price charged being 30 kreuzer per lb at the works.

The introduction of the production of malleable cast iron necessitated a substantial extension of the plant. A steam boiler and a turbine replaced the water wheel (1868). The old foundry was rebuilt and new furnaces were installed. More workers had to be engaged. Many of them came from the villages of Merishausen and Hemmenthal. In 1868 Georg Fischer II erected his first hostel to provide accommodation for his workers. There is a photograph, taken in 1895, which shows several workers who were with Georg Fischer II in his early days and were still serving the firm. The most senior of them was the veteran file cutter Johannes Germann who did not retire until he reached the age of 75. The others included Ulrich Werner (a master founder), Bührer (a crucible maker), Blum (furnace fireman), Gantert (a maintenance man), Baumer (locksmith), Pante (a polisher), and Krug (who prepared the sand for the moulds). The preparations which Georg Fischer II made in 1868 to increase his labour force came just in time for the boom in iron and steel that followed the Franco-Prussian war. In 1871 Georg Fischer II had 141 men on his books while in the following year 210 were employed. But the slump which began in 1873 necessitated a quick reduction to 153 workers.

In 1864, a year after he had married Emma Pfister, Georg Fischer II purchased the three Mühlental works from his father. At about the same time he began to make 'tube fittings', for which the firm eventually became world famous. In the early 1860s many gasworks and waterworks were being established in Switzerland. There was an increased demand for tube fittings to join lengths of iron piping together either in a straight line or at an angle. At first such fittings were made of puddled wrought iron and were hammered and pressed into shape. The American Stanley G. Flagg had realised that malleable cast iron fittings would be just as efficient as wrought iron fittings and would be cheaper. He had produced malleable cast iron fittings at Philadelphia in 1854 and some ten years later Georg Fischer II began to make them in Switzerland. Georg Fischer II was the first to make these fittings on the Continent. By putting his grandfather's invention of malleable cast iron to a new use he had laid the foundations of the future growth of the firm.

Georg Fischer II's catalogue for 1868 offered 91 different malleable cast iron fittings for sale. A group of English artisans who visited the Paris Universal Exhibition of 1867 reported that Georg Fischer II had shown 'a good assortment of malleable fittings' which were 'quite new in the gas tube and fitting trade.' They were said to be 'very serviceable' and were cheaper than rival products. Georg Fischer II's catalogue for 1878 listed 387 different sorts of malleable cast iron fittings—both polished and galvanised—suitable for joining together gas pipes, water pipes, and steam boiler tubes. The fact that prices were quoted in roubles as well as in francs shows that Georg Fischer was aiming at an international market.

The many samples of his files, steel castings, tube fittings and other malleable cast iron products which Georg Fischer II displayed at the Zürich industrial exhibition of 1883 showed what remarkable progress his firm had made since he had become its owner 19 years previously. Though files and fittings were the most important products of the Mühlental plant Georg Fischer II was also making steel castings in sand moulds, which had been invented in the 1840s by Jacob Mayer in Germany and by J. C. Fischer in Switzerland. The plans which Georg Fischer II was making for the future included the manufacture of really large steel castings and the establishment of a branch factory in Germany to increase his output of fittings. But he died suddenly in August 1887 at the age of 53. His life's work had been to turn his grandfather's little workshop into a well equipped modern steel plant employing 183 men. Many years later his daughter Emma recalled that in his early days her father had overcome many difficulties and misfortunes such as the loss by fire in 1868 of a newly opened fittings workshop and model room. Stamm wrote that 'by making fittings Georg Fischer II had embarked upon a very promising field of industrial activity. His malleable cast iron fittings found a ready sale both at home and abroad.' Georg Fischer II was 'a man of highest intelligence and principles, a man of culture who had an enormous capacity for hard work.' He left his son an efficiently run business and 'a respectable fortune.'

2. GEORG FISHER III: STEEL CASTINGS AND ELECTRIC FURNACES

On the unexpected death of Georg Fischer II his son Georg Fischer III gave up his studies in Dresden and returned to Schaffhausen. Although only 23 years of age he took charge of the family business which now consisted of four plants—the file manufactory, the malleable cast iron works, the fittings plant, and the plant in which small crucible steel castings were made. He promptly carried out his father's plans for the extension of the steelworks. He decided to give up the manufacture of files to make room for an expansion of the output of other products such as fittings and crucible steel castings. Although Fischer steel files had an excellent reputation he realised that the challenge of competition from cheap German and Swedish imitations would be increasingly difficult to meet in the future. In 1888, therefore, he gave up the manufacture of files and set up a new foundry (two cupola furnaces) to produce fittings and a new screw cutting plant. These new works were constructed in accordance with specifications drawn up by his father.

At the same time Georg Fischer III also expanded his output of steel castings to meet the ever growing demands for such products from railway companies, tramway undertakings, and the rapidly growing Swiss and German electrical industries. Within a year or two Georg Fischer III was casting large steel wheels for locomotives and electrical installations. For a time he still used a process that was not very different from that invented by J. C. Fischer in 1845. But in 1890 a Siemens-Martin open-hearth furnace replaced the crucibles of the original Fischer technique. This enabled Georg Fischer III to make castings which were much bigger than the horse shoes produced by his great grandfather.

Meanwhile the firm's output of fittings and malleable cast iron continued to increase. Gas was now being used for cooking as well as for lighting and new fittings were needed for gas stoves. Georg Fischer III extended his foundry plant to make room for two new copula furnaces and a furnace capable of holding ten

FOUNDRY OF THE BUTTERLEY IRONWORKS AT ALFRETON, DERBYSHIRE
Source: W. H. Chaloner and A. E. Musson,
A Visual History of Modern Britain—Industry and Technology (Vista Books, 1963)

THE MIDDLETON COLLIERY RAILWAY NEAR LEEDS
Source: C. F. Dendy Marshall,
A History of British Railways down to the Year 1830 (1930)
By courtesy of the Clarendon Press

J. C. FISCHER—1830
By courtesy of Georg Fischer A. G., Schaffhausen

J. C. FISCHER'S SIGNATURE AND SEAL
By courtesy of Georg Fischer A. G., Schaffhausen

crucibles. At the Geneva industrial exhibition of 1896 Georg Fischer III showed numerous samples of his products made from both malleable cast iron and cast steel. By this time his assets amounted to nearly 3·5 million francs and he was employing 550 workers. He was well served by the senior members of his staff including Tague (the business manager), Buchmann (the plant supervisor), Bucher (the accountant), Meier (the head traveller), Schneckenburger (the senior technician) and the veteran foreman Germann.

In the autumn of 1895 the expansion of the firm of Georg Fischer was carried a stage further by the opening of a new plant for the production of fittings. Although only 20 kilometres away from Schaffhausen these works were in Baden. Georg Fischer III purchased 70,000 square metres of land and the first buildings—grouped round the foundry—were built close to the railway station at Singen am Hohentwiel. Before long over 200 men were employed in the new plant and it was soon necessary to erect houses for the workers. The Fischer collection of some 2,000 patterns was transferred to Singen.[7]

In a letter to a friend Georg Fischer III explained why he had opened a new plant on the other side of the German-Swiss frontier. He wrote that 'owing to the growth of competition, many imitations of Fischer fittings have appeared on the market, particularly in Germany. These fittings are certainly no better than ours but they are cheaper. We have had to do something to meet this threat to our sales in Germany. On the one hand the lack of space at Mühlental would make it very difficult for us to extend our works there. On the other hand the Reich's import duties hamper our exports to Germany. My late father had considered the possibility of establishing a branch factory in Germany for the manufacture of fittings. Owing to his unexpected death he had not been able to put his idea into practice and I have now taken up the plant again.'[8]

In the spring of 1896—shortly after the opening of the Singen steelworks—the need to raise new capital for still further expansion made it necessary for Georg Fischer III to turn his family firm into a joint stock company[9] but he—and his old colleagues Tague, Buckmann and Schneckenburger—continued to run the firm for a time.[10] In its early years the new company flourished. There were ample opportunities in those days for selling steel castings—despite the fierce competition from powerful rivals such as Krupp of Essen—as well as fittings and malleable cast iron products. The boom in the electrical industry on the Continent

89

—particularly in Germany—led to an increased demand for steel castings of various kinds.

Within a year of the establishment of the company the directors decided that they would have to double the capacity of both their plants. Owing to the foresight of Georg Fischer III ample space was available at Singen for this purpose. In the narrow Mühlental, however, land for new works was much more difficult to secure. The directors discussed various possible solutions of the problem, including a plan for the establishment of a new foundry in the parish of Berlingen on the Basel-Schaffhausen railway. Although a piece of land was purchased at Berlingen it was eventually decided that the new plants should be built at Mühlental. They were erected in 1898 and 1899 and included a building to hold a Bessemer converter. After 1899 the Fischer works turned out Siemens-Martin steel, Bessemer steel, and crucible cast steel, but in 1902 the making of crucible cast steel came to an end exactly a hundred years after a method of making steel as good as that of Huntsman had been invented by J. C. Fischer. Owing to the continued expansion of output it was decided in 1900 to increase the share capital from 3 million francs to 4·5 million francs.

In 1902 Georg Fischer III could look back with some satisfaction on his achievements in the twenty years that had elapsed since he had assumed responsibility for the running of the Fischer steelworks. He had greatly expanded the Mühlental plant and he had successfully established a flourishing branch factory at Singen. He had substantially increased the output of fittings and had installed both Siemens-Martin and Bessemer furnaces to enable larger steel castings to be made. When the financial strain of continual growth proved to be too great for his own resources he had turned the family firm into a joint stock company, and under his direction the company had increased its assets from nearly 3·5 million francs (1896) to 9·2 million francs (1900) and its output of steel products from 1·7 million kilogrammes to 7 million kilogrammes.

Then came the depression of 1902–4.[11] On the Continent, particularly in Germany, the sudden recession in the electrical and machine building industries was a severe blow to the firm of Fischer. A contemporary observer remarked that over-optimism in the electrical industry led to disaster. 'There is a tendency even for well established branches of manufacture with long experience to indulge in over-production. It is, therefore, understandable that the electrical industry in the first flush of its youth should throw prudence to the wind in expanding its productive capacity. The output of the big companies was inflated to such an extent that one might think that each of them was hoping to provide the whole world with electricity. And when these concerns had exhausted their own credit they established a number of subsidiaries as a means of raising yet more money for themselves. Finally they started to accept orders on which no profit could possibly be made. Losses were indeed inevitable.'[12]

There was also a decline in Fischer's sales overseas. The depression in these markets was—at any rate partly—due to the Boer war and the Boxer rising. There was a serious fall in the prices of steel castings and fittings. Before long the output of the Fischer plants was only one third of the capacity of the steelworks. In two years the reserve fund was exhausted and a trading loss of 750,000 francs had been incurred. These losses made a radical financial reconstruction imperative. A quarter of the firm's capital (1,250,000 francs) was written off and new preference shares were issued to the same amount. The shareholders elected a new board of directors early in 1901 and on April 1 of that year Ernst Homberger took charge of the company's affairs. He saw the firm through the dark days of the crisis and presided over its fortunes for many years afterwards.

So J. C. Fischer's great-grandson gave up the control of the firm that had been associated with his family for a century. A hundred years previously Johann Conrad Fischer had set up his little workshop at Mühlental. Now one of his descendants left the great steelworks that had been built up after the death of J. C. Fischer by Georg Fischer II and Georg Fischer III.

But this was not the end of Georg Fischer III's career. In association with Dr. Berthold Schudel[13] he devoted his abundant energies to the solution of problems connected with making steel in an electric furnace. Before long he had built an experimental station on the Geissberg near Schaffhausen where he installed a Héroult-Lindenberg electric furnace.[14] This little furnace was fired for the first time on October 24th 1907. A small steelworks developed from this research station and in due course a larger electric furnace came into operation (1910).[15] The steelworks were soon turned into a joint stock company. Then Georg Fischer III set up another small steelworks—with two electric furnaces[16]—at Giubiasco near Bellinzano in the canton of Ticino, which was operated by a subsidiary company called the St. Gotthard Electric Company.[17]

During the first World War Ernst Homberger and his colleagues realised that the future of high quality steel production lay with the new electric furnace and not with Bessemer or Siemens-Martin furnaces. And they turned to the pilot they had dropped in 1902. Georg Fischer III was now one of the leading Swiss experts on the electric furnace and he placed the results of years of research at the disposal of his old firm. In 1917 the Georg Fischer Company of Schaffhausen acquired a controlling interest in Georg Fischer III's two little steel works at Geissberg and Giubiasco. The plants themselves were of little significance but the technical knowledge on steelmaking by the electric furnace was an invaluable acquisition. The success of the Schaffhausen steelworks after the first World War was in no small measure due to the scientific achievements of Georg Fischer III.

Few families can have made so considerable a contribution to the science of metallurgy—and particularly the production of iron and steel—as the Fischers of Schaffhausen. Members of this family were responsible for the production of crucible cast steel, malleable cast iron, steel alloys, steel castings, fittings, and the electric steel furnace. Many of their processes were not original inventions. The Huntsman and Marshall families had made crucible cast steel in Sheffield long before J. C. Fischer invented his own process at a time when English steel was not available on the Continent. Malleable cast iron was made in England before J. C. Fischer made it at his son's plant in Austria. Jacob Mayer made steel castings a year or two before J. C. Fischer made them. Steel fittings were an American invention and the electric furnace on which Georg Fischer III experimented was a French invention. The Fischer family was important because its members spread the knowledge of metallurgical discoveries in relatively underdeveloped industrial regions on the Continent. The high quality of their steel products enabled the Fischers to challenge great rivals such as Huntsman, Krupp, and Mayer. They played a significant rôle in the industrial development of Switzerland and, in particular, of their home town of Schaffhausen.

---

[1] Ernst Ackermann and Walther Meier, *Dreissig Jahre Aktiengesellschaft der Eisen-und Stahlwerke vormals Georg Fischer, Schaffhausen, 1896–1926* (1926); F. Aschinger (ed). *Hundertfünfzig Jahre Georg Fischer Werke 1802–1952* (1952); Karl Schib, *Geschichte der Stadt Schaffhausen 1045–1945* (1946) (see appendix on the Georg Fischer Steelworks); and A. Stamm, *Georg Fischer Werksentwicklung von der Kupferschmiede zum Grossbetrieb* (typescript in the Fischer archives).

[2] For Henry Bessemer see W. H. Chaloner, *People and Industries* (1963), pp. 74–85; Alan Birch 'The early Development of Bessemer

Steel' (*Edgar Allen News*, Sheffield, Vol. XXXII, February & March 1953, pp. 41–2 and 64–5); 'Henry Bessemer and the Steel Revolution' (*Nachrichten aus der Eisen-Bibliothek der Georg Fischer Aktiengesellschaft*, December 1963 and June 1964). For Émile Martin see André Thuillier, *Émile Martin* (Nevers, 1964).

3 On November 5th, 1855 Georg Fischer I applied to the Schaff-hausen authorities for the recognition of his son's right to be regarded as a citizen of Schaffhausen and therefore not liable to Austrian military service. See the letters of Georg Fischer I in the *Ausgangsbuch* in the Museum zu Allerheiligen (Schaffhausen). This correspondence was not used by the author of *Hundert-fünfzig Jahre Georg Fischer Werke 1802–1952* (1952). It may be added that Seraphine (sister of Georg Fischer II) acted as her brother's housekeeper until his marriage to Emma Pfister of Schaff-hausen. Seraphine Fischer married Dr. Sigmund Schudel.

4 It is stated by H. Pfister in 'Entwicklung der Industrie der Stadt Schaffhausen' (*in Festschrift der Stadt Schaffhausen zur Bundesfeier*, 1901), that Georg Fischer II began to manufacture malleable cast iron products in the Mühlental works immediately after his grand-father's death. This is incorrect.

5 From the correspondence of his father Georg Fischer I it is clear that the plan to establish a plant to make malleable cast iron products had been considered as early as 1856. See Karl Schib 'Gies-sereigeschichtliches aus dem Kanton Schaffhausen' in Hans Boesch and Karl Schib, *Beiträge zur Geschichte der schweizerischen Eisengiessereien*, (1960) pp. 182–3.

6 The documents concerning the early manufacture of malleable cast iron products and fittings by Georg Fischer II have been col-lected by Walter Liechti. See the collection of documents in the Georg Fischer archives entitled *Kurzbericht und Belege unserer Nachforschungen über den Beginn der Temperguss- und Fitting-fabrikation bei Georg Fischer I und II im Mühlental Schaffhausen*.

7 After 1896 new patterns were made in duplicate—one copy for Mühlental and one for Singen—in a new workshop established in Schaffhausen in the Frauengasse.

8 Quoted by F. Aschinger (ed), *Hundertfünfzig Jahre Georg Fischer Werke, 1802-1952* (1952), p. 50.

9 *Aktiengesellschaft der Eisen- und Stahlwerke von Georg Fischer.*

10 L. Erzinger was elected chairman of the board of directors in 1896 and B. A. von Ziegler was elected vice-chairman.

11 For a brief account of the depression of 1902–4 see W. J. Ashley, *The Progress of the German Working Classes in the last Quarter of a Century* (1904) pp. 142–153.

12 Quoted in *Dreissig Jahre Aktiengesellschaft der Eisen- und Stahlwerke vormals Georg Fischer Schaffhausen* (1926), p. 38.

13 Dr. Berthold Schudel was the son of Dr. Sigmund Schudel-Fischer who had been managing director and part owner of the Fischer steelworks at Traisen in Austria (1879–94). These works had been

founded by Georg Fischer I of Hainfeld and had been operated first by him and later by his younger brother Berthold.

14 This was a one-phase alternating current electric furnace. Paul Héroult (1863-1914) was one of the pioneers of the electric steel furnace. The first electric furnace appears to have been that invented by William Siemens as early as 1879. In the early 20th century various types of electric furnaces were built on the Continent. For example those of Kjellin of Sweden, Stassano of Italy and Héroult of France. See Sir John Clapham, *Economic History of Modern Britain*, Vol. 3 (1951) pp. 149–150.

15 This was a 2 ton three-phase current Héroult electric steel furnace.

16 This was a 5 ton alternating current electric steel furnace.

17 For Georg Fischer III's steelworks at Giubiasco see Hans Boesch. 'Fonderie nel Cantone Ticino' in H. Boesch and Karl Schib, *Beiträge zur Geschichte der schweizerischen Eisengiessereien* (Schaffhausen, 1960), p. 269 with an illustration on p. 263. In 1920 the steel output of this plan was 4·3 million kgm.

APPENDIX I

Documents

1. AN EARLY NEWSPAPER ACCOUNT OF FISCHER'S CAST STEEL PROCESS[1]

In the last twenty years significant advances have been made in the iron foundries owing to the efforts of men with experience in this industry. Iron and steel have been produced more efficiently and more cheaply partly by introducing better smelting processes (based upon correct chemical principles) and partly by using improved mechanical devices and securing a stronger blast of air. The result has been that the technique of iron and steel production has been raised to a higher level than ever before. But one aspect of the refining of this useful metal—the making of cast steel in sealed crucibles—has, so far as the general public is aware, been virtually confined to England where Huntsman earned a deservedly high reputation for the excellent quality of his steel.

It is true that in France in the Year VI M. Clouet made known a process by which iron bars could be melted and turned into steel of the required hardness and strength. However much one may honour the inventor of this excellent process the fact remains that no one appears to have used it to make steel on a large scale. According to Herr Fischer those who have used M. Clouet's method have come to the conclusion that it is an interesting laboratory experiment but not a practical industrial process.

It will therefore be of interest not only to experienced steelworkers but also to the general public to know that, after four years of intensive research, Herr Johann Conrad Fischer has succeeded in making genuine cast steel. Fischer is a young man who holds the office of director of the iron mines in the Canton of Schaffhausen. He is a man of great ability with a profound knowledge of physics and chemistry. His experiments have been numerous and have been conducted on a large scale. Fischer's cast steel is equal to that produced in England from every point of view—hardness, durability, and uniformity of grain.

Fischer's process has been described to me by a careful and experienced observer. It appears that Fischer, like Clouet, makes cast steel by melting bar iron in sealed crucibles. But he employs a quite different technique from that recommended by Clouet. The use of this technique reduces the time and labour involved and—other things being equal—a greater quantity of steel is produced at each melting. One aspect of Fischer's method is of particular interest from both a metallurgical and a chemical point of view. To make cast steel Fischer fills his crucibles with bars of iron and not with pieces of blister steel previously made by the cementation process.

One of the most difficult and costly problems that the inventor had to solve was how to make crucibles that would withstand the great heat employed in his steel making process. Neither the crucibles made in Hesse nor those made in Passau proved to be entirely satisfactory. The former are liable to burst. The latter are less likely to do so but they become soft when subjected to great heat. Consequently before the iron has begun to melt these crucibles collapse either from their own weight or from that of their metal contents.

After numerous failures Herr Fischer at last managed to discover the materials best suited to the manufacture of his crucibles. He also found out the correct proportions in which these materials should be combined. Moreover he has actually found such materials in the Canton of Schaffhausen and most of them are available close to the iron ore mines of which he is the skilful director.[2] Fischer now makes his own crucibles and they withstand for as long as necessary the greatest heat that he uses in his furnace.

It is not known if Fischer inserts one or more crucibles into his furnace and it is not clear how the necessary heat is obtained. He may secure a sufficient draught through his furnace or he may use the bellows which were originally installed for the foundry and the hammer fires. Whatever the method employed, Fischer makes a very fluid steel which flows into the smallest crevices of his moulds. But when the white hot steel leaves the furnace it is sufficiently malleable to be shaped by a powerful hammer. Steel strips about two feet long and two inches thick were seen in Fischer's works.

Experimental chemists and practical ironmasters will both be interested to know that a step forward has been taken on the Continent in the processing of iron and that Fischer's efforts—so costly in time and money—have been crowned with success. We wish that Fischer himself would give an account of his achievements. A first-hand description of this process might well be a decisive landmark in the history of the iron industry and might point the way to improvements in its manufacture.

2. J. C. FISCHER TO ALEXANDER I OF RUSSIA, JULY 4, 1814

C'était avec le plus grand regret qu'au moment où votre Majesté daignoit voir ma manufacture d'acier fondu je n'avois aucun fabricat digne d'être présenté à votre attention. La fonte que je fis à ce jour si mémorable et si encourageant pour moi me parut d'être d'une importance plus haute que de l'employer pour d'objets ordinaires et je l'ai conservé religieusement à l'exception de ce qui me falloit pour la confection de cette arme qui a été fabriqué entièrement à Schafhouse sous ma direction et dont la qualité pour la justesse du tir et le très peu de poudre qu'il faut pour la charge doit prouver qu'il n'y a pas de matière plus convenable pour des pareilles armes que l'acier fondu. Veuillez donc daigner l'accepter comme l'hommage le plus sincère et comme un souvenir des jours heureux que le séjour de votre Majesté et de votre soeur auguste ont causé à ma patrie qui doit tant à la bénévolence particulière d'un Monarque dont les actions glorieuses parlent plus haute que les éloges les plus éloquentes.

3. FISCHER TO YEATES BROWN, OCTOBER 15, 1814

Dear Sir,

Being arrived again at my own home though somewhat later than I intended, first on account of a longer stay at Paris, I think it my duty to express my most grateful feelings for the friendship I experienced from your part by means of this letter, as a fatality of circumstances did not permit me to do it by word of mouth. Your honoured father whom I had the pleasure to see before I left London and to whom I beg to pay my best compliments, will no doubt have told you how much I was satisfied with my voyage through England, which I extended as far as Leeds, and that all the interest and instruction I gathered from this tour was owing to your kind recommendations which I found were attended to even beyond my expectations. I am therefore, dear Sir, under very great obligations to you and I only wish to be able one day or other and in some manner to retaliate them. If therefore you yourself should not happen to visit my native country so soon again as I greatly wish for, any person you will be pleased to recommend to me shall meet with as friendly a reception as if it was yourself, as far as my power (permits)[3] and the sooner I shall have occasion for this the more glad I shall be, as it will procure me the pleasure of learning[4] from you.

I cannot forbear but to mention once more the kind reception I met with at Soho. And as I suppose that you write now and then to these gentlemen you will have the goodness to tell them how much I am beholden to them for their friendship, especially so to Mr. Watt who did me the pleasure to accompany me himself and to introduce me into several of the most famous ironworks of England where I did not know whether I should more admire their extent or the dexterity and perfection with which everything is performed.

As on my further progress I had an opportunity to make the acquaintance of Mr. Wedgwood at Etruria, of Mr. Lee at Manchester, of Mr. Gott at Leeds whom and his lovely family I ever shall remember, and of Messrs. Walker and Booth at Rotherham, you will find that it was a most fortunate accident for me when I first met you at the foot of the hill between Zürich and Schaffhausen. Little did I then guess its future importance.

Before I left London Mr. Schenk, a friend and countryman of mine, engaged himself to forward at all times to me whatever I wanted to get from England. If therefore you should wish to send anything to Switzerland as I shall be often in the case (?) of having goods from London, you need but to trust it to the care of that gentleman who is at the counting house of Messrs. Reed and Bell, Throgmorton Street, Angel Court and I shall with the greatest pleasure fulfil your ultimate directions. Before I conclude this letter, which I am afraid is becoming too long already, permit me to desire you to pay my profoundest respect to your beloved lady and to agree at the same time the assurance of the most sincere esteem with which I have the honour to be

Your obedient Servant

J. C. Fischer

Yeates Brown Esq.
Lombard Street, No. 66
London

Schaffhausen in Switzerland
the 18th October 1814

4. J. C. FISCHER TO JAMES WATT (JUNIOR), MARCH 6, 1815

Sir,

It is with those agreeable feelings that I take the liberty to address these lines to you, which always arise from the acquirement of something that's precious, and as such I shall ever consider the honour of having made your personal acquaintance and your kind permission to write to you when returned to my own home. The great obligation I am under towards you would have made it my duty to make my acknowledgments much sooner than I do now, had it not been for the apprehension of intruding upon your time on one hand, and on the other for waiting the departure of a Swiss gentleman and friend of mine, Mr. Studer of Winterthur, who will be so good as to charge himself with this letter and whom I take the liberty to recommend very much to your good favours, as his extensive travels to different parts of the world will render you his personal acquaintance both agreeable and interesting. Mr. Studer will at the same time deliver you two samples of cast steel[5] into which I have converted according to my promise the two different specimens of English iron you had the goodness to furnish me with. These samples which I have the honour to get submitted to your examination will prove I hope sufficiently that the English iron whether good or bad will be as fit as any other iron for being converted into a very good sort of cast steel provided the composition of the flux be calculated according to its nature and properties. By the great number of experiments I have made already on the iron and the different modifications it is apt to undergo, I was so sure of success with respect to this, that immediately after the casting of the bars I presented them to the action of a tilting hammer of 150 lbs weight, going at the rate of 216 strokes in a minute which they bore so well as if made from the best Swedish or Russian iron.

If I was not afraid of having entertained you too long already with an object of fabrication which, in comparison with the importance of those I have seen in your manufactory, shrinks to nothing, I should say still some words on the different manner of proceeding as they are in use at Rotherham and Atterclif(fe) and my own little laboratory. My only and most hearty wish is that you might realise your intention of coming this spring to Switzerland which would procure me the pleasure of talking with you at large on subjects that greatly interest me, and of which I know no more competent judge than yourself. As Mr. Lee of Manchester is expected within a few months here (Mr. Love whose acquaintance I made a few weeks ago told me so) you would meet I fancy a very agreeable companion of voyage, besides young Mr. Gott of Leeds, whom and whose respectable family I shall never forget.

I don't remember whether I have told you that the Russian

Emperor visited my steel foundry when at Schaffhausen. I have been presented since by his Majesty with a very precious ring set with 91 brilliants sent from Vienna (date 18 Nov. 1814) accompanied with a letter whose contents greatly enhanced the value of the gift. Before I conclude this letter I think it my duty to mention to you that Mr. Wedgwood has done the highest honour to your kind recommendation. I only regret the very little time that was left upon my hands for making a long stay in your sweet isle, as it was not above a month. My consolation is however that it has furnished me with matter for contemplation these twenty years to come, and I have not yet given up the idea of treading English ground again. Be pleased to remember me to Mr. Bo(u)lton and Mr. Murdock and believe for ever to be entirely

Yours

J. C. Fischer

Schaffhausen
the 6th March 1815

5. J. C. FISCHER TO BENJAMIN GOTT, FEBRUARY 20, 1816

Dear Sir,

Though it was very often in my thoughts with you while you was travelling on, and always entertained the agreeable hopes of hearing you were well and safe arrived in England again, yet I never could have flattered myself to be remembered by you in such a manner as I now experienced, by receiving the box you had directed to Mr. Keller at Stuttgardt to be forwarded to me. In opening it I was most agreeably surprised to find that you had extended your kindness even as far as to my friend Mr. Pfister and the good Abbot of the Monastery at Rheinau. The next day after I had received these estimable presents (which was a Sunday) I went immediately to Rheinau to have the pleasure to deliver the razor-case destined to the Abbot into his own hands.

I should wish very much you had been a witness of the pleasure it gave that worthy old man. He could not conceive that he should be remembered so far off, nor that he ever should get something from England. He not only charged me to render you his most cordial thanksgivings, but to prove in some measure his satisfaction, he ordered (as I stayed for dinner) a particular sort of wine called straw wine on the table, with which he not only regaled all the monks, but the first toast he gave was your and your beloved family's health, to which I heartily pledged.

The highly finished needles and scissors which your beloved lady and most amiable daughter had the goodness to present my spouse with, gave her an immense deal of pleasure. She only grieves that it is out of her power to make any retaliation, at least for the present, and she begs to agree meanwhile the expression of her grateful sentiments conjointly with those of my own for the beautiful and most convenient razor case, which for its excellency and as it came from persons I honour so much, I immediately appropriated for my own use, though not without some remonstrances from Mrs. Fischer, who thought it was a pity to use it at all.

Mr. Pfister, who is not very well this winter, reserves for himself the pleasure of testifying you his gratitude by a letter of his own, and only begs me meanwhile to thank you most heartily in his name.

As for the book of Hope, containing the costumes of the ancient Romans and Greeks, I was highly pleased to find you had had the goodness to execute my commission, and I shall thank you very much to let my son know what it costs as I am till this moment without any direct news from your part and where I am to refund its amount for your account. All the persons to whom I showed this work, admire with me the beauty and correctness of the engravings and the interesting choice of the objects, which become still more interesting by the perusal of the prefatory discours(e), so meritoriously embellished by typographic art and elegance.

A few weeks ago I received from Mr. Lee a small treatise on gas light, wrote by Mr. Murdock. I found its contents so very interesting that I immediately translated it into German, in order to be published, as I thought Mr. Lee, to whom I wrote about it, would not take it amiss my doing so.

I should not forbear to mention at the same time an establishment which I had seen in England and which I consider of as much importance as the former, or perhaps still more, on account of the more general application it is subject to in domestic life, viz. the heating with steam, which your sons had the goodness to show and explain to me, when I was favoured with the introduction into the numerous establishments of your extensive manufactory, which most likely, has not its mate in the kingdom. Indeed it was not a trifle to operate on so large a scale an idea, for which mankind must be beholden to you, on account of the great benefits resulting from, and that you did it in spite of the prejudices and the ridicule of the public, which is always in opposition with the introduction of novelties, be they ever so well founded on sound reasoning or the most decisive experiments.

And now, Sir, before I conclude my letter give me leave to beg two things of you as a favour. First, if ever I can be of any service to you, or that you have any person who is travelling to Switzerland to recommend to me, to dispose of me in the most unreserved manner, and secondly, that young Mr. Gott, who gave me hopes when I was at Leeds of visiting my country also, will be so good when arrived at Schaffhausen, to come directly to me, and to live and stay with me as long as he pleases.

Indeed, Sir, this favour will make me quite happy as it gives your son as well as me the opportunity of making the most of our time, during his stay here. In this pleasant expectation I beg you will agree of Mrs. Fischer and myself our most respectful salutations to you, your beloved lady and family and to believe to remaining with the most distinguished esteem.

Yours
Fischer.

Schaffhausen
the 20th February, 1816

6. J. C. FISCHER TO WILLIAM MURDOCK, FEBRUARY 20, 1816

Dear Sir,

Though the time was so very short during which I had the advantage of enjoying your society, and profit of your conversation, yet it was long enough to establish and consolidate with me that high esteem I always think myself owing to men, who not only excel in talents and skill, but also are so happy as to become benefactors of mankind in the application of them, and I only regret that imperious circumstances did not permit me to stay longer in a country where by autopsie and conversation I might have learnt more in a month, than anywhere else in a couple of years.

Pardon me Sir this expectation! and let it serve as an apology for intruding upon you, and desiring you at the instance of a friend of mine to be so good as to send to Mr. A. Schenk,[6] at Messrs. Reed & Bell, Throgmorton Street, Angel Court, London, two or three ounces of your platina wire of about two lines in diameter, which I think will be sufficiently thick for to line the touch holes of guns with it.[7] The amount of the said wire will be paid at sight of the bill.

Mr. Lee of Manchester, who did me the honour of visiting me at Schaffhausen, since I left England, had the goodness to send me a few weeks ago your most interesting treatise on gas light and its application to economical purposes. On perusing it I could not help thinking that though it is a great fortune that Nature that has so many treasures in her store, yet they would avail us very little if there were not persons endowed with peculiar faculties that enable them to show to their (contemporaries how to)[8] use and how to apply them properly.

If ever I should be honoured by a few words from your part, be pleased to let me know whether there exist long ago in England nail manufactures by mechanical means? Within a short time there will such a one be established here by a gentleman who has one already in Austria, and where all sorts of nails, with and without heads, are manufactured without anvil and hammer in a most perfect manner. As much as I remember there was one Mr. Dudley of Sheffield who got a patent for the same object in the year 1790 but I doubt whether he ever succeeded so far. But perhaps since that time there may have been made a great many improvements in that sort of machinery. Be pleased to remember me to Mr. Watt whose undeserved friendship and hospitality I never shall forget as long as I live and to dispose if to them or to you I should be able to render an agreeable service begging you meanwhile to agree the assurance of my most perfect esteem with which I have the honour to be

Yours

Fischer

Schaffhausen the 20th February 1816
to William Murdock Esq.,
at Messrs Boulton and Watt at Soho near Birmingham.

7. J. C. FISCHER TO G. A. LEE, JUNE 16, 1817

Dear Sir,

Mr. Näher, proprietor of the iron foundry at the Lauffen near the fall of the Rhine, the bearer of the present, had the goodness to offer me his readiness for charging himself with any letter or parcel I should wish to send to England where he intends to go in a very short time.

I would not let pass this opportunity to thank you again to

your kind remembrance of which you was pleased to give me a proof, by communicating to me Mr. Murdock's most interesting treatise on the use of gas light, which I translated into German and inserted into my diary written during my tour through France and England of which Mr. Näher, whom I take the liberty to recommend to your kindness, will have the honour to transmit to you an exemplar, which I beg you will be pleased to accept as a token of my gratitude and high esteem.

A few months ago several beds of pit coal have been discovered in the neighbourhood of Schaffhausen and especially a very promising one near Constanz, the exploitation is, what I have learnt, already begun, and as our Canton abounds with iron ore Mr. Näher intends to avail himself of the advantages of this sort of fuel, unknown hitherto with us, seems to present. But as the reduction as well as the refining and puddling process carried on with coaks and pit coals, differs entirely from that with charcoal, he should think himself very happy if by autopsie he might enable himself to establish on his return a similar mode of proceeding now in general use in the United Kingdom.

But as this requires the admittance into one or other of the numerous iron foundries, Mr. Näher would think himself infinitely obliged to you, if by your kind advice he should obtain an opportunity of gratifying his curiosity and also if possible that of nail rendering manufactory by mechanical means, as he himself has established such a one of late.

Young Mr. Gott of Leeds has done me the favour of visiting me last autumn. I was highly pleased with that young gentleman and knew not whether I should more admire his learning and parts or his modesty. I only regretted his parting so soon.

Before I conclude my letter give me leave to desire you to remember me and also Mrs. Fischer to your beloved sister, and so tell her that I have taken the liberty to translate into German some of those fine novels her modesty called but Canterbury tales, but which deserve far another name. Hoping that You and your beloved family are well I beg to agree the assurance of the high esteem with which I have the honour to remain

Your devoted

J. C. Fischer

Schaffhausen
the 16th June 1817
to S. Lee Esq., at Manchester.

8. BLUMHOF'S DESCRIPTION OF FISCHER'S CAST STEEL, 1817[9]

As early as the year 1809 Fischer of Schaffhausen sent to the *Société d'encouragement pour l'industrie nationale* in Paris some samples of his cast steel which possessed the qualities that we have already discussed. According to various experts, such as Ullrich, Schenk and others, the best quality of Fischer's steel is much superior to the best quality of English steel. As long ago as the year 1804 Fischer's achievement in making cast steel was justly recognised at an industrial exhibition held in Berne. Fischer's methods are different from those used in England. First, he does not smelt blister steel (made by the cementation process) as is the English practice but he uses bar iron with some additional materials. Secondly, he uses a cylindrical blast furnace in which he places several crucibles made of highly fire-resisting clay. The smelting is done with charcoal. Subsequently Fischer made a cast steel capable of being welded, which is also of high quality. In addition Fischer makes 'yellow steel' which is an alloy of one part of copper and three parts of steel.

9. ARTICLE ON THE ALLOY OF CERTAIN METALS WITH CAST STEEL, 1823[10]

M. Fischer, Lieutenant Col. of Artillery at Schaffhausen, states when bar-iron, steel, and particularly grey cast iron, surrounded by a great deal of carbon are exposed to a violent fire for several hours, there is formed on the surface of the fluid metal a kind of graphite or carburetted iron, which appears in very thin scales, brilliant like ologist iron, but soft, and capable of marking paper, like pencils. Their form is very irregular.

The author took an ounce of this artificial graphite, and an equal weight of pure alumine pulverized, and exposed this mixture, in a well luted crucible, for half an hour, to a degree of heat strong enough to melt malleable iron, which answers to about 160° of Wedgwood's pyrometer. After having removed the crucible out of the furnace, and suffered it to cool, a regulus or button was found in the bottom weighing exactly half an ounce, and the fracture of which was granular, of a silvery-white inclining to yellow. The residue was a black powder, weighing likewise half an ounce exactly, and giving off a strong smell of sulphur.

The author melted this regulus again in another well luted

J

crucible, with five ounces of cast steel. The mixture being very liquid, instead of running it into an ingot mould, M. Fischer contented himself with laying it out of the furnace, the covering being sufficiently luted, to prevent the liquid metal from running out, which on cooling took the lengthened form, resulting from the situation of the crucible. When the whole was become cold, he broke the crucible, and found the ingot crystallised at its surface in rays diverging from various centres, an impression of which had been taken by the scoria which covered it. The upper surface of this was, as it were, silvered, or rather covered with a metallic varnish, resembling the coating of pottery made with platina.

The fracture of this ingot, which weighed exactly five ounces and a quarter, was found highly crystallised in vertical laminae, some brilliant, some dull. This ingot yielded to the hammer without breaking, but exhibiting extraordinary resistance and hardness. After having been drawn out into a bar eleven inches long, heated only to a brown red, and afterwards hardened, the grain became so fine that it could no longer be distinguished by the naked eye. The fracture was greyish white, resembling that of porcelain. The hardness which this bar had acquired by tempering was surprising: it scratched the best tempered steel, and resisted the action of a very good graver. The polished surface was damasked very speedily when exposed to the action of dilute sulphuric acid: but nitric acid gave it a deep dull grey colour. Some penknives made of this steel preserved for a long time the sharpest edge.

The author has likewise attempted to form the alloy of steel silver in the large way, according to the process of Mr. Faraday. For this purpose he filled two crucibles, each with twenty five pounds of cast steel. Presuming that all or a part of the silver to be added was liable to be volatised by the powerful heat, he put it together with the steel in one of the crucibles only. For the other he waited the complete fusion, and then threw the silver upon the liquid steel, into which it fell immediately on account of the excess of its specific gravity. The mixture was stirred with an iron bar covered with a thin coat of refactory earth, and afterwards run into an ingot mould. The crucible into which the two metals were put before fusion, was allowed to cool in the furnace.

After having drawn out these two masses by hammering, there was not the smallest difference found between them; and what is very remarkable is, that the alloy welded very readily.

10. MEMORANDUM ON FISCHER'S STEEL BY EBENEZER RHODES, 1825[11]

Sheffield
June 30th 1825

We have this day manufactured a pair of razors from the steel brought to us by the gentleman to whom we give this memorandum. It is of a very fine quality, extremely hard and admirably calculated to sustain a durable cutting edge. We have of course not used the razors, but we speak from the manner in which the steel works under the hammer, and the fineness of the polish of which it is capable and the beautiful and fine texture when broken etc.

E. Rhodes & Co.,
Razormakers

11. FISCHER'S VISIT TO ENGLAND IN 1825[12]

As I had invented meteor steel (a steel-nickel alloy) which possessed qualities of remarkable excellence, I decided to visit England so as to make it known there. In the circumstances I was able to make contact with leading ironmasters, chemists, engineers, and skilled mechanics and I secured a knowledge of their industrial establishments from the inside.

What struck me most was the progress that had been made in the iron furnaces and foundries and the skilful way in which the English were taking advantage of their ability always to have molten iron at their disposal.

The English can not only cast iron products of any weight up to 150 cwt and more but also the finest and most delicate cooking utensils such as those which you now see before you. These utensils are not only light and unbreakable but they are protected against rust by a thin coating of tin. They are of excellent quality. The English also make the smallest nails, barely $\frac{3}{4}''$ long for knocking in shoes and plaster. A man and a boy can make 450,000 nails a day. A pound of nails is sold for seven kreuzer in Swiss money (i.e. one shilling). The iron for both kitchenware and the nails is smelted in cupola furnaces which have entirely replaced the more expensive reverberatory furnaces.

These cupola furnaces usually have a capacity of twenty cwt but by increasing their height this can be raised to thirty cwt. Several furnaces are used simultaneously to make large castings. Once the iron has been heated it is usually possible to smelt fifteen —indeed even twenty—cwt in an hour.

England was the pioneer in the introduction of cotton spinning machinery. The use of such machinery has now spread to such an extent that it marks an epoch in the industrial history of civilised peoples. It has had consequences that no one could have anticipated when mechanical spinning was first invented. For a long time the achievement of mechanical cotton spinning stood alone except for wool, the spinning of which by machinery did not present serious difficulties. But now flax too can be spun by machinery. This apparently intractable problem was long discussed and very high prizes were offered for its solution. The advantages of mechanical spinning are attested by the rapid development of flourishing textile mills in England. There may well be some justification for the doubts and anxieties that have arisen concerning this new industrial phenomenon and I would not like to express a definite point of view on the question as to whether this invention should be regarded as a piece of good fortune or not. But my observations have made it clear to me that no one can hold back the march of progress or alter the changes that accompany it. In my view it is most sensible to adapt oneself to changing conditions—and not to leave it too late to do so.

Weaving by power driven machinery is closely linked with spinning by machinery. In England the mechanical looms can handle all the textile yarns. Not only are ordinary cloths woven by machinery but also large artistic carpets which have as beautiful designs as the silks of Lyons woven on a Jacquard loom.

The use of coal gas for lighting has been a welcome improvement but now it is gratifying to be able to report that gas made from oil has great advantages over its rival. We are now spared the most unpleasant odour of coal gas and the generators are simpler, cheaper, and more efficient.

Not satisfied with inventing oil-gas the English have discovered how to compress it into a space thirty times smaller than its normal volume and they now store it in metal containers and cylinders capable of withstanding great pressure. By this means it is possible to transport oil-gas to individual households and to small factories where there is no space to erect a gas generator. According to information supplied to me the oil-gas needed to give a light for 16 hours of a brilliance equal to seven table candles costs about 38 kreuzer (i.e. 4/-). In their plant in City Road, London, Messrs. Taylor and Martineau are making the very best types of oil-gas generators as well as ingeniously constructed compression pumps and gas-holders.

12. MARTINEAU AND SMITH'S SPECIFICATION CONCERNING THE MANUFACTURE OF FISCHER STEEL, 1825

TO ALL TO WHOM THESE PRESENTS SHALL COME, I, JOHN MARTINEAU the younger, of the City Road, in the County of Middlesex, Engineer, and HENRY WILLIAM SMITH, of Lawrence Pountney Place, in the City of London, Esquire, send greeting.

WHEREAS His present most Excellent Majesty King George the Fourth, by His Letters, Patent under the Great Seal of Great Britain, bearing date at Westminster, the Sixth day of October, in the sixth year of His reign, did, for Himself, His heirs and successors, give and grant unto us, the said John Martineau and Henry William Smith, His especial licence, that we, the said John Martineau and Henry William Smith, our exõrs, admõrs, and assigns, or such others as we, the said John Martineau and Henry William Smith, our exõrs, admõrs, or assigns, should at any time agree with, and no others, from time to time and at all times during the term of years therein expressed, should and lawfully might make, use, exercise, and vend, within England, Wales, and the Town of Berwick-upon-Tweed, and also in all His said Majesty's Colonies and Plantation abroad, the Invention of "CERTAIN IMPROVEMENTS IN THE MANUFACTURE OF STEEL," communicated to us by a certain Foreigner residing abroad; in which said Letters Patent is contained a proviso obliging us, the said John Martineau and Henry William Smith, by an instrument in writing under our hands and seals, or under the hand and seal of one of us, particularly to describe and ascertain the nature of the said Invention, and in what manner the same is to be performed, and to cause the same to be inrolled in His Majesty's High Court of Chancery within six calendar months next and immediately after the date of the said recited Letters Patent, as in and by the same, reference being thereunto had, will more fully and at large appear.

NOW KNOW YE, that in compliance with the said proviso, I, the said John Martineau the younger, do hereby declare the nature of the improvements so communicated to us as aforesaid to consist in adding to and mixing or combining with blister steel, or such other steel as is ordinarily used in cast-steel works, such alloys, and in such proportions, as will greatly improve the quality of the said steel, and will enable the manufacturer to produce, in goods made of the said alloyed steel, the beautiful wavy appearance exhibited on the best Damascus sword blades. This said alloyed steel we call meteor steel. And in further compliance with the said proviso I, the said John Martineau, do hereby describe the manner in which the said improvements so communicated to us as aforesaid are to be performed, as follows (that is to say): —

Twenty-four parts of zinc, four of purified nickel, and one of silver, are put into a black lead or other refractory crucible, the surface being covered with charcoal powder; the cover is to be luted on and the whole subjected to the heat of a steel furnace until it is fused; the mixture when melted, is then poured out into cold water, so as to render it brittle and more easy to pound into small pieces for use. This we call meteor powder, and although we have found proportions of the different metals be the best for general purposes, yet we do not confine ourselves to these precise quantities, a small variation affording a scarcely perceptible difference in the results.

Having produced our meteor powder in manner aforesaid, we next proceed to make our meteor steel, in the process of making which we charge our crucibles, which are of the usual size, form, and fabric, with the following ingredients, and in the following proportions (that is to say): — Twenty-four pounds of blister steel, or such other steel as is used in cast-steel works, eight ounces of meteor powder pounded very small, six ounces of pounded chromate of iron, one ounce of charcoal powder, two ounces of quick-lime, two ounces of porcelain clay. The above proportions produce a steel of an excellent quality, and capable of exhibiting the said wavy appearance in a beautiful manner, but we vary somewhat the proportions of meteor powder, according as more or less of this wavy appearance is required. The quantity of charcoal must also be somewhat varied, according as a harder or softer steel is required, and according as the blister or other steel used for charging the crucible is more or less converted; these are points which may be safely left to the experience of any ordinary steel caster. The quick-lime and porcelain clay being only used as fluxes, may be varied in quantity without injuring the process, but the proportions herein-before described are the best we have as yet discovered. The furnaces and crucibles at present in use in cast-steel works may be used in the manufacture of the meteor steel, and the said steel, when made as aforesaid, may be cast and tilted in the usual manner, in order to draw out and exhibit the said wavy appearance upon any article manufactured with this steel. The surface, when polished, should be rubbed over with any acid which readily acts upon the steel, and according as the wavy lines are required to be more or less conspicuous, so the surface is to be kept moistened with the said acid

for a longer or shorter period; as soon as a sufficient effect is produced, the acid must be carefully washed off. Various acids will
answer for this purpose; but we prefer a mixture of one part
nitric acid to nineteen parts of distilled or French vinegar.

Now, whereas we do not claim exclusive right or privilege to
any of the apparatus herein-before described as used in the manufacture of the said meteor steel, but only to the mixed metal produced by the combination of steel, zinc, purified nickel, and silver,
and chromate of iron, in manner herein-before described, and
which mixture constitutes the said improvements so communicated to us as aforesaid; and such improvements being, to the best
of our knowledge and belief, entirely new and never before used,
I, the said John Martineau the younger, do hereby declare this
to be our Specification of the said improvements, and that I do
verily believe this our said Specification doth comply, in all
respects, fully with the proviso in the herein-before recited Letters
Patent. Wherefore we do hereby claim to maintain exclusive right
and privilege to the said improvements.

In witness whereof, I, the said John Martineau, have hereunto
set my hand and seal, this Fifth day of April, in the year of our
Lord One thousand eight hundred and twenty-six.

JOHN MARTINEAU, Jr. (L.S.)

AND BE IT REMEMBERED, that on the Fifth day of April,
in the year of our Lord 1826, the aforesaid John Martineau came
before our said Lord the King in His Chancery, and acknowledged the Specification aforesaid, and all and every thing therein
contained and specified, in form above written. And also the
Specification aforesaid was stamped according to the tenor of the
Statute made for that purpose.

Inrolled the Fifth day of April, in the year of our Lord One
thousand eight hundred and twenty-six.

13. FISCHER'S VISIT TO ENGLAND IN 1827[13]
(Fischer arrived in London on Monday, September 17, 1827).

Tuesday, September 18
Visited Conrad in the morning, went with him to Mr. Lane,
Smith and Martineau, and wrote home.

Wednesday, September 19
Conrad came to see me and we went to Mr. Lane's clerk.
Went to the smelting plant in the afternoon.

Thursday, September 20
Made various purchases. Wrote to Mr. Gott at Leeds and
sent him my diary to be bound.

Friday, September 21

Went to Johnson and Thomson's London Steel Works and offered him ordinary cast steel at 45 and ordinary steel from Styria at 28 per ton . . . Spent the evening with Martineau.

Saturday, September 22

In the morning I saw Smith junior and Martineau on business and spent the afternoon writing home and writing a description of the Thames Tunnel . . .

Sunday, September 23

Wrote a statement concerning my business with Martineau and Smith. Lunched with Conrad in the City Road and went for a walk with him in the evening.

Monday, September 24

Conrad and I went to Smith junior in the morning. Afterwards I went on my own to the banker Rothschild with an introduction from Berger . . . Went to the London Steel Works in the afternoon . . .

Tuesday, September 25

Wrote to Japy. In the morning Conrad and I came to an understanding with Smith junior. I called on Mr. Prévost[14] and asked him for an introduction to Woolwich. Saw Mr. Martineau and offered him my invention concerning bricks in return for a one third share (of the profits).[15]

Wednesday, September 26

Went to Woolwich with Conrad to the foundry and the boring machine as well as the artillery tests . . . Spent the evening with Conrad.

Thursday, September 27

. . . Saw N. M. Rothschild . . . Went with Conrad to Thurn and Omrod. Went previously to Perkins . . .

Friday, September 28

Called on Mr. Brande in the morning but did not see him. Afterwards saw Mr. Faraday at the Royal Institution. Lunched with Conrad and went with him in the evening to Mr. Martineau to tea . . .

Saturday, September 29

. . . Went again to Perkins with Conrad . . . Visited the Haymarket theatre with Conrad . . . Got home from the theatre at 1.30 a.m. Perkins' metal for pistons is 20 parts of copper and $4\frac{1}{2}$ parts of tin . . .

Sunday, September 30

Conrad came to lunch . . .

Monday, October 1

Lunched with Conrad . . . Spent the evening at home writing an account of my visit to Woolwich.

Tuesday, October 2

. . . Went to Piccadilly and Charing (Cross) enquiring after Lämlin.

Wednesday, October 3

In the morning again saw Smith with Conrad . . . Wrote home in the evening.

Thursday, October 4

In the morning saw Smith again and gave him a draft for 750 francs . . . At 3 p.m. left for Leeds, via Sheffield.

Friday, October 5

Had breakfast in Nottingham. Arrived at Sheffield at 2 p.m. . . . Went to steel rolling mills and met Huntsman who was having his steel—made from ore from India—rolled. Afterwards went to Sanderson's cast steel works. Was with him in the foundry and saw the casting. Afterwards went to Bixley and Green . . .

Saturday, October 6

Left for Leeds at 6 a.m. . . . Arrived in Leeds at 11 a.m. and went to Mr. Gott. Made various purchases at the new market in Leeds and afterwards went with Mr. Gott to his house for lunch. Returned in the evening.

Sunday, October 7

Had breakfast with Mr. Gott and went with him and his family to church. Went to church again in the afternoon. Back at 9 p.m. . . .

Monday, October 8

Went to Mr. Gott in the morning and we saw his solicitor and discussed my business with Smith and Martineau . . . Left for London at 1 p.m. Saw Sanderson for a moment in Sheffield.

Tuesday, October 9

. . . Returned to London safely thank God at 4.30 p.m. . . . Spent the evening with Conrad . . .

Wednesday, October 10

Went with Conrad to Mr. Smith. Agreed with him and with Mr. Martineau on the main points of the contract. May God bless this enterprise. Wrote home in the evening.

Thursday, October 11

In the morning I went with Conrad to Lane and drew up the new contract with Richard Smith and Martineau. Afterwards made various purchases . . . Lunched with Conrad. In the afternoon went with Conrad to Hammersmith to see the suspension bridge.

Friday, October 12

Went with Conrad to Lane to examine and approve the new contract . . . Wrote home and to George . . . Wrote to Gott in Leeds . . .

Saturday, October 13

Went with Conrad to Lane and signed the new contract with Richard Carter Smith and Martineau . . . Left for Dover in the evening.

Sunday, October 14

Sailed to Calais on the steamship *The Sovereign* . . .

At the end of October Fischer wrote in his notebook in English:

'The 27th, 28th and 29th Oct. was (*sic*) three very pleasant days for me. The 27th I wrote to my friend, the 28th a considerable sum of money was paid (*sic*) to me, and the 29th I refer to the note opposite and the same day begun (*sic*) a very interesting construction in the brook near the foundry.'

14. FISCHER'S AUSTRIAN PATENT FOR STEEL CASTINGS, DECEMBER 1845[16]

(A patent is granted to) Johann Conrad Fischer, Lieutenant Colonel and City Councillor, owner of a cast steelworks and a file factory in Switzerland, for an invention for melting bar iron while keeping its malleable tenacity. The iron is melted in crucibles into a thin fluid and it is then cast in clay, sand or iron moulds. This invention eliminates the need both for a subsequent conversion process (as is the case with malleable iron) or a tedious softening process which may last for several days—processes which have hitherto been necessary to ensure that the metal can be properly used. In Fischer's process the steel is ready for use immediately after it has been cast, just as when bar iron or forged iron is made. Fischer's steel castings may be improved by using a file, a chisel, a drill, a hammer, or the tools used by a turner. The duration of the patent is for two years.

15. W. T. BRANDE TO FISCHER, JANUARY 1, 1846

Royal Mint,
London,
1 Jan. 1846

My dear Sir,

We have made some trials with the bar of steel you sent us, and are well pleased with it. Will you be so good on the receipt of this to prepare for us two bars of the same quality each 3 *inches square* and two bars 1½ *inch square,* and forward them to us without delay.

Will you also inform me who are your London agents and to whom I am to pay the amount of our debt to you. I should also wish to make some arrangement for a further supply of your steel, which, if you can furnish of the same quality as the sample bar and of such sizes as we require we should use here in preference to any which I have lately been able to procure.

Pray let me have an immediate answer to this and if you should come to London let me see you upon your arrival here.

Yours faithfully

W. T. Brande

The sizes of the bars to use for our common dies are 1½ inch by 1¼, and if you can send us some 3 or 4 bars of that size they should be immediately tried.

16. J. C. FISCHER'S DESCRIPTION OF HIS DISPLAY CABINET AT THE GREAT EXHIBITION, 1851

View of the interior of the exhibitor's cast steel and bar iron foundry, in illustration of the method of making cast steel, which differs in three points from that in general use in England, viz. the melting furnaces are portable; they contain six crucibles, instead of only one or two and hot blast is employed to produce an intense degree of heat, scarcely obtainable by high chimneys and a simple draught of air. By this process it is stated that with 120 lbs. of coke, 126 lbs. of steel may be melted, thus effecting a considerable saving of fuel.

Ingot of meteor steel, a kind of steel invented and named by the exhibitor in 1825; the upper part of this ingot exhibits a fine specimen of crystallisation. An ingot, of which a part has been cut off in a transversal direction, to show the interior crystallisation, as well as its density and purity. Four bars of the same steel exposed to the action of acids, to discover their damask; the quality may be estimated from the aspect of the grain at the end of each bar.

Two daggers and four razors of meteor steel, which, with the exception of one, have been put into an acid, to discover their watering, and to show their polish.

Ingot of Swiss iron, converted by direct fusion into very soft cast steel; part of this ingot is tilted out for a rifle gun, flattened at the top into a bar of nearly three eighths of an inch thick, and bent to show its tenacity. Ingot of English scrap iron, converted by direct fusion into good cast steel. The butt end of the ingot, when tilted out into a box, was broken off, to show the grain, hardened and unhardened. This steel is particularly adapted for files.

Gear-wheel, cast in sand, of the same scrap iron converted into cast steel.

Two crucibles, with their lids, differing in form and composition from the ordinary ones: in one of them, bar iron has been melted.

Two small ingots, consisting of two parts of scrap iron and one part of copper; showing that these two metals may be united, and that a useful and cheap alloy is thus obtained.

17. J. C. FISCHER'S DESCRIPTION OF HIS CAST STEEL PROCESS, 1851

Supplement to the Notices about my Articles mentioned in the Catalogue of the Exhibition of Industry in London.

It would be very presumptuous of the undersigned to enter into a competition with the English manufacturers of cast steel whose credit in excelling in this branch of industry was established everywhere nearly a century ago, by sending, as he does, such scanty and unseeming articles to this memorable and unparalleled Exhibition.

It was only at the request of the principal members of the Government of the Canton of Schaffhausen, which, as a wine-growing and agricultural country is but poorly provided with manufactures, that at least some signs of industry might be given, that he ranged himself among the Swiss senders, and a further excuse he thinks it might be, that manufacturers of cast steel could have perhaps some interest in getting acquainted by the draught of the interior of his melting house (joined to the box containing his articles) with his method of producing cast steel, invented by him some forty years ago, and deviating from the ordinary way, as far as it has come to his knowledge, even till now.

The advantage which he thought might arise from diminishing the diameter of the crucibles and increase their number, without enlarging the dimensions of the furnace in the same proportion, has completely been obtained, and with good coke, no more than 115 pounds are required to melt 126 pounds of steel (each of the six crucibles being charged with 21 pounds) within about three hours time, whereas, as he has been told, nearly three times as much fuel must be consumed to produce the same quantity of steel, in the way generally used. A second advantage, which his method procures him, as diminishing the expenses of making cast steel, is in producing it directly from the bar iron without prealable cementation, of which process, of course, time and expense is entirely saved; and a third and also very considerable advantage he has obtained by the introduction of hot blast, some years ago, into his portable melting furnaces, whose construction is far more cheaper than that of the thick walled wind furnaces with their high and costly chimneys, besides the possibility they procure, to carry the intensity of heat to a degree not attainable by the simple action of the atmosphere, so that it has enabled him to melt in one of his experiment furnaces, constructed upon the same principle as mentioned above, nearly three ounces of pure platina to a perfect lump or regulus, only under a cover of pulverised glass, without any other flux whatsoever which the most distinguished chemists of England, Mr. Faraday at the Royal Institution and Mr. Brande at the Royal Mint, who both have seen it, will attest.

Being convinced that all sorts of bar iron must become of a good quality, when they are thoroughly refined and purified, which in the crucible is far more easy than in the hearth or puddling furnace (though even there he thinks it practicable) and that furthermore by addition of fluxes or certain metals (as the most interesting discoveries of Mr. Faraday with respect to the combination of silver with steel, and again aluminium with steel have sufficiently proved) they might still be ameliorated, he was in consequence of this supposition led to the discovery of his meteor steel, which as far as he may be allowed to judge, is in quality second to none, besides the peculiar property it possesses to show a fine damask or what is called watering on the polished surface when exposed to the action of acids a property which is in high esteem in the eastern countries of our globe.

Pursuing the above mentioned idea of a posterior refining, he has also succeeded to his entire satisfaction to convert the offals of coke iron in one direct fusion into a good, useful, and cheap sort of cast steel, and in consequence of the different contrivances alluded to, he is enabled notwithstanding a ton of coke from St. Etienne near Lyons, which he uses at Schaffhausen for melting, amounts to £3 10s English money to sell the meteor steel in bars of one shilling per pound, the ordinary weldable cast steel in ingots, five pence if large quantities are commanded, and of the cast steel manufactured from the above mentioned scrap iron, the costing price amounts to about three pence a pound. It is to be understood that all here is said regards only his manufactory at Schaffhausen; in England each ton of steel would cost so much less with respect to the fuel as the price of coke differs there from that at Schaffhausen, viz £2 15s. Captain Hale, engineer at Woolwich, inventor of the tangential Congreve rockets, who visited him two years ago, and was present at the foundry during the melting and casting of bar iron and steel, and quite recently Mr. Baird, engineer at the manufactory of Messrs. Robinson, Russell & Co. at Greenwich, who puts together a steam boat, furnished by these gentlemen, for Schaffhausen, might perhaps be pleased to give some further notices that might be wished for, which the undersigned suppresses for brevity's sake, thinking himself sufficiently honoured when this sketch about cast steel should be deemed worthy of some attention, as contributing to the history of this useful metal, and concludes with the wish, that choice, quality and cheapness of his articles, sent to the Exhibition, may in some manner compensate for bulk, show or quantity.

John Conrad Fischer
Cast Steel and File Manufacturer
at Schaffhausen in Switzerland,
January and May 1851.

18. ROBERT WUNDERLICH'S ACCOUNT OF J. C. FISCHER'S DISPLAY AT THE GREAT EXHIBITION, 1851[17]

Steel is undoubtedly one of the most important industrial products of the modern world. The improvement and the expansion of the manufacture of steel has an immense influence because of the present exceptionally heavy demands of the engineering industry. For a long time—and in many quarters even today—it has been assumed that the hardness, elasticity, purity and all the other desirable qualities of English steel could never be matched by anything that could be made on the Continent. Consequently enormous sums are being paid to England every year to buy this valuable material from which machinery of high quality can be made. In many countries far-seeing statesmen and economists have urged governments to take energetic steps to promote the production of this important material. Aided by the gigantic scientific advances of our day it has been possible for many an inventive engineer to achieve good results in this respect.

Probably no one has been so successful as Colonel J. C. Fischer of Schaffhausen in challenging English supremacy by producing really high-quality steel. Indeed Switzerland can be proud of the fact that Fischer can be described as the leading manufacturer of steel on the Continent. His name is known not merely in local business circles but his reputation has spread even as far as England itself. Moreover, the leading Swiss firms—Escher, Kurz, Rieter & Co. and others—buy Fischer's steel products for their own use.

There is an anecdote about old Colonel Fischer which is told by furnace-men and engineers. It is perhaps rather a tall story and we cannot vouch for its authenticity. Yet the fact that such a story is repeated—and we heard it from a practical engineer—does illustrate the reputation that Fischer has gained for himself among his colleagues. The story goes that on one occasion when he was in England—he lived there as a young man and still goes there from time to time—he called at a cutler's shop and asked to see a razor of the best and hardest English steel. When he was shown a razor he looked at it and expressed his doubts concerning its quality. The cutler assured him that he would not find a better razor in England. To test the quality of the steel Fischer took a pen-knife from his knapsack and began to cut at the edge of the razor. He sliced off one piece after another until the razor was ruined. The cutler, completely taken aback, exclaimed 'Damn you, Sir, if you aren't the devil then you must be Fischer himself!' We repeat that we cannot guarantee the truth of this anecdote but *se non è vero, è bène trovàto*.

Fischer has displayed some very interesting samples of his products at the Great Exhibition. First, as the key to his display cabinet, he shows a picture of the interior of his steelworks and ironworks. The picture illustrates the technique that he uses to make cast-steel—a technique which differs in three respects from the methods employed elsewhere:

(i) His furnaces are not fixed as in most other ironworks but can be moved from one place to another.

(ii) His furnaces can hold six crucibles and not merely one or two as is customary in other plants.

(iii) He uses the hot blast for the smelting process to secure an extremely high temperature, which could not be secured merely by using the draught provided by a high chimney. By this method Fischer is able to smelt 123 lb. of steel with 120 lb. of coke and this results in a great economy of fuel. This probably explains Fischer's assertion that he is in a position to make steel more cheaply than in England although his fuel (coke) costs nearly five times as much in Schaffhausen as in England.

Fischer has sent to the Exhibition the following samples of his steel products:

(i) An ingot of meteor steel—a kind of steel which he invented and named in 1825. The top of the ingot shows a fine crystallisation which is the mark of genuine damascened steel. Meteor steel has all the other superior qualities of damascened steel.

(ii) Another ingot of meteor steel which has been cut across so that the interior crystallisation—and also the firmness and purity of the sample—can be seen.

(iii) Four bars of meteor steel which have been treated by acids in some places so as to show the damascene effect. A small piece of steel was chipped off each sample so as to show the quality of the heart of the bar.

(iv) Two daggers and four razor blades made from Fischer steel. With one exception all are damascened so as to show the effect of polishing this steel.

(v) An ingot of Swiss bar iron converted into very soft cast-steel by direct fusion. A part of this ingot is in the form of a rifle-barrel and the upper part has been smelted into a flat bar. This bar has been bent back to form a ring and this illustrates its great—its almost incredible—elasticity. This is certainly remarkable and such steel is obviously well suited to the manufacture of rifle-barrels.

(vi) A cast-iron ingot made from English scrap iron and also produced by direct fusion. The scrap iron was bought from Escher, Wyss & Co. of Zürich. A part of the ingot has been cut away to show both the soft and the hardened grain.

(vii) A gear-wheel made from the same scrap iron, cast in sand and so turned into cast-steel at the same time.

(viii) Two crucibles for smelting and their lids. They differ from normal crucibles both in shape and in the way in which the different parts have been put together. One of these has already been used to smelt bar iron so that it is possible to appreciate how resistant it is to heat.

Finally

(ix) Two small ingots made from two parts of scrap iron and one part of copper, to illustrate the possibility of combining these two metals into a cheap and useful alloy.

Colonel Fischer's steelworks were established as long ago as 1807. In the year 1804 he made his first successful experiments, though only on a small scale. Cast-steel is really an independent invention. At that time the English method of making such steel was a closely guarded secret and Fischer had to discover his own technique to produce it, which was determined by the use of a different fuel. There is no catalogue giving a price list of Fischer's products. His customers on the Continent and in England know them already. Fischer has given details of his process in a private memorandum which he has sent to the Commissioners of the Exhibition.

19. DESCRIPTION OF THE GEORG FISCHER STEELWORKS AND THEIR PRODUCTS, 1857[18]

We now come to the exhibits displayed (at the Berne Industrial Exhibition) by Georg Fischer of Schaffhausen. It has already been observed that the products displayed (by this firm) are of very high quality. They include wrought, rolled, and unwrought cast-steel ingots as well as forged bars of all types and sizes. Georg Fischer has also shown various parts of machinery and tools including an unwrought circular saw-blade, a finished saw-blade, two hardened rollers of the best cast steel, and some anvil stocks for the use of goldsmiths and metal workers. In addition there are four other cabinets in which the firms display a large assortment of files—flat, smooth, and semi-smooth and also rasp files and saw files. Finally there are two large arm files. All these products are made from cast steel produced in Georg Fischer's plant. The steel is very good and the workmanship shown in making the steel products is of the highest quality. Above all the files are so good that they equal those made anywhere else—even those manufactured in Sheffield, which is the main centre in England for the production of steel. Fischer's files are admirably adapted to the various uses to which they may be put. They are hard enough to have a very long life and their surfaces are absolutely smooth. We have tested Georg Fischer's products and have satisfied ourselves that they are of the highest quality.

K

It is true that we have not tested the actual steel itself because its excellence is evident both from the fracture in the rolled ingots and from the high quality of the various tools and machine parts made from it. Georg Fischer's price list shows that he charges no more than English firms. The best proof of this is the fact that Georg Fischer can compete successfully with English and other foreign rivals. We sincerely wish that this firm will soon be able to make Switzerland independent of other countries in the manufacture of these steel products. From information that we have received it appears that the necessary steps have been taken to expand and to increase the efficiency of Georg Fischer's plant. It is proposed to install good crucibles and furnaces so that it will be possible to make a great variety of cast steel products. Moreover it is the intention of the firm to make improvements in its equipment for forging and grinding the metal as well as for softening it or hardening it as may be required.

When the new buildings are completed the firm will increase its labour force from 4 to 80 or more. At present from $2\frac{1}{2}$ cwt. to 3 cwt. of cast steel products are made every day. Some are in the form of steel blocks or patterns while others are files or tools of various kinds, and already between one and two hundredweight of old files are resharpened daily. The firm of Escher, Wyss & Co. of Zürich orders between 7 and 8 cwt. of new files from Georg Fischer every month and sends him between 12 and 15 cwt. of files for resharpening. This is indeed the best proof that, under their present owner, these steelworks are making only goods of high quality that are sold at competitive prices.

20. SCHMIDT'S DESCRIPTION OF THE FISCHER PROCESS FOR MAKING MALLEABLE CAST IRON 1860[19]

The excellent steel products made by Georg Fischer of Schaffhausen enjoy a well deserved reputation throughout the world of technology. For rather more than a year the firm has added really first class malleable cast iron to its other products.

The raw material which is used is a unique kind of fine grained iron ore found in peat. It is smelted in crucibles placed in a circular blast furnace. At the moment the firm has only one of these furnaces. It holds five crucibles each of which contains on the average about 35 lbs of iron ore. The output of the daily smelting is between 170 lbs and 180 lbs of iron. In a year 400 cwt of malleable iron are produced from 500 cwt of iron ore. Some iron is lost in the smelting and tapping processes. The thick sand moulds are heated before tapping takes place. When the maximum heat in the furnace has been attained and when the molten iron is in its most fluid condition, the iron is poured into the moulds as quickly as possible.

The cast iron is now turned into malleable iron by placing pieces of cast iron—with appropriate additional material in the form of powder—in cylindrical crucibles 6″ in diameter and 12″ high. The crucibles are inserted into a reheating furnace which is very similar to a potter's upright furnace. Here they are fired until they are red hot and they remain in the furnace for some time. Small pieces of iron are heated for 8 or 10 hours while larger pieces require from 40 to 60 hours. The firm has three reheating furnaces holding respectively 9, 28 and 48 crucibles. Normally one reheating process is done every fortnight. The size of the reheating furnace which is used depends upon the amount of cast iron to be turned into malleable iron.

The malleable iron made by this process is of excellent quality and can be hammered or welded. Since it is superior to other products of this kind, both in softness and tenacity, it is much sought after. It can easily be bent. A turner can make screws from it. This malleable iron can be welded with other soft iron or with steel. By being polished this iron acquires the same brightness and colour as pure wrought iron made in the forge. The proof of this lies in the numerous tests which have been made with this iron. These tests have shown that holes and slits in malleable iron can be enlarged or chased in just the same way as holes and slits in ordinary wrought iron.

The price charged for this malleable cast iron varies according to the shape and size of the product. The average price is 30 kreuzer per lb in Schaffhausen. From 24 to 26 kreuzer are charged for parts of large locks and scales, for big keys, for horse shoes and for parts of harness trappings. From 28 to 30 kreuzer are charged for smaller parts of locks and guns, for secateurs, and for large scissors used by tailors. From 36 to 48 kreuzer are charged for small cash box locks, for large decorated keys, and for the handles of swords.

---

[1] *Morgenblatt für gebildete Stände,* March 23, 1808.
[2] Iron ore (bean ore) and clay (kaolin) were found at Lohn near Schaffhausen.
[3] The words in this sentence have been rearranged. The original reads 'as far as if it my power' and 'was yourself' appears over 'my power'.
[4] In the original the word 'hearing' is written above 'learning'.

5 Fischer added: 'and observe the smooth cast bar is from the cold short and the porous one from the tough iron.'

6 A Mr. Schenk was mentioned by Fischer in his *Tagebuch* for 1814 (p. 77). See below p. 125.

7 According to Fischer (*Tagebuch*, p. 107) Murdock sold platinum to gunsmiths at 15/- an ounce.

8 The words in brackets were crossed out in the original.

9 Extract from J. G. L. Blumhof, *Versuch einer Encyclopädie der Eisenhüttenkunde* (Giessen, 1817), pp. 507-8. Schenk, mentioned in this document, was the armourer David Schenk of Schaffhausen.

10 Article in the *London Journal for Arts and Sciences*, November 1823, pp. 275-7. A photostat of the article is in the Fischer archives. Fischer, then in London, wrote in his diary on June 10, 1825: '. . . When I returned home I was surprised to find that an unknown person had left me a copy of the *London Journal for Arts and Sciences* for November 1823. There was no covering letter. On reading the article I found that it was an exact translation of a paper that I had read two years previously (i.e. 1821) to the Swiss Natural History Society . . .' (*Tagebuch*, 1825, p. 230). The paper had been printed in the *Annalen der Physik* (edited by L. W. Gilbert), Vol. LXIX, 1821, pp. 257-263.

11 Fischer's *Tagebuch*, 1825, pp. 325-6.

12 Extract from Fischer's address to the Swiss Natural History Society at Solothurn in 1825: *Verhandlung der allgemeinen schweizerischen Gesellschaft für die gesammten Naturwissenschaften in ihrer elften Jahresversammlung zu Solothurn . . . 1825*, pp. 54-56.

13 Extracts from Fischer's note book (*Schreibkalender*) for 1827 in the Fischer archives. Details of Fischer's daily expenditure have been omitted.

14 Alexander-Louis Prévost (1788-1876) of Geneva was the Swiss consul in London at this time.

15 Fischer had made fire proof bricks with clay found at Lohn near Schaffhausen and had secured an Austrian patent for this invention (1827).

16 *Encyclopädische Zeitschrift des Gewerbewesens*, Vol. VI (Prague, 1846), p. 552.

17 R. Wunderlich, *Der Beobachter und Berichtstatter in London . . .* (Winterthur, 1851).

18 Report on the third Swiss Industrial Exhibition in Berne, 1857, in A. Stamm, *Georg Fischer Werksentwicklung von der Kupferschemiede zum Grossbetrieb* (typescript in the Fischer archives).

19 Carl Heinrich Schmidt, 'Die Fabrication von hämmer- und schweissbarem Gusseisen bei Georg Fischer in Schaffhausen' (*Polytechnisches Journal*, fourth series, vol. vii, 1860, p. 236). The author refers to an article in the *Württembergisches Gewerbeblatt*, 1860, No. 32. Schmidt's article has been reprinted by Karl Schib in 'Giessereigeschichtliches aus dem Kanton Schaffhausen' in H. Boesch and K. Schib, *Beiträge zur Geschichte der schweizerischen Eisengiessereien*. (Schaffhausen, 1960), p. 185.

Extracts from Fischer's Diaries

1. LONDON IN 1814

August 22, 1814

Although I had not been in London for twenty years I had no difficulty in finding my way about. I cannot honestly say that there have been any great improvements in the interval. That is certainly true of the shops and their contents. The great difference is that everything has become fantastically expensive. A good many prices, including those of the main necessities of life, have risen between 20 per cent. and 50 per cent. So far I have been unable to discover the cause, perhaps because people did not *want* to tell me. It may be that the Continental System has been an indirect cause. Again, the complete disappearance of gold coins, which were once so common, and their replacement by paper money may have been an immediate cause of the rise in prices. The English say that the impact of world events has depressed industry and trade but they hope that there will soon be a turn for the better.

As I had no urgent appointment, I decided to deliver my letters of introduction and renew my acquaintance with the London banker Mr. Y(eates) B(rown)[1]. This gave me a good opportunity to look round London and to undertake a detailed inspection of the shops, as I wished to make some purchases. In the evening Herr Schenk[2] visited us in our lodgings. At the end of the day I sent a letter home. I had learned many things that I wanted to know on my first day in London. In particular I had discovered that the price of cast steel was from 1/- to 1/8d (per lb?) delivered in London. I had also found out that in the whole of England there are only three plants making cast steel and that the process is still kept secret. I also learned that in public houses the drinks are raised out of the cellar by a little pump and the glasses are filled in that way. This admirable improvement greatly simplifies the task of the innkeeper. I had an opportunity of examining the machine in some detail and I made a sketch of it.[3]

August 23, 1814

On the morning of August 23 I visited several shops and I had a long and interesting conversation with Mr. Morris of Ludgate Hill, who is a famous gunsmith. In the light of his experience he laid down the following principle governing accuracy of fire. He argued that the greatest accuracy is secured if a rotatory motion is imparted to the bullet. He had no use for the new method of firing with hypochlorite, because this powder corrodes the inside of the barrel and soon burns it. The gunpowder which he sells is smooth and powerful. Its grains are neither round nor of uniform size. I came to an agreement with him that I should test his powder and compare it with powder made in Berne which I had brought to England with me, because he refused to accept my suggestion that the efficiency of the Berne powder was due to the roundness and the uniformity of its grains. Mr. Morris, on the contrary, thought that if the grains were angular and coarse, the powder would ignite more quickly, as there would be more points of contact. This argument seemed rather far fetched to me, but it all goes to show that a case can be made out for any point of view.

Leaving Mr. Morris I went with Ringk[4] to the British Museum. Here I was fortunate to meet Mr. Planta[5]. I was lucky to find him, as he usually lives in the country during the summer. I showed him a letter from Professor Müller[6] and also enquired after Mr. Boone. Mr. Planta was unable to give me any information concerning Mr. Boone but he promised to make some enquiries. Mr. Planta took the greatest interest in the work of Johannes von Müller[7] who now lives only in his books. Mr. Planta told me that Müller's *History of the World* would shortly be appearing in an English translation.

Mr. Planta kindly arranged for the museum to be opened for me. I have not the space to give a detailed description of it here, but it has changed very much for the better in the last twenty years. Much rubbish has been thrown out. Everything is much better displayed and more systematically arranged. There is now a fine cabinet of minerals. For the most part it contains the choicest specimens, which are classified on the principles laid down by Hauy[8] and Werner[9]. The antique busts, statues, and bas-reliefs are displayed in fine rooms. From an antiquarian point of view the best exhibits are undoubtedly the objects found in the course of excavations in Egypt and Herculaneum. The exhibit which interested me most was the famous wall painting (from Herculaneum) depicting the worship of Isis. As far as I know it is the only monument which has inscriptions in the Greek, Coptic and ancient Egyptian languages.

On leaving the museum I visited the most famous pencil factory in London. This is Bookman[10] and Layton of (28) Great Russell Street, Bloomsbury Square. I had already visited J(ohn) Middleton & Co. of Shoe Lane, Fleet Street,[11] who also makes pencils, but is in a cheaper line of business. In both factories I had an opportunity of seeing how the pencils were made. I satisfied myself that the outstanding quality of the pencils was due solely to the high grade graphite which is found only in (Cumberland).[12] The graphite is carefully graded so that both soft and hard pencils can be made.

A journey of several miles took me to Messrs. Bouverie[13] and Antrobus and then I went to call on Herr Huber in Green Street, Grosvenor Square, whom I had hoped to see before his departure. However, I look forward to seeing him and Frau Huber in Switzerland, and this to some extent compensates me for my disappointment at missing him in London. He would have been most helpful to me.

At six o'clock in the evening I fulfilled an engagement to dine with Yeates Brown of Manchester Street, Manchester Square. He and his wife received me in that friendly and hospitable manner which was often to occur again during my stay in England. The splendour of the house reflects the wealth of its owner. In the dining room there were not only arm-chairs but also a kind of low sofa like an eastern divan. All the furniture was made of rich, highly polished mahogany and the coverings were of the very best embroidered taffeta. There was a Gothic stained glass window in the alcove facing the garden. Silver cutlery and choice crystal glasses completed the picture. The wines were very good, the madeira being of exceptionally high quality.

After dinner, at 10 p.m., tea was served. Mr. Brown showed me several magnificent books from his splendid library. A particular rarity was a copy of *One Hundred Merry Tales of Shakespeare*. The original manuscript was once lost and it has only recently been discovered by chance. In accordance with a custom peculiar to England it was reprinted in a limited edition of only 50 copies. On looking through this book I seemed to recall having read the first two or three stories before and then I remembered that I had read them when I was a boy in an old German book illustrated with woodcuts and bound together with Aesop's fables. It was the work of a certain Hofmann and philologists would no doubt be interested to know whether the English or the German version was printed first.

As I was leaving Mr. Brown was good enough to invite me to call at his office on the following day, so that he could give me letters of introduction which would help me in the journey which I proposed to make to the north of England.

August 24, 1814

On the morning of August 24 my first task was to secure a visa for my passport at the Aliens Office, Crown Street, Westminster. Here, as elsewhere, I noticed that Englishmen were much politer to foreigners than they had been 20 years before, particularly to those asking their way. It rained heavily without interruption all day long, so I could not go far afield and I confined myself to paying a few calls in the centre of London. I collected my letters of introduction from Messrs. Brown and Siordet.[14] Next I visited Dollond, the famous optician,[15] (Samuel) Fenn, steelmerchant of (105) Newgate Street[16] and (Edward) Stammers the cutler of 99 The Strand.[17] Stammers makes knives which are plated on both sides with silver and have a fine permanent cutting edge. These knives do not get rusty or lose their brightness.

August, 25, 1814

I assumed that in the evening I would be able to catch one of the many mail coaches which run daily to Birmingham. In the morning I did a little more business with Dollond. I discussed various matters with him, including the merits of the alloys used by Short and by Herschel in the manufacture of mirrors and in the differences in the refractive power of crown glass and flint glass. On the whole he seemed to share my view that—assuming equal efficiency in the smelting processes—iron would prove to be better than copper, as it would give the reflector greater brightness and a whiter colour. It is well known that it is just as easy to alloy iron with tin as it is to alloy copper with tin. Arsenic is not required for the tin-iron alloy.

At 2 p.m. Mr. S.[18] called for us at our lodgings and we lunched with him at the Queens Arms in Cheapside. During our stay in London he has been most helpful to me and to my travelling companion.[19]

Before we had lunch Mr. S. was kind enough to go with us to five different places from which coaches leave for Birmingham, but we were unable to book a seat, as they had all been taken. So I paid £2 to book a seat for the following afternoon at 4 p.m. I called at the shop of James Tringham, a crucible dealer of 3, Cary Lane, Foster Lane, Cheapside.[20] I was very pleased to discover that English crucibles of black iron are just the same as my own in height, breadth, and thickness. They do not in any way resemble the crucibles made in Germany. I thought that these English crucibles were very expensive since they cost 4d a lb or about 32 kreuzers in our (Swiss) money for a crucible weighing 3 lb. At home one would pay only 15 kreuzers for such a crucible.

After lunch we went to the Strand, where I hoped to make the acquaintance of Mr. Berola, the watchmaker, but as he was not at home I called at the cutler whose shop was next door to Berola's and gave him two razors made nine years ago by Kym of Berlingen from my steel. At that time I was making steel only in very small quantities. I asked the cutler to sharpen and polish these razors himself, so that he could tell me what he thought of the quality of the razors and the steel.

On the same evening I discovered the workshop of an important firm of tool manufacturers at 10, Cockspur Street, Charing Cross. The owners were Germans named Holtzapffel and Deyerlein. Herr Holtzapffel was most helpful and showed me his stock of lathes. The cheapest cost 30 guineas, the most expensive—fitted with devices for performing basset work and engine turning—cost 250 guineas. I admired the beautiful finish of these lathes, and saw two simple but effective attachments for cutting threads and hollowing out. These attachments were quite new to me . . .

It was too early to have a look at the gas lighting in Pall Mall, but in order to find out how to get there eventually, we went past Wedgwood's showrooms near St. James's Square. Then we returned to our lodgings where we entertained Mr. S. to tea in the English fashion until ten o'clock in the evening.

August 26, 1814[21]

Early on the morning of August 26 I took a walk to Snow Hill in the hope of seeing a brewing apparatus which can be used in the home. I found out, however, that the inventor has moved to Piccadilly with his machine. Next I called upon Mr. Berola and showed him the rolled steel for watch springs which I had brought with me to London. He was delighted with it.

Berola and I fetched the Berlingen razor on which Mr. Stammers had passed a very favourable opinion. We then called upon the mechanic who supplies Mr. Berola with watch springs so that he too could see my rolled steel. Like most Englishmen he had a prejudice against all foreign products. I drew his attention, however, to the merits of my steel and pointed out to him how laborious—one might almost say how unnecessarily tedious—was the method employed in England to make watch-springs. English makers of watch-springs buy their cast steel wire costing 6s 8d (a reel) and cut off what they require [by] hand. Every spring has to be heated six or seven times before it is thin enough. In the end Mr. Berola's spring maker showed signs of being convinced and actually promised Mr. Berola to make some springs from my rolled steel that very day.

On the way back to my lodgings I called upon Mr. (Samuel) Fenn, a watchmaker at (105) Newgate Street.[22] He, too, was delighted with the rolled steel strips for watch springs which I showed him, and told me that in his opinion no similar product was made in England. It may be added that the very high price of English watches, as compared with Swiss watches, proves how laborious are the methods used to make English watch springs. A single English watch spring costs nearly as much—half a crown—as a dozen of similar quality made in Locle or Fleurier (in Switzerland).

As I had to be at the Swan with Two Necks to catch the Birmingham coach I only had time to have my lunch and pack the bare essentials for my journey. Herr Ringk and Herr S. were good enough to see me off and I asked Herr S. if he would kindly give Herr Ringk any assistance that he might require in my absence.

The outside of the coach was already occupied by nine people and I had an inside seat. My travelling companions were a type-founder and a pharmacist, both of London, and a gentleman farmer from the neighbourhood of York. He wore a coat of fine cloth and had a silver tipped cane. Despite his well dressed appearance he had the unpleasant habit of squeezing the contents of his nose onto the floor of the coach before making use of his handkerchief. I was astonished at such conduct from one who was no mere peasant and I was equally surprised that no one in the coach showed the slightest concern.

The company seemed pleased that I joined in the conversation and the type-founder regaled me with an account of the antiquities of St. Albans, through which we passed. He said that some of the houses had been standing since Julius Caesar's day, and from their dilapidated condition I could well believe it.

The coaches in this part of England travel unusually quickly. Their speed is between 8 and 9 miles an hour, whereas elsewhere they only go between 7 and 8 miles an hour. Consequently we reached Coventry in good time. This is an important town, but it is not a beautiful one. We reached Birmingham on the morning of August 27.

2. BOULTON AND WATT'S WORKS AT SOHO

August 28, 1814 (Birmingham)

I spent the morning writing and at two o'clock in the afternoon I went from Birmingham to Soho, which is a good hour's walk away. Mr. Watt's house is situated in a very large and charming park. It is a much superior dwelling to the others in the neighbourhood, for it is built of stone and has a slate roof. Most houses in Birmingham and elsewhere in England are built of clay and red bricks. The interior of Mr. Watt's house shows that the owner is a very wealthy man, for it contains all the English demand for their comfort. A servant conducted me to a sitting room, and Mr. Watt came in almost immediately. Mr. (Yeates) Brown in his letter of introduction to Mr. Watt had referred to me as the director of our (Schaffhausen) iron-ore mines and so the conversation was quickly directed to this topic. Mr. Watt wanted to know the location and state of our mines. He produced an excellent map by Weiss[23] and I was able to show him all that he wanted to know from it. The conversation then turned to a consideration of different kinds of iron and also to steam engines.

Much to my surprise Mr. Watt showed me round that part of his plant in Soho which is devoted to the manufacture of steam engines. I was dumbfounded at what I saw. No description could do justice to the building in which these works are housed. I was amazed both at the great masses of iron and at the skill which the workmen had devoted to the construction of the building. What might have seemed impossible has now been achieved. What was once a confused pile of piping and cylinders has become an elegant iron building of Doric and Corinthian pillars.

I was shown a collection of Swedish, Siberian, and English iron. Mr. (Matthew Robinson) Boulton, who is Mr. Watt's partner, joined us while we were looking over the smithy and turners shop. I greatly admired the wonderful craftsmanship of the smiths although they were engaged only in the humble task of making a chisel. The cutting blade was fixed in a hazelwood shaft and was secured with wire so that no joins were visible. These chisels rarely break and never recoil in the workman's hand. I visited a workshop next to the counting house, which contained a large number of copying machines and here again I could not help admiring the characteristically high standard of craftsmanship of the workers.

Choice wines were served at lunch and the conversation was animated. In his letter of introduction Mr. (Yeates) Brown had mentioned that I could speak English fluently and this fact stood me in good stead with the assembled company. The conversation came round to the composition of metals in ancient times and I could not refrain from mentioning my discovery of yellow steel.[24] Those present were very interested in a sample which I showed them and they at once invited a certain Mr. Murdock to join us for tea. I was told that he had an exceptional knowledge of metallurgy and that he had long been engaged in working on metal alloys. The dessert was very plentiful by English standards and included bunches of large muscatel and other grapes which cost at least half a guinea and sometimes a whole guinea.

Tea and coffee were served together and the conversation again turned to the composition of metals. Mr. Murdock proved to be a very competent metallurgist but he had not got beyond making an alloy composed of equal parts of copper and iron. When a big ironworks in the neighbourhood was mentioned Mr. Watt said to me: 'Stay the night. I assume that you can ride. Tomorrow we will get our horses saddled and we will ride over to visit some of the more interesting ironworks (in the district). They include one which employs 5,000 men.' I declined the invitation to stay the night since I did not wish to appear to be too forward, but I gladly agreed to visit the neighbouring ironworks on the following day. When I left Mr. Watt went with me as far as the entrance to his park . . .

On the following morning (August 29th, 1814) I left Birmingham at 7.30 a.m. and walked five miles to Soho. During breakfast a certain Mr. Low of Trinidad appeared . . . Mr. Low soon left us and went to the foundry and engineering workshops where he wanted to discuss matters with Mr. Murdock. Soon afterwards Mr. Watt said: 'Let's go. I am never sure when people are going to buttonhole me'. We had excellent horses and were attended by a groom and a Danish dog . . .

After we had ridden for nearly a mile, Mr. Watt suddenly pulled up his horse and said: 'I am going to take you to a plant to which no foreigner is usually admitted. Do not tell anybody, not even Mr. (Yeates) Brown, that you have been there. Do not give anybody a letter of introduction to me asking me to admit them because it will be of no avail.' We continued down a long road which contained pleasant cottages for the workers, all built exactly to the same plan and each with a very nice garden. We dismounted at a big gate leading to a drive.

During her stay in England the Grand Duchess Catherine, famous for her learning and interest in scientific progress, considered these ironworks to be sufficiently remarkable to be honoured with a visit. She had asked Mr. Watt to let her see the entire establishment. Mr. Watt drew my particular attention to the fact that the Grand Duchess had been graciously pleased to discuss with him at some length the construction and mechanism of the many steam engines which she saw there. These ironworks are situated on the canal linking Birmingham with Hull, Portsmouth, London and Liverpool, the four main English seaports. The works are completely enclosed by a high wall and consist of several separate buldings, each of which is many hundreds of feet in length. The most important are the foundry, the pattern shop, and the new workshop. Four furnaces produce enough molten iron to enable castings to be made up to a weight of 200 cwt. The plant containing the stores for drying the moulds is situated opposite the foundry. The whole space between these two buildings forms a pit in which the largest cylinders are cast upright. The sand for the moulds is dug on the site. It contains some ferrous dust and a great deal of mica. The whole of Birmingham is built on such sand.

I visited what I would call the Iron House because the floor, the stairs, and the roof are made entirely of cast iron. The floor and the stairs are not slippery, but are rough cast like a carpet. They are painted black and are kept spotlessly clean. In this and other buldings steam engines of 6 to 50 h.p. are at work. They perform their allotted tasks quietly, regularly and efficiently—a tribute to all that human ingenuity has contributed to their construction. Among other things these steam engines strike money, roll lead into sheets, stamp out plated wares and move hammers. They move large piston rods and winches. They also bore out cylinders but it often takes many months to turn out a pair of them. Dozens of boilers were to be seen made of black iron plates . . . and beautifully rivetted together.

All the workshops and even the big courtyard were lit by gas which had been installed by Mr. Murdock. Mr. Watt was good enough to show me the installation and to explain how it worked. The coking—strictly speaking the distillation—of the coal takes place in two large furnaces. The separation of the gas from the bitumen and other substances takes place in two other containers nearby. The gas is conveyed in pipes from the containers into two iron holders with a capacity of about 3,000 cubic feet of gas. These holders—closed at the top —are open at the bottom but are sealed by the crater in which they stand.

In order to show me how the installation worked Mr. Watt had the counting house cleared, and then he lit the gas. The light on every desk came from glass lamps containing four jets. It burned brightly without any odour. No one has yet made known publicly the method by which the smell of the gas can be removed and the blue part of the flame can be eliminated, but many attempts to do this have been successful.

July 4, 1851

I wished to go to the Soho plant which was once so famous. In 1814 Mr. Watt, the owner of the works at that time, had received me in a most friendly manner. So I took a cab and Mr. Weiss was good enough to accompany me. He had already told me that this great plant for the construction of machinery had suffered a complete decline since the deaths of Mr. Watt and his partner Mr. (Matthew Robinson) Boulton—whom I also knew well. When we got to Soho no one was in the office. The many workshops were quite empty, deserted, and decayed. What a difference from what I had seen when this plant was at the height of its glory and when the two partners enjoyed an income greater than that of many a prince. I would never have believed so rapid a change possible had I not seen it with my own eyes. Here as in many another place the inscription 'sic transit gloria mundi' would indeed be appropriate.

3. THE WEDGWOOD POTTERY WORKS 1814

September 1, 1814 (Newcastle under Lyme)

On the following morning, September 1st, I booked a seat on the mail coach to Manchester which was due to leave at

4 p.m. Then I set off for Etruria, which is three miles distant from Newcastle under Lyme. As in Soho (Birmingham) so in Etruria, the approach to the works is along a pleasant road lined with workers' cottages. This factory, too, is situated on a canal and there are numerous iron waggon ways in the vicinity.

Mr. Wedgwood was already in his office (when I arrived). When I presented Mr. Watt's letter of introduction he said: 'Mr. Fischer, if you would like to see the factory I will get someone to show you round at once, and then you can come to my house for lunch.' I was shown everything from the working of the steam engine to the storing and packing of the china.

Wedgwood's flint comes from the Gravesend district. It is first calcined, then crushed, and finally ground by millstones. These are similar to those used for grinding watch glasses, but they are between six and nine feet in diameter. The same process is used for the various types of clay, such as pipeclay. When these operations have been completed the flint and clay are mixed in equal proportions. Next the mixture is fed into somewhat smaller mills where water is added, so that the material can be kneaded into pulp which is passed through sieves. These sieves are made from the finest silk thread and they are subsequently shaken by a crank mechanism. Eventually the mixture attains an almost incredible degree of fineness. The silk threads are so fine and so close together that the particles which pass between them are only one thousandth of an inch in diameter. The mixture flows into receptacles and is then transferred to drying beds of soft bricks which are 60 feet long, 20 feet broad and 9 inches deep. The mixture is heated in a small flame and is continually stirred. After some 24 hours it is thick enough to be transferred to the cylinders.

It is perhaps not strictly accurate to apply the term 'cylinders' to these vessels since their shape is that of inverted truncated cones. These cones are five feet high. At the top they are three feet wide and at the bottom they are two feet wide. At the base of each cone there is a short gutter, one foot inside and nine inches deep. The cones move on wheels and an iron shaft passes through them. So called 'knives' are fixed to the upright iron shafts. The knives are so arranged that they fit neatly between the shaft and the inside of the cone. Their flat sides lie in the form of a spiral so that anyone who looks down into the cone appears to see something resembling the inside of a snail's shell. Clay is thrown into the cone from time to time and it is eventually pressed out from a hole at the bottom. It is cut by a wire into square blocks which are thrown on to a heap near at hand. The clay ferments or rather the moisture spreads uniformly through the clay. Then the clay is passed through the cones again and it is once more cut up into blocks of regular size. The blocks are placed by the workers on planks. It may be added that the waggonways or iron roads which are to be found all over the factory are mainly used for transporting these materials. They are moved in small open boxes on little waggons. A waggon of this kind, with its load, weighs nearly twelve hundredweights but it can be pushed by a woman. A loaded waggon was weighted in my presence to satisfy my curiosity.

The clay has now been prepared for use, and the next process is performed on the ordinary potter's wheel. The making of flat plates, however, is different and will be described later. The potter's wheel in use in England differs in only two respects from that used in Switzerland. It is made of mahogany to prevent warping and it is driven by machinery and not by manual power. This lightens the labour very considerably and enables output to be almost doubled.

I saw a very simple but very efficient device by which the speed of the potter's wheel can be varied despite the fact that the steam engine works at a constant rate. The device consists of two hollow cones a foot apart. One is in the normal position while the other is upside down. One cone is driven directly by the machine itself while the other is driven by a leather belt which links the two cones. A pulley passes down the spindle of the potter's wheel and the worker operates a treadle which controls the motions of an iron fork. This fork moves the leather belt up or down as desired. When the belt moves upwards the blades in the cone move more slowly and when the belt is moved down then the blades revolve very fast. This arrangement, of course, will work satisfactorily only if nothing happens to loosen the belt and so change the relative positions of the two cones. The same elegant device of parallel cones—one upright and one reversed—is used to regulate the lathes which I will describe later.

After leaving the potter's wheel the clay is placed in receptacles in a drying room which has a temperature of 80° Réaumur (100° Centigrade). The clay soon attains a consistency which is rather firmer than the 'air dried' clay of our (Swiss) potters. In this state the clay comes onto horizontal turning lathes. The clay has now sufficient consistency to be handled without any danger of losing its shape and it is mounted—in a very simple manner—on a wooden chuck or pattern. The only tools which are used for throwing are thin scrapers which are bent into various shapes. These instruments are also used to polish the crockery when the throwing process has been completed. When one considers how fine a materials is being used the success achieved in the throwing and polishing processes is really remarkable.

When the crockery has hardened sufficiently to be ready for the kiln it is placed—according to its size—in appropriate receptacles. These receptacles (saggers) are made from the coarsest firebrick. At this point I noticed something which is perhaps not generally known outside England, but is nevertheless of great importance. In order to prevent the distortion of the dishes and plates, some rough quartz sand is poured into the receptacle (sagger) so that all the spaces between the pieces of crockery are filled and each piece is safely covered and protected. Moreover this sand is a good conductor of heat and yet—owing to the size of the grains—the moisture generated by the heating process is able to escape.

Next the crockery is placed in round kilns (12 feet high and 12 feet wide) which have a dome or cupola at the top. The Germans would call them upright kilns. The heat which is required for this process comes from ten furnaces which are arranged—equidistant from each other—in the form of a circle. One fire heats the centre of the kiln. In this way the heat is distributed in a uniform manner so that the crockery can be baked properly. The process can be carefully regulated, since there are peep holes through which the crockery can be observed while the baking is going on. This initial process takes 60 hours, and is called 'overfiring'. I was struck by the fact that the kiln was opened immediately the firing was completed, with the result that the crockery had already cooled by the following day when it was taken out. I should add that each kiln is protected by an outer structure in the form of a sugar loaf.

The manufacture of plates (is different). It is a simple process. A sufficiently large lump of potter's clay is placed on a slab of plaster and beaten with a hammer of roughly the same size. These pieces of clay are then placed in a plate-mould and are sponged all over. Later, when the plate is dry enough, it is turned on a lathe and is polished in the same way as other pieces of crockery.

L

After the firing process comes the glazing process. The glaze is not poured over the pottery. Instead the pieces of crockery are dipped into a tub full of glaze. This is a very quick method. An even greater advantage of this method is that the glaze is applied in a uniform manner and is not put on too thickly. Once it has been glazed the crockery is dried on thin circular clay rests which resemble the grindstones used to sharpen knives. The crockery is now again placed in receptacles (saggers) which are heated for 12 or 14 hours. This is what takes place when the crockery is to be glazed in one colour. On the other hand if the glazing is to be ornamental in character then the crockery has to go through a further process. A mineral dye is made into a thick paste with linseed oil and is then warmed and rubbed on to engraved copper plates. An impression on silk paper is taken from these plates. The silk paper is wrapped round the chinaware which has been varnished with turpentine. By this means the decoration is transferred from the copper plate to the crockery. Next the crockery is dipped in water so that the silk paper is washed off and the impression is left behind. To remove the oil and the turpentine the crockery is lightly fired and then glazed. If the decoration is in some colour other than black, a second application of mineral dye is necessary before the last firing. This method of decorating earthenware pottery by means of (engraved) copper plates was first invented some 35 years ago by Adam Spengler, a native of Schaffhausen.[25] His name is now almost forgotten. He was the director of the former porcelain factory near Zürich which he founded. Owing to the poverty of his parents he never had a good education and his talents were not fully developed. In other circumstances he would have been an outstanding figure in his trade. As it was—although born in dire poverty—he nevertheless raised himself from the position of an ordinary potter to that of a skilful manufacturer.

In Wedgwood's factory I saw a very efficient—though probably little known—method of quickly putting small decorations, such as names or coats of arms, on to pottery. The dye is smeared on to a small engraved copper plate (leaving a residue on the lines of the engraving). A piece of very flexible rubber of suitable size is placed over the engraved part of the plate. In this way an impression from the engraved lines (on the copper plate) is transferred to the piece of rubber. Next the piece of rubber is wrapped round the chinaware so that the names or coats of arms are transferred to the crockery.

Over thirty people are employed in the workshop for decorating chinaware. They include some very competent artists, particularly in landscape painting. Girls are employed to paint common subjects such as borders. The methods used to apply enamels and drawings of concentric rings are just the same as those in other porcelain factories.

I was greatly impressed by the skill with which both black and coloured crockery were embellished with charming embossed decorations and figures. The hollow moulds are derived from a metal casting. The pipe clay from which they are made is of very fine quality and has only been very lightly fired so that it absorbs a great amount of dampness. The clay, which is fairly soft, is pressed into these moulds and all the surplus clay is removed. If a very thin or fragile area requires trimming it is simply scraped smooth with a spatula. The ornaments made in this way are fixed to the main piece of chinaware by wetting the spot to which they are to be attached. They are then pressed into position with the finger and the process is completed by means of a fine brush of camel hair.

I also noticed that the clay, or the material from which the black crockery is made, has a dark rust colour before it is fired. This shows that the material used for securing a black colour is oxide of iron. Several hollow metal cylinders are used for making different kinds of moulded handles and other decorations which are fixed to chinaware. Holes can be made in the cylinders if necessary. A cylinder is filled with a length of soft clay and a piston or metal ramrod is pressed upon it by means of a screw. In a short time many feet of shaped strips come out of the cylinder. One strip can be used at a time or alternatively several strips can be interlaced as is done when china fruit dishes are made.

Throughout my visit I was greatly impressed by the simplicity of the technique used and the skilful division of labour employed. When I had seen everything I wished to see I went to the showroom in which many articles were displayed. I selected for my own use a dinner service and a black tea service.

I then called on Mr. Wedgwood at his house which is pleasantly situated on a little hill half a mile from the factory. The conversation at dinner was mainly on scientific and industrial topics. Mr. Wedgwood appeared to be unwilling to discuss his own inventions, though he did say something about the pyrometer (furnace thermometer). He gave me the astonishing information that the contraction (which takes place) in this instrument no longer follows the same laws as it formerly did. Mr. Wedgwood ascribed this to changes which had taken place over a period of time in the mass of clay, as well as to internal fermentation. I told Mr. Wedgwood that I would like to select a porcelain tea service for my own use, but that I had not yet found anything suitable. To my surprise he replied: 'I cannot advise you to buy porcelain here. You are going home through France and you can get better and more beautiful porcelain in Paris. I shall probably soon give up the manufacture of porcelain.' I expressed my astonishment, and Mr. Wedgwood said that France had much better materials for making porcelain than England. I talked about Chinese kaolin and pé-tun-tzé.[26] Mr. Wedgwood replied that nothing of importance had been written about Chinese porcelain since the appearance of Father Halde's book.[27] Mr. Wedgwood also observed—and this is fairly well known—that this remarkable mixture will stand a greater degree of heat than European porcelain . . .

The time at my disposal had come to an end. I took my leave of Mr. Wedgwood, a man whose father—a common Staffordshire potter—had established a factory which, because of the excellence of its products, had sent its goods all over the world. Now his son is doing his best to increase the established reputation of the firm.

4. MANCHESTER IN 1814

September 2, 1814

On the morning of September 2nd I reached Manchester which has now become a large town with a considerable population. Formerly it was so unimportant that it did not send members to Parliament.[28] At a suitable time in the morning I presented my letter of introduction from Messrs. Boulton and Watt of Soho to Mr. (George Augustus) Lee, who owns a spinning mill which is so large that there can be few to equal it in size. Mr. Lee was just going to the Exchange and he took me with him. He said to me: 'I will find a gentleman (Mr. Willoughby) on the Exchange who is associated with me in the spinning mill and he will take you round Manchester and show you the sights. Mr. Parienta, a Portuguese gentleman who called on me yesterday, will join you. At 4 p.m. we will go to my house in the country for dinner.' But it took us two hours to find Mr. Willoughby and I was getting anxious lest the time at my disposal should slip away. Mr. Willoughby was a highly intelligent man and he understood that we[29] wanted to see the things that really mattered.

He first took us to a factory in which the so-called 'Manchester cloth' or fustian is woven and cut. The cutting is done by rapier like instruments about two feet in length . . . The cloth—6 feet broad—is stretched on a frame and the operator cuts it with a single thrust. By long experience the operator can do this with remarkable skill and speed.

Next we visited a teazling mill, a singeing furnace, a bleach works—in which a very rapid method of bleaching was employed—and also a dyeworks for finishing the fustian cloth. Power is supplied to the teazling machine by a steam engine. The machine consists of wooden cylinders encased in tin plates in which holes have been punched to roughen the surfaces. These cylinders draw the fustian between long hard brushes which move backwards and forwards with great speed. By this means all the fibre which has not been woven into the cloth is brushed away. The cloth now goes to the singeing furnace where it is exposed to the heat emitted by a large number of semi-cylindrical cast iron pipes. These pipes are heated by flames from a coal fire which are continually fanned by a draught. Each pipe is 8 or 9 inches in diameter. The length of the pipes is a little more than the width of the cloth. The teazled cloth, which has to be absolutely dry at this stage of the process, is kept moving over the glowing iron pipes at the rate of about $3\frac{1}{2}$ feet every 5 seconds. The cloth is pressed firmly onto the iron pipes. Next the cloth passes through a rapid bleaching process in which oxygenated hydrochloric acid is used. This method is well known and has often been described. It immediately removes the brown marks which are frequently caused by the singeing process. The only comment that occurs to me is that this method of bleaching cloth has no bad effects provided that the acid is thoroughly washed out of the cloth afterwards.

The only aspect of the dyeing operation which was particularly noteworthy was the use of steam power to supply water to various boilers and square receptacles. In the preparation of grey cloth it should be observed that the singeing process takes place after the cloth has been dyed (and not before). I asked Mr. B, the owner of this factory, for information concerning the price of these cloths but I do not know enough about the trade to be able to say if the English cloths are cheaper or dearer than those made on the Continent. Mr. B said that the cloths of lower quality cost 1s. 4d. a yard or 44 kreuzer for 1½ ells and cloths of better quality cost 4s. 6d. (2 gulden, 28 kreuzer) per yard. Mr. B. was a gentleman of excellent manners who did not adopt a superior attitude towards his workmen but lent a hand himself with any job that was being done. Mr. Willoughby told me that Mr. B. was worth at least £50,000.

We went from this factory to Mr. C's mechanical spinning and weaving shed. Here every mule jenny is driven by steam power and has 240 spindles. When the carriage of the mule jenny is as far back as it can go it stops of its own accord to allow time for the twisting operation. Why is this still a purely manual operation in Switzerland?

The carding machines are very similar to those used in Switzerland. But—like the spinning machines—they are not very well finished. It is worthy of comment that the spindles are made entirely of steel and that the yarn is wound directly on them whereas in Switzerland the yarn is wound first onto a bobbin and then onto a spindle. The cotton is very thick, dirty and knotted together and is wound round a thin cloth-covered wooden cylinder from which it is fed into the carding machine. I found it difficult at first to understand how a fine thread could be produced in this way. But when I examined the preliminary spinning of the cotton which I have never seen on the Continent . . . I appreciated the reason for the high reputation of English yarn and English cloth. It was a No. 40 yarn which was being spun here . . . and it was woven immediately afterwards.

Some years ago one read in the newspapers about the rising of the (handloom) weavers at Nottingham and one or two other places. The weavers had destroyed power looms and weaving sheds. And when one sees these power looms for oneself it is easy to appreciate the bitter feelings of the men who have been thrown out of work (by them). Fifty of these looms —operated by one and the same steam engine—stood in a medium sized room. Each was no more than about 4 feet in height, length and width. They were operated by 15 artisans and one foreman. The movement of the shuttle to and fro (by a spring) and the passing of the thread (into the machine) take place rather more quickly than could be done by hand. Consequently the output per hour by the power loom is rather more than by the handloom. Moreover as the foreman rightly observed the power loom does not get tired in the same way that a handloom weaver gets tired. Consequently the cloth produced by the power loom is more uniform—and therefore of higher quality—than cloth made by hand. I proved this to my own satisfaction by taking away with me samples of the cloth woven by the power loom and grey Manchester cloth woven by hand.

I would have liked to have seen a calico roller printing works but there was no time for this. On the way to Mr. Lee's house I learned something of a process which removes from workrooms in factories the unpleasant smell of hydrogen gas while at the same time changes the flame from a blue to a bright colour. This process is still kept secret.

We travelled to Walnut Cottage which is Mr. Lee's country house. It is three miles away from Manchester and is situated in pleasant grounds. Mr. Lee's sister keeps house for him. She is a very well educated and highly cultured woman and is the author of the 'Canterbury Tales'. Our lively conversation came to an end at eight o'clock when a special messenger from Manchester brought Mr. Lee a letter. Mr. Lee left for Manchester immediately and Mr. Parienta and I accompanied him.

I asked Mr. Lee where in England a locomotive was used instead of horses to draw waggons. He said it was in Leeds. As I knew nobody there Mr. Lee was kind enough to write a letter of introduction in all haste to Mr. Gott, the greatest cloth manufacturer in the country. As I had already booked my seat on the Leeds coach for the following morning I no longer had an opportunity of going to Mr. Lee's spinning mill, although he offered to show me over his works himself in the evening. I was, however, able to admire the brilliant lighting of the dining room by means of hydrogen gas which streamed out of the jets of crystal gas holders. I left Manchester on September 3 delighted with the new and remarkable things that I had seen. I had not originally planned to go to Manchester as the time at my disposal was limited. My visit was due to the friendly advice of Mr. Watt and to the letter of introduction (to Mr. Lee) which he gave me.

I might add that Mr. Lee is an expert in many branches of knowledge and he is certainly one of the most outstanding Englishmen of today. He was the first to have the courage to introduce gas lighting on a large scale. For this purpose he availed himself of the services of Mr. Murdock, the inventor of the apparatus for generating hydrogen gas for lighting which was made at Boulton and Watt's works.

5. AN IRONWORKS NEAR WEDNESBURY

June 15, 1825 (at Birmingham)

After a breakfast which made it easy to forget about another meal until six in the evening we went in the direction of Wednesbury to the great iron foundry on the canal. We entered a huge hall at the end of which were two cupola blast furnaces each about 10 feet high and 30 inches broad. They were operating continuously, the blast of air being injected from two nozzles fixed at opposite sides of the furnace. Over a hundred men were at work most of whom being stripped to the waist because of the extreme heat. They were engaged in a series of non-stop operations—casting the iron into moulds; rubbing the sand from the red-hot cast iron wares as they came from the moulds; removing or breaking the moulds, and carrying the ironwares to the annealing furnace. I was amazed at the precision with which these operations were carried out and at the way in which everybody went about his appointed task so that order emerged from apparent confusion. The products made here include kitchen utensils of all kinds, ornaments, and even nails of as small a size as one inch in length. The nails are softened and are sold for 7 kreuzer a pound in our money or one shilling for five pounds.

It would be appropriate to describe in greater detail the methods used in these works where thousands of products are accurately moulded and successfully cast. Any professional ironmaster knows that the scraping of the moulding-boxes and the removal of ironwares from the sandy mould normally entails the destruction of the mould. But when small cheap objects are being made, this is impracticable. The moulds in which the nails are to be cast are made in form of metal plates constructed on the same principle as stereotype or bas relief. The heads and upper parts of the nails are cast in holes sunk into the plate which is attached to the furnace. In the middle of one half of the mould are four holes which fit exactly into the four taps of the other half of the mould. Before the two parts of the mould are joined everything is carefully cleaned and then covered with a layer of coal dust so that the nails now form part of the mould. One half of the nails protrude out of the mould. Both the heads of the nails and the channels through which the molten metal flows are slanted at an angle so that none of the fluid metal is lost. In this way a number of half nails are made in one portion of the mould. Then the taps on one half of the mould are joined to the holes in the other half of the mould so that complete nails can be cast.

It may be added that all the moulds are made of strong solid iron. On the other hand the moulds for kitchen utensils are often complex in character. They are placed one on top of the other according to size and are formed into moulds which are divided vertically into two sections. Some moulds are divided into several parts. These moulds are made of copper toughened under the hammer.

They are able to smelt as much as 12 hundredweights of very grey Staffordshire pig iron an hour using a powerful blast and good coke. Even after resmelting it remains grey in colour and granular in texture provided that it is not cast too thin and is not cooled too quickly.

As a precaution, however, everything is put into the softening or annealing furnaces. The iron products are placed in large cast iron cylinders which are five feet high and two feet broad. Six of these cylinders are inserted in a furnace and are packed with powdered cement. After twenty four hours really soft iron is produced which can be drilled, filed and bored. But the nails are treated rather differently. The utensils which come out of the annealing furnaces go next to the lathes where the turner's work is made easy because the iron is now smooth and the sand falls off easily. After the turning process the utensils often have a silver appearance.

From the turning lathes the utensils go to the locksmiths' workshop for scouring, for the drilling of holes, and for the fixing of handles. The method of scouring the cast iron utensils is the best that I have ever seen. It is economical in fluid and fuel and there is no danger of the workers burning their hands because they use fine strong tongs to hold the scouring material.

Finally when their products are shining brightly these workers in cast iron—like coppersmiths—tin the bottoms of the utensils so as to prevent coagulation. After the tempering process the outsides of the utensils are tarred as to prevent rusting and to give them a fine black finish. Before they are packed for despatch the utensils are dried at a heat which does not melt the tin and they are also provided with lids made of tinned sheet iron. On every utensil the number of pints which it holds is clearly marked, which is very convenient for many users.[31]

6. THE WOOLWICH ARSENAL, 1825-7

I

October 22, 1825

Major Johnson, Royal Artillery, received me in a very court-eous manner and instructed an officer of the watch to show me round. This officer was quite young but he was anxious to give me all the help that he could.

We first visited the foundry. Two Miller's cannon[32] were just being cast by a new system that I shall describe later. These 24 pounders were in the pit ready for casting while six others were being moulded.

The metal that was being used was an alloy consisting of 100 parts of copper to 11 parts of tin. I was impressed by the method of casting. The metal is poured into the mould through a funnel shaped like a cone. The advantage of this method is that the metal entering the mould is quite pure. Moreover it is especially advantageous that the metal, which is very hot, flows into the mould very slowly.

On leaving the foundry we went into the boring workshop. There is no need to describe this workshop in detail since it lacks many of the amenities to be found in several recently established plants of this kind. Nevertheless I am bound to say that I have never seen better boring or turning than in this workshop. The bore of one of the Miller 12 pounders was polished as brightly as if the work had been done by a gold-smith. The base of the gun was semi-spherical in shape. The flash vents are not quite so narrow as in French artillery but they are made of copper and are firmly screwed into the cannon.

Next we went to the little workshop where signal rockets, for use on land and at sea, were being made. I thought it was a good idea to cover the sticks and tongues of the rockets so as to prevent them from deteriorating owing to dampness. In this workshop some very big rockets are made which are capable of being fired to a great height and for a long distance. One type —the 'star rockets'—fire 22 rockets at a time. Having seen all this I could understand how Congreve came to have the idea of inventing his rocket, and how Shrapnell came to invent his spherical case shot.[33]

Our next visit was to the so-called Repository where all kinds of weapons are displayed. Some—like Congreve's rockets—are real weapons which can be used, while others are small models of original weapons. I was most interested in Shrapnell's spherical shots, Congreve's rockets, and a machine for quickly mixing different kinds of gunpowder in a uniform manner. The British government gets its gunpowder from seven different powder mills and no two types are exactly the same. I also found it of interest to compare the very remarkable results of exploding gunpowder when it is simply put into linen sacks and hung on walls, gates, or fences, with the results obtained first by a petard and then by a fire ship. I saw how petards were made and filled and also how their sulphur sticks work.

I examined Shrapnell spherical case shots of various sizes. These explosive projectiles are fired from howitzers and are also used as war heads of the larger types of Congreve rockets. Neither in their outward appearance nor in their construction do they differ very much from our own grenades. But I did notice that the fuze[34] hole has a sharp worm in it which effecttively prevents the fuze from falling out. This also ensures safety when the fuze is rammed into the hole. I also observed that before the aforementioned fuze is screwed into place the grenades are filled with small lead or iron pellets and that the cavities are then filled with gunpowder. My guide was an experienced veteran of Leipzig and Waterloo where he had been attached to a Congreve battery. He was very communicative and told me that the gunpowder which was poured into the cavities is adequate not only to explode the grenade but also to scatter the shot over a large area.

The Congreve rockets stood against a wall in order of size from so called 3 pounders to 32 pounders. The latter, which has a sheet iron cylinder about 5 feet long and 9 inches in diameter is said to weigh about 300 lbs when it is fully charged. The 12 feet sticks for the bigger rockets were not attached to them, but the smaller sticks were fixed to their rockets. All of them were fixed by three iron clips to their unprimed cap shells. Only the larger types are used as incendiary projectiles to set ships or buildings on fire. The smaller rockets are used as offensive projectiles against small groups of the enemy in the field, particularly cavalry. The ends of the larger rockets are conical in shape. There are little holes all round the cone for about a quarter of its length from the cap downwards as well as at the base of the cone. These holes are covered with pieces of parchment and are varnished. So called 'Greek fire', which cannot be extinguished, pours out of these holes. The Greek fire is contained in the rocket itself—and in two sealed tubes attached to the rocket—and it is only ignited by the gunpowder when the rocket is close to its target. The medium sized rockets, on the other hand do not have a cone at their apex. They have a Shrapnel spherical case shot from which the fuzes project outwards near the side of the cap. They too are ignited by the fire from the rocket as it approaches its target. The little rockets have solid iron egg-shaped heads. I was told that if they were shot at an angle of 45 degrees the largest rockets could reach a distance of 3,000 yards and the smallest 1,500 yards.

I would gladly have learned more about these very effective weapons of war—particularly the construction of their interiors and the composition of the powder that supplied the driving force. I hesitated, however, to make any further direct enquiries—the answers to which I could already guess from the character of my guide—and I hoped that some happy chance might enable me to glean some more information about the rockets.

There are two reasons why I propose to describe the machine which mixed the different kinds of gunpowder which came from the seven powder mills in the kingdom. The first is because it is a very simple machine. The second reason—and this is important for my own country—is that it is hard to secure uniformity in this chemical preparation without using such a machine. Uniformity in gunpowder is essential if we are to prepare accurate tables based upon experiments concerning the distance that a particular type of shell can be fired.

The machine consists of seven square vessels on a block. These vessels are funnel shaped and are open at the top. At the bottom of each of them is a rather narrow pipe to which a valve has been fixed. All these pipes reach to within a short distance of the broad upper base of an inverted cone which terminates in a relatively large hole . . . and is capable of being rotated. One operation suffices to open all seven valves at once and the various powders then run through the pipes as sand flows in an hour glass. The different powders are mixed by the rotary motion of the funnel. Finally the mixed powder falls through a hole in a large vessel. So far all tests with the new mixture of powders have been most successful.

I was astonished at the force of a gunpowder explosion even when the powder is not placed in a strong container. I was shown how a hundredweight of gunpowder was put into nothing stronger than a linen sack which was hung up against a lattice iron gate and then fired. The whole gate and the latticework was blown to pieces. But when one of the larger petards was fired only a small hole, no larger than the petard itself, was made in the gate. A petard and its base are expensive to produce and are so heavy that six men are required to move them into position. On the other hand a hundredweight of gunpowder can be placed in position by one man. This information appears to me to be important from the point of view of the science of war.

I formed a high opinion of the efficiency of the sulphur fuze which has replaced the match in firing cannon. The great advantage of this method is that the artilleryman knows at once for how many minutes a fuze will burn. He also knows how many fuzes he will need for a particular purpose or in a particular action which may last for hours. The fuzes are covered with white paper on which distances are marked with strips of black paper to show how much of the fuze will burn away in a particular length of time. This might be regarded as a sort of pyrotechnical clock which can be used both by night and by day.

There were other curiosities on show but they are hardly worth describing since they serve no practical purpose. My guide, whom I was probably keeping from his lunch, gave me little information about the flint locks fired by percussion caps except that tests made with them had been just as satisfactory as those made with cannon.

Later I learned that the officer could have taken me to the Rotunda which is a good fifteen minutes walk from the arsenal. The Rotunda contains a very big new model room which has models both of fortifications and of old and new pieces of artillery. But the officer excused himself at the guard room and gave me back my letter from the Board of Ordnance so that I could show it at the Rotunda. I did not do so, however, as the person in charge of the Rotunda was not in uniform but in civilian clothes . . .

In the Rotunda I was again interested mainly in the Congreve rockets . . . There is nothing further to report upon the larger rockets except to mention some evidence of their effectiveness that I saw for myself. One of these rockets after flighting 1,500 yards accidentally struck a square column eight inches thick. The rocket went right into the column but was embedded there because the tail end blew up. I discovered that there must have been a paper cap in the rocket or rather that some paper padding had been inserted in the sheet iron cylinder. I asked the man in charge if this was done with all the rockets and he agreed. This seemed to me to be of some importance in amplifying my information concerning the construction of the rockets.

As I was discussing these rockets with the man in charge, a gentleman in mufti came to me. I realised that he was a soldier, though. not in uniform. He asked me if I was Lieutenant Colonel Fischer and I said that I was. He said: 'Did the officer who showed you round the arsenal accompany you to the Rotunda?' 'No' I replied. 'I am sorry', he said, and introduced himself. 'This gentleman', he said, pointing to the man in charge, 'will show you all that you wish to see.'

It was getting late but I continued for a time to examine the rockets. I also inspected a field workshop for saddlers and gunsmiths which seemed to me to be more likely to be useful in the steppes or in a desert rather than in our more populated lands, but I saw that it was fitted out in a very ingenious and practical manner.

I was satisfied with my visit, although I had not been able to see everything. Night had fallen and it was very dark. I crossed Blackheath which has a bad reputation for footpads but I was not molested in any way. I hailed a patrol and was told that the Dover coach—on which I had provisionally booked a seat for the first part of my return journey to Switzerland—would soon be in the vicinity of Morden College, where I had planned to catch it. The coach arrived within a few minutes . . .

II

Wednesday, September 26, 1827

On September 25 Herr Prévost, the Swiss chargé d'affaires (in London),[35] secured from the Board of Ordnance a permit for my eldest son and for myself to visit the Woolwich arsenal. On September 26 we went together to see the arsenal, the foundry, the workshops, and the model rooms. I was familiar with the arsenal but I was glad to have secured permission for my son to see it since he is both a gunsmith and an artillery officer. On showing my permit to the Commandant, (Major) General (G. Bulteel Smith)[36], an officer was detailed—as on my previous visit—to show us round. As we left the office by the foundry I heard the sound of heavy gunfire. I asked the officer if this came from gun practice or from troops on manoeuvres. He said that the noise came from experiments that were being carried out to test the usefulness of a suggestion put forward by General

Ford. He proposed to strengthen a part of the defences of a fortress against siege guns by means of an iron mesh made of bars one and a half inches thick. He wanted to find out how such an iron curtain—with a total thickness of three inches— would stand up to the fire of a heavy calibre gun. As I was very interested in this experiment I asked the officer if I could see it and he readily agreed.

I saw three iron 24 pounders drawn up in batteries. As is usual in England the fire locks were secured onto the guns. When the command was given to shoot, the triggers of the fire locks were pulled by a fairly long cord. The cartridge cases were made of linen and were probably soaked in a solution of alum to make them less inflammable. The charge consisted of eight pounds of powder which was one third of the weight of the cannon balls and these were absolutely spherical in shape. As the line of fire was slightly uphill the balls were loaded without a wad of felt and without overcharging. In any case there is little space in English cannon for wads because the barrels are bored so accurately and such excellent ammunition is used. But bundles of broken-up ships-cables were available for overcharging if required.

In Switzerland we fix a sight at the end of a gun barrel to secure an accurate aim. But on these cannon—as on all metal cannon of whatever calibre—the English put a slit on a flat oblong piece of metal at the head of the cannon. Accurate shooting depends upon really correct aiming and this is a much better method than ours because there is little danger of an apparent displacement of the target owing to an actual change in the point of observation and there is certainly no danger at all of any obstruction in the view of the target. In this case the target consisted of earthworks 8 feet long and 6 feet high pro- tected by stone blocks covered with an iron mesh which has already been described. The gunners frequently hit the target at a distance of 1,890 feet.

Two cannon were fired so accurately that one shot often hit exactly the same spot as the previous shot, but one cannon was generally firing high and somewhat to the left of the target. Although the cannon balls were made of excellent material they split into many fragments on hitting the iron mesh. I received permission to keep one of these fragments. The outer layer of iron rods took the first shock of the impact of the cannon ball and these rods were generally broken, but the inner layer was

151

unharmed. Only a single rod of the inner layer was split by a ball which ricocheted but it remained in position.

I could not wait to see the end of this test—50 rounds or 250 shots were to be fired—as I had to return to London. On the next day it was proposed to reduce the firing distance by a half, but I saw enough to be satisfied that even although the iron mesh might eventually be destroyed it would be of great value against siege guns if it were used to protect the weakest point of a blockhouse.

My son and I went on the familiar tour of the two model rooms, the foundry and the boring plant. We saw several cannon displayed in front of the so-called Rotunda. These trophies of campaigns in various countries are preserved because of their beauty or excellence of construction. I was particularly pleased to see two exceptionally large mortars, cast by Schalch of Schaffhausen in 1726. Schalch was only a young apprentice when he was promoted to the position of Master Founder of the Royal Foundry because he had foreseen an accident which occurred when his warnings were ignored. He had a long and distinguished career in this post which he held until he was an old man. He was a rich man when he died.

Nothing new of any importance has been added to the exhibits in the Rotunda since I wrote about them two years ago except for a model of an apparatus invented by Colonel Congreve. This is an apparatus for carbonising wood for gunpowder. The oxygen freed by this process is piped under retorts and is used again as a fuel. But, as I recall, Professor Lampius of Freiberg in the Erzgebirge (Ore Mountains in Saxony) had thought of this a long time ago. I was also interested to have the opportunity of inspecting two little wrought iron pieces of artillery or swivel guns—firing balls weighing three quarters of a pound—which were captured by the English from the ruler of Burma at the same time.

These two little cannon are undoubtedly very remarkable pieces. An expert can see how far these by no means uncivilised people are behind their conquerors in technical knowledge. Yet from the peculiarity of their construction one can see that —though only in a somewhat primitive and inartistic manner —even the Burmese possess the universal striving of the human spirit towards perfection and beauty.

The need to introduce breech loading for heavy artillery seems to have been felt just as keenly in the Far East as in Europe where such great progress has been made in military science. In so far as I am qualified to pass an opinion upon breechloaders I would say that the method used in Burma is an original one and has not been borrowed. It is at least as good as—if not better than—any technique employed elsewhere since these guns, although loaded from the rear, also possess complete and solid breech plates.

The method employed by the Burmese is as follows: That part of the cannon which is called 'the area of loading' is much thicker than in European cannon and the calibre of the bore is proportionately larger. The top half of the barrel at the rear is cut away on the line of the longitudinal axis so that a semi-circular groove is opened up. A short dolphin shaped loading rod, operated by a hand lever, is inserted into the groove which is also conical in shape. The breech plate is then closed so that the charge is kept firmly in position. The cannon are con-structed in a somewhat rough and ready manner and one could say that every stroke of the hammer is completely Indian in character. But whoever made these pieces did try to decorate them with an open lotus flower.

I have called these pieces of artillery 'swivel guns' since their two trunnions[37] are encircled by a pointed spoke on a bracket which enables the cannon to be firmly fixed in the ground or in a piece of wood.

In the fragments of my journal for 1825 I wrote about the most interesting exhibits of the model room of the arsenal. There is little to add now to this description, but there is on show a new machine for firing rockets which has been con-structed by the officer in charge of the model room. The machine fires a dozen ordinary rockets simultaneously and—what is more important—they are all aimed in a uniform and accurate manner. The machine consists of a wooden frame into which twelve wooden hammers are fixed. The hammers are attached to a winch by arms which are long enough to make the hammers strike with sufficient force. The machine is oper-ated manually by turning the handle of the winch. Each hammer strikes a stamp which in turn strikes a percussion cap of the rockets. The rocket sticks, like the hammers, are fixed in the wooden frame.

As far as I know this idea had not been tried out anywhere else. This is an admirable and safe method of letting off fire-works or of shooting rockets in wartime. Normally large struc-tures are erected in which fire-works are let off and serious damage can be done to persons and to property if there is an

M

accident because the explosive and inflamable objects are close together and many workers are confined within a small space. But the new appliances that I have described can be erected on a wide open space in little wooden cabins just big enough to hold the two workmen who operate them. Such an arrangement would make it impossible—as has happened in the past —for an entire hall to go up in flames in a few moments.

The foundry is in no way remarkable in comparison with foundries elsewhere. The furnaces are not even particularly large. In my opinion, however, there is an advantage in having relatively small reverberatory furnaces since the great heat produced by a coal fire facilitates the complete combination of the tin and copper which are to be alloyed. This in turn produces a more compact fusion of the two metals. The alloy is of really excellent quality and, judging from its colour, I think that it contains rather more tin than the alloy used by French cannon founders.

There are two boring machines in the workshops of the arsenal. The larger one bores cannon while the shorter one bores mortars and howitzers. No expert should miss a chance of seeing them. He will leave the plant marvelling that such simple machines can make such fine pieces of artillery with bores of so remarkable a finish.

England, so rich in money and technical skill, has squandered her iron and other metals to construct thousands of machines and other products. Yet these boring machines—and as usual they serve also as turning lathes—are simply constructed from oak. Only in those places where it is necessary are iron slats screwed on to the wooden machine. As is customary elsewhere the workers gradually pushed the slats forward by means of cog wheels. In this way the slats make a groove on the two gauges and the boring rod runs on this groove.

The first step in the boring process is to make a small indentation in the centre of the barrel with a hand brace. The point of the centre bit is then put into this little opening and a hole, some 3 inches in diameter, is made in the barrel. Next the hole is made absolutely circular by means of a specially constructed chisel and its diameter is so adjusted that the first spoon bit can be precisely inserted. This spoon bit has a flat top and a semi-circular base and it is used to make the first hole running through the whole length of the barrel.

Once the pilot hole has been finished it is enlarged by inserting one flat boring rod after another. At the front end of each rod there is a steel ring. The diameter of each ring is that of the rod previously inserted and acts as a guide so that the barrel is always both straight and concentric. Finally a polishing rod is used. This differs from those previously employed in as much as it has no guide ring and is rounded at the end. English cannon and mortars always have hemispherical chambers and this is a good idea since it simplifies the cleaning of the barrel (after firing) and the removal of every fragment of the cartridge. Moreover the (final) polishing is done in such a way that there is a breech at only one side of the barrel—namely the side which is adjacent to the half-rounding at its mouth. It is against this side that the barrel rubs when it is turned. The other side, however, has a rounded polished edge and this too serves its purpose admirably.

Measures are taken to avoid what is called 'the shakes'. These can be a very unpleasant—though normally not a really dangerous—phenomenon. In the final operation the borer not only removes an exceptionally fine metal shaving but he also screws into the barrel two semi-circular pieces of beechwood about 6 inches in length. Beneath each piece of beechwood a playing card is fixed. In this way the hole in the barrel is filled. It is then smeared with oil and receives a final polish.

I was surprised to find that this boring machine had no sliding tool. I was told that the first stages of the boring of a barrel were performed with quite simple turning tools which the artisan rests upon a wooden support. The tasks was completed with the aid of slats set at right angles to each other. Moreover the cannon is correctly shaped by using an iron filed model which the mechanic has previously fixed at either end of the cannon for this purpose. On it is drawn a circle of the correct diameter.

In the course of a lengthy conversation the mechanic said to me: 'In this way we can finish making a piece of artillery more quickly than with sliding tools. It is true that we have such tools but—as you can see—we do not use them.' When the barrels of mortars or howitzers are manufactured the first opening is made in the same way as when cannon barrels are bored, but in the production of mortars and howitzers an apparatus is used when I have never seen before. By employing this tool the mechanic can accurately bore a barrel of any desired calibre.

7. SANDERSON BROTHERS OF SHEFFIELD

July 4, 1825 (at Birmingham)[38]

As I had an appointment with Mr. John Sanderson[39], a Sheffield manufacturer of cast steel, at one o'clock in the afternoon I was able to go out for only a short time in the morning. I had made the acquaintance of this very respectable gentleman on the mailcoach (from Sheffield) to Birmingham. With his two brothers he operates the largest cast steel plant in England. They trade with North and South America. He was very surprised that I had exact and detailed information concerning his methods of manufacture—from the materials used to make the crucibles to the moment when the cast steel finally comes under the hammer. On the other hand he did not have the slightest idea concerning my method (of making cast steel). He began to believe me when I showed him a sample of my 'meteor steel,'[40] the articles made from this steel,[41] and the testimonial from (Ebenezer) Rhodes (of Sheffield), whom he knows well, concerning the quality of my steel. He now realised that this product,[42] the manufacture of which is still kept secret in England, is not only made elsewhere but is made in as good a quality as in England. We got on so well together that he actually confided in me the extent of his weekly output which would have appeared incredible to anyone who did not know industrial conditions in England.

October 5, 1827 (at Sheffield)[43]

. . . I hurried to Mr. Sanderson[44] at the cast steel works in distant West Street. He was in his office and greeted me in a very friendly manner as did his two partners to whom I was introduced. He offered to put me up for the night if I were staying in Sheffield but I declined. We had a discussion about methods of making steel and then I decided to take my leave. But instead of showing me out he took me to his coal warehouse and let me see the fine light coke that he uses. To my immense astonishment he then took me to the melting plant which was in full operation. For a time I watched the melting and the casting and then I went to the cementation works where they make steel by the cementation process from Swedish iron which is marked with the letter L and is therefore called 'Hoop L'. This iron is the best material for making steel by the cementation process which is then turned into cast steel. Sanderson's steel made by the cementation process is a really first class product and its uniformity leaves nothing to be desired. I

156

told him what I did with the steel that was left over after the casting process in order to make the best use of it and this interested him very much because he too had a large amount of this steel on his hands. Finally I made some observations on the steel which Huntsman is alleged to have made from Indian iron ore. I said that from my own inspection of this steel I would regard it as a poor imitation of a steel nickel alloy. I added that I believed the gentlemen of Sheffield would agree with me. He smiled and said: 'They can't throw any dust in your eyes.'[45] Although we are competitors we parted on friendly terms.

July 31, 1845 (at Sheffield)[46]

. . . After lunch I went to my old friend Mr. Sanderson. Sandersons are the biggest manufacturers of cast steel in Sheffield for they have 36 melting furnaces and 6 cementation furnaces in which they make steel from Swedish iron. As I anticipated I received a warm welcome from old Mr. Sanderson whom I first met twenty years ago on the coach from Chesterfield to Sheffield[47] and he showed me right through his plant which he is not prepared to do for everybody.

We first went to the cementation furnaces. One had just been fired while the other was in full swing. In each of these furnaces there are two receptacles—each containing about 160 hundredweights of Dannemora iron—and three fires. What happens is this. One flame heats the front of the first receptacle, one flame heats the back of the second receptacle, and a third flame heats the space between the two receptacles. There are holes which create a draught of air through the furnace. Mr. Sanderson gave instructions for an 'eye' to be opened for me. This is a little peep hole in the front of the furnace that is covered by a piece of fireproof clay. When the slab of clay is removed I could see the play of the flames and I could estimate the heat inside the furnace. I thought that the maximum temperature had not yet been attained but this is far from easy to determine as things look very different on a sunny day and on a cloudy day.

From here we went to the plant in which cast steel is made. For the last twenty years—indeed I might say for the last fifty years since Huntsman's works first got into full swing—absolutely no change has occurred in the process of making cast steel. One sees the very same furnaces and the very same crucibles. And—cold or warm—the same methods of filling and emptying the crucibles are employed though funnels are now used for the emptying process.

The casting was very carefully done. Every furnace contains two crucibles each holding between 30 lb and 35 lb of steel. One of the first two crucibles to be tapped had a little hole in it and over half the steel had leaked out. The caster very sensibly poured the steel that still remained in the crucible into the second crucible. This was possible because no crucible is quite full when it comes out of the furnace owing to the fact that the crucibles are covered by flat heavy lids. The caster then poured out the steel from the second full crucible in a very careful manner. The next furnace was opened shortly afterwards. This time both crucibles were in good order and they were cast in the same way (as the other). Three men perform the casting process. The first lifts the crucible and carries it to a receptacle which is partly buried in the ground. The second worker holds the crucible with a pair of tongs. The third worker removes the crucible lid with a pointed iron bar and then uses a small rake to remove the few pieces of slag that are floating on top of the liquid steel.

As several baskets of coke were standing by the furnaces, I asked Mr. Sanderson how much coke he used to make a hundredweight of steel. He gave me the exact figure. I thought that I had not understood him correctly and repeated the question. He gave me the same answer as before.[48] And his answer pleased me. Now I told him how much coke—on the average—I used. He exclaimed three times: 'You beat us! You beat us! You beat us!'[49] I gave him one reason—the most important of several—for his greater consumption of coke (as compared with mine) and he agreed with me.[50]

October 30, 1846 (at Sheffield)[51]

I walked a long way from Cammell's steelworks to Turton's plant[52] looking in at Huntsman's hammerworks on the way and as no one was available I made an almost equally long journey to West Street to see my good old friends Messrs. Sanderson who have the biggest cast steel works here. But they too were not at their works. I was told that they would be back after 5 o'clock after they had had their lunch.

October 31, 1846 (at Sheffield)[53]

. . . At 11 a.m. I went to Messrs. Sandersons' works. The younger gentleman was available. He took me to the firm's rolling mills[54] which are a very long way away from the casting plant. They have 11 rolling mills and some furnaces. The rolling mills turn out steel ingots in various forms—square, flat and round. They are beautifully made and have no blemishes. You will always find that Englishmen are never satisfied until they have got a thing absolutely right.

July 7, 1851 (at Sheffield)[55]

... I went ... to West Street to the steelworks of my old friend Mr. Charles Sanderson. I was sorry to learn that he was suffering from gout and arthritis—as he had been four years ago—but he was not actually bedridden. I had to walk nearly a mile to his home but this did not prevent me from visiting him. He greeted me in his own house in the most friendly fashion. His wife at once invited me to tea and as I was very thirsty and felt far from well I was very glad to accept. She is a very pleasant and well read lady. The general conversation was about the Great Exhibition at the Crystal Palace. At the moment this is the one topic that people in England want to discuss—at any time of the day—with foreigners. And indeed one cannot blame them for talking about this miracle which has so suddenly appeared to dazzle the inhabitants of our globe!

I was very pleased when Mr. Sanderson promised me that, as soon as his hand is better, he will give me some exact information concerning the minimum of coke that is necessary to smelt our (Swiss) bean iron ores into grey pig iron fit for a cupola furnace. He is an able mineralogist who had a good knowledge of Swiss iron ores and he has had a very long experience of the smelting process. He also promised to let me have a drawing of a furnace sufficiently small for the purpose that I had in mind.

We spoke of a furnace of which there is a model in the Exhibition. This has a ventilator at the top which is opened only to receive the funnel through which the necessary coal and ore are inserted and then it is immediately closed again. The flames and gases are taken to the side (of the furnace) by closed pipes and are then used again for other purposes. This furnace—like Wilkinson's furnace—has three blast pipes and it is certainly the best type of furnace now available. But, owing to ill health, Mr. Sanderson has not yet seen it. I mentioned that I had seen another—and much larger—model of a furnace at the Exhibition which had six blast pipes. But that is certainly too many because they greatly weaken the mouths of the furnaces. It was over fifty years ago that the mining official von Reden erected a furnace of this kind in the Harz with six blast pipes but he did not derive any more advantage from it than he would have done from three.

After a visit which had lasted over two hours I left this family with which I have always been on friendly terms. I expressed the hope that they would soon visit me in Switzerland.

8. LONDON IN 1851

June 19, 1851

I had hoped to make an early call on Dr. Bolley and Mr. Colladon, the two Swiss commissioners for the Exhibition. They both live in Finsbury Square which is a long way from the Crystal Palace and therefore not very convenient from the point of view of the efficient discharge of their duties. Neither of them was at home. On the other hand at the Royal Institution I received a very warm welcome from Mr. Faraday, the leading English chemist. I had a most interesting talk with him and this was ample compensation for my long walk from Finsbury Square where the compatriots to whom I have referred, lived.

We talked for nearly an hour on metallurgical and pyrotechnical problems. Then I walked for another thirty minutes to get the exhibition to which I had sent a display cabinet at the request of the (Schaffhausen) authorities . . . As a father I may be forgiven for having devoted to-day's visit to the Austrian section to see the exhibits sent by two of my sons who have settled in that country which is beautiful and so richly endowed with natural resources.

Georg Fischer of Hainfeld had sent six boxes of files made from cast steel. In a seventh box he displayed samples of cast steel bars. The jury will have to decide on the merits of the shape, cutting quality, and efficiency of these files and bars. Berthold Fischer of Traisen has sent an excellent collection of malleable cast iron products. At one time the process of making malleable cast iron was kept secret in England but I discovered how to make it and secured an (Austrian) patent from the Emperor Francis in 1829.[56] In addition to these malleable cast iron products Berthold Fischer also showed some samples of his spindles which are made for textile mills. I went to one of the attendants, who are to be found in little offices all over the exhibition, to explain that my son's display had no ticket on it. The tickets indicate the name of the manufacturers and the number of the display as listed in the catalogue. The attendant was quite agreeable to my making out a ticket myself. But as these exhibits are in the Austrian section I thought it proper not to do this myself but to write to Herr von Buschek, the Austrian commissioner to the exhibition.

People here are very well disposed towards foreign visitors. This is particularly true of the police. An experience of my own may serve to illustrate this fact. My own display cabinet had with it an engraving of a picture of my works made by Herr Beck. There were also two very fine damascened daggers made of the steel nickel alloy which I call 'meteor steel'. But now I could not see these daggers although they had been packed in a place that was easy to find.

I was almost sure that they had been lost so I asked an attendant about them. He at once sent a policeman to the official in charge of the Swiss section. This official came to me and produced the daggers from behind a big piece of meteor steel where they had been placed for greater safety. They were now displayed in their proper place . . .

June 20, 1851

Big cities, with few exceptions, ruin the people who have to spend all their lives in them. They are indeed no better than prisons. Lucky is the man who can live all his life in our beautiful Switzerland and can earn a decent living there. Rarely, if ever, does a bright sky smile on the Londoner as it does upon us. For nearly the whole year the Londoner sees only the smoke and dust which spreads a dull cloud far over this metropolis. The Londoner never sees our fine meadows, running streams or green woods let alone our alps crowned with silver snow. In London one sees endless rows of grey and dark brown houses and one hears the continuous noise of countless vehicles. In hotel dining rooms and even in ordinary public houses there are only brief conversations or actually complete silence. Everyone who enters a restaurant looks for an empty table and then quickly hides himself behind a newspaper. This is only a brief—but not exaggerated—sketch of life in London today.

On the other hand, the English devote more of their time to their homes than is customary among their neighbours on the other side of the Channel. And their lack of conversation promotes the spirit of enquiry and invention in relation to the most unexpected subjects. And this gives them the skill which has made them great and is ever adding to the success that they have already achieved. These reflections and comparisons came to me after a day which began and ended in a tedious way, though I must add that I did have an interesting talk with a steel manufacturer from Newcastle-on-Tyne. I could not go to the exhibition and I could not go to the Chinese collection which is not far from the Crystal Palace. I only met the banker from whom I drew the money that I needed—and one needs plenty of it here. It is a good thing to have earned it previously!

June 21, 1851

I went for a walk early in the morning and in England at the height of the summer 'early in the morning' means half past seven when most of the shops have not yet opened and not many people or vehicles are in the streets. Yesterday I received a cheque for £30 payable at the banking house of Payne and Smith. I reached the bank at an early hour so that I could give instructions that the cheque should not be honoured unless I presented it myself. The only bank officials who were available were junior clerks who noted my request and suggested that I should return at 9 o'clock when the cashier would have arrived. What had happened was this. On the previous evening, while I was away, my tailor had fetched my coat to repair it. My notebook and the cheque were in the overcoat. It was after 9 o'clock when I got home and there was nothing that I could do about it then. So this morning, after I left the bank, I went all the way to the shop where the tailor worked. The proprietor said: 'If your notebook was in your overcoat you will certainly get it back and its contents as well'. He immediately accompanied me to the tailor who quickly produced the notebook. There is much dishonesty in London but plenty of honesty as well. In fact I think that honesty is commoner than dishonesty. It is drink that makes this city poor and wretched and this applies to all classes of society.

In all business offices there is the greatest punctuality. Indeed punctuality is a matter of mathematical precision. This certainly has its advantages. I might add that when I returned to the bank a little before 9 o'clock I was shown to a seat facing a counter where five cashiers conducted their business. At five minutes to nine the official to whom I had to give my cheque took his place behind the counter. I had it in my hand and showed it to him. He did not say a word but emptied several little bags of gold coins into a drawer. Then he produced the well known little cash shovel that is used for coins in the banks. And then he just waited.

At the stroke of nine he asked me if I wanted gold or banknotes. I said I wanted gold. He did not count any of the sovereigns and half sovereigns but simply weighed them on his scales and then put them on the counter without taking any further notice of me. I counted the money and it was quite correct.

When I arrived at the Glass Palace—that surely is the best name for it—I asked a policeman to direct me to Professor Wilson's office. He told me to go to another part of the building. I found the office in due course but Professor Wilson was not in. Half an hour later when I had decided to go home I saw a policeman approaching me from a distance. I wondered what he could want with me and I hoped that I had not been guilty of some breach of the law. The policeman politely enquired if I had found the office that I was looking for, I told him that I had found it all right. This shows how sharp the police are in remembering faces for I was dressed quite in the English fashion in a black suit. It was from this policeman that I learned that the exhibition would stay open until about the end of October. I was glad to hear this since two of my sons, who live in Austria, intend to come to England later in the year. I have already said that these policemen are polite and far from aggressive in their manner. They are selected with great care. They wear dark blue jackets with a registration number stitched on the collar. They have dark blue trousers, smart round hats and white gloves. If there is any likelihood of rain the police carry rolled up india-rubber coats under their arms. The police here do not wear swords. Nor do they have pointed beards or meerschaum pipes. They know this great city—or at any rate their own district—very well. If you want to know the way you cannot do better—provided that you speak English—than to ask a policeman who will not only give you a polite answer but will sometimes actually accompany you for part of your way.

As today is a Saturday the price of admission (to the Exhibition)—as on all Fridays as well—is raised from 1s to 5s.[57] But the rooms were almost empty. As I have already said the wealthier visitors can accustom themselves to the popular shilling days just as easily as their less affluent neighbours . . .

June 22, 1851

Today is a Sunday and I began by finishing writing what I started yesterday but had been unable to finish owing to sheer exhaustion. Afterwards I walked down Cheapside which is quite a long street. I would have liked to have gone into a coffeehouse for a glass of ale or claret but all the shops were hermetically sealed and their doors were firmly closed. Even the front door of my own hotel was locked and only if one knew the secret could one turn the right knob and effect an entry. Otherwise there would be nothing for it but to ring the bell.

On returning to my hotel I asked for my bill as I have been accustomed to settle my account every day. But the innkeeper politely asked me to wait until Monday. I do not know if this is the practice elsewhere or if my innkeeper is a member of one of the dissenting sects. But I do know that on the Continent innkeepers are quite prepared to make out a bill on a Sunday and they do not take long about it if the guest wants to get away quickly. Of course no one criticises the observance of the Sabbath. Indeed those who observe the Sabbath should be honoured—so long as their observance is the outward expression of a truly thankful heart. For such people every day would be a Sunday. Christ himself gave the best advice on this matter when he answered a question put to him by the Pharisees—whose representatives are still with us today.

I got into an argument with a young lady who strongly criticised Parliament for allowing trains, omnibuses, and cabs to run on Sundays. She explained that her own pious family always observed the Sabbath strictly. To illustrate this she explained that since her papa's funeral had taken place on a Sunday—and in England a coffin its conveyed by a hearse and is not carried by pallbearers—his hearse had been drawn by hired horses and not by the family's horses. I thought to myself —the hired horses had to break the Sabbath so that the family's horses might be saved from the dread consequences of a breach of God's laws.

The rest of the day I spent in writing to my youngest son Berthold who, like his two elder brothers, has earned his living and has made a name for himself in Austria by his skill and hard work. Horace's dictum 'Ubi bene ibi patria' has been proved correct for all three of them so far. On the other hand it is true that most Swiss who emigrate eventually come home again. In the course of my letter to Berthold I wrote: 'Yesterday I visited the old inn where I used to live; it is the Cross Keys

in Wood Street, Cheapside. I also walked down the little alley
—Shoe Lane off Fleet Street—where I worked for the mechanic
Rhee 57 years ago.'

London does not change like other towns. It simply grows
bigger. Its brick houses remain as black, grim and monotonous
as ever. There are always two sides to every coin. England has
its industrial exhibition which is something temporary. We in
Switzerland have all the varied beauties of nature which are
continually renewed by their own creative forces . . .

June 30, 1851

Last week the sailors serving on the two royal yachts were
brought to London at the Queen's expense to see the Exhibition. They came by special train from Spithead where I believe
the yachts are lying at present. They all looked very smart in
blue jackets, white trousers and low broad-brimmed oilskin
hats. Many of them were wearing good conduct ribbons. It is,
I think, a good idea and it fosters a spirit of emulation . . .
The example of the Queen in sending her sailors to the Exhibition has been followed by others for the benefit of those
who cannot normally get to the Crystal Palace because of the
nature of their work, because they live too far from London, or
because they have not enough money. Orphans and schoolboys,
for example, have been taken to the Exhibition. As I was
sitting at breakfast I saw on two occasions parties passing in
five coaches. The members of one party were standing in so
called 'vans' while others were in coaches provided with seats.
All the coaches were decorated with flags and boughs of trees.
Each was drawn by four horses. Over 300 persons—they were
workers from two factories—were accommodated in each group
of five coaches. For good or ill many others must be coming to
the Exhibition in the same way and this must substantially increase the revenues from admission tickets . . .

1 Fischer had previously met Yeates Brown in Switzerland.
2 See also pp. 98 and 102.
3 Presumably an early type of beer engine.
4 Georg Carl Ringk von Wildenberg (1794–1860) of Schaffhausen.
5 Joseph Planta (1744–1827), who was of Swiss origin, was the
Principal Librarian of the British Museum between 1799 and
1827.
6 Professor Johann Georg Müller (1759–1819) of Schaffhausen.
7 Johannes von Müller (1752–1809) of Schaffhausen, the famous
Swiss historian.

[8] René Juste Hauy (1745–1822), a French mineralogist.

[9] Abraham Gottlob Werner (1750–1817) a German mineralogist and geologist.

[10] Fischer wrote 'Brockman'.

[11] The London *Post Office Annual Directory* for 1818 lists John Middleton as a black lead pencil maker of Vine Street, Piccadilly, p. 227).

[12] Fischer wrote 'Cornwall' in error.

[13] Fischer wrote 'Bouvie', The banking firm of Bouverie and Antrobus of 35, Craven Street, The Strand, was listed in the *Triennial Directory of London, Westminster, Southwark . . . for the years 1817, 1818, 1819*, p. 111.

[14] The firm of J. M. Siordet & Co., merchants, of 8 Austen Friars, was listed in the *Triennial Directory of London, Westminster, Southwark . . . for the years 1817, 1818, 1819*.

[15] Peter & George Dollond, 59, St. Paul's Church Yard.

[16] Fenn's firm was described in the London *Post Office Annual Directory* (1818) as a 'watch, clock, and mechanical tool manufactory.' (p. 114).

[17] *Ibid*, p. 313.

[18] Perhaps the Mr. Schenk mentioned above.

[19] i.e., G. C. Ringk von Wildenberg.

[20] James Tringham was listed in the (London) *Post Office Annual Directory* (1818) as an assayer of ores and metals (p. 336).

[21] The date given in the diary is August 27th but it should clearly be the 26th.

[22] Fenn's shop was described as a 'watch, clock and mechanical tool manufactory' in the (London) *Post Office Annual Guide* for 1818, (p. 114).

[23] J. H. Weiss, *Atlas Suisse*, Bâle et Strasbourg, 11 maps, (1796 *et seq.*), Map 3, Schaffhausen.

[24] A copper and steel alloy.

[25] Fischer was mistaken in supposing that the method of decorating chinaware that he described had been invented by Spengler. Sadler and Green had used the process in England before it had been used by Spengler.

[26] i.e. the clay from which Chinese porcelain was made.

[27] Father Jean Baptiste du Halde (1674–1743), a Jesuit priest had written a book entitled: *Descriptions historiques, géographiques et physiques de l'empire de la Chine et de la Tartarie Chinoise* (4 volumes 1735): English translation 1736.

[28] Manchester was enfranchised in 1832.

[29] i.e. Fischer and Parienta.

[30] Fischer's *Tagebuch*, pp. 250–254.

[31] On his return to Switzerland Fischer showed samples of English cooking utensils to a meeting of the Swiss Natural History Society at Solothurn.

32 'Miller's cannon' was at that time a popular name for these cannon, but they had been invented by General Robert Melville and not by Patrick Miller.

33 At this time Shrapnell's invention was known as a 'spherical case shot'. Its name was officially changed to 'Shrapnell shell' on June 11, 1852.

34 'Fuze' is a contraction of 'fuzee'.

35 Alexandre-Louis Prévost of Geneva had been Swiss consul and commercial agent in London since 1817.

36 Major General G. Bulteel Smith, Royal Artillery, had been appointed Commandant of the Woolwich Garrison in February, 1827.

37 Trunnions are supporting cylindrical projections on either side of a cannon or mortar.

38 Fischer's *Tagebuch*, pp. 336–7.

39 Fischer wrote 'Sanders' in mistake for Sanderson.

40 i.e. a steel-nickel alloy.

41 i.e. a pair of razors.

42 i.e. cast steel.

43 Fischer's *Tagebuch* pp. 441–3.

44 Fischer wrote 'Sanders.'

45 'They can't throw any dust in your eyes' was in English in the original.

46 Fischer's *Tagebuch*, pp. 528–30.

47 It was on the coach from Sheffield to Birmingham.

48 Later Fischer stated that Sanderson was paying 14/- a ton for coke at that time. See Fischer's *Tagebuch*, p. 532.

49 'You beat us' is in English in the original.

50 Fischer saw Mr. Sanderson again on August 2, 1845 (*Tagebuch*, p. 538).

51 Fischer's *Tagebuch*, pp. 605–6.

52 Fischer wrote 'Messrs. T.'.

53 Fischer's *Tagebuch*, p. 607.

54 At Attercliffe.

55 Fischer's *Tagebuch*, pp. 726–8.

56 The actual date of this Austrian patent was December 24, 1828.

57 Fischer's *Tagebuch*, 1851, p. 662. A little later he wrote 4s. (*Ibid*, p. 701).

APPENDIX III

Money, Weights and Measures in Switzerland, 1815-48

MONEY

1 South German Gulden or Florin (60 Kreuzer) = 1/8
1 Reichstaler = 1¾ Gulden   = 3/-

MEASURES (in metres)

1 Fuss (foot)	=	0·30
1 Elle	=	0·60
1 Zoll (inch)	=	0·03
1 Linie	=	0·003
1 Klafter	=	1·8
1 Rute	=	3

AREA (in square metres)

1 square Fuss	=	0·09
1 Juchart	=	3·600

WEIGHTS

1 Pfund (pound)	=	500 grammes
1 Zentner (cwt)	=	50 kilogrammes
1 Loth	=	$\frac{1}{32}$ Pfund = 15·6 grammes

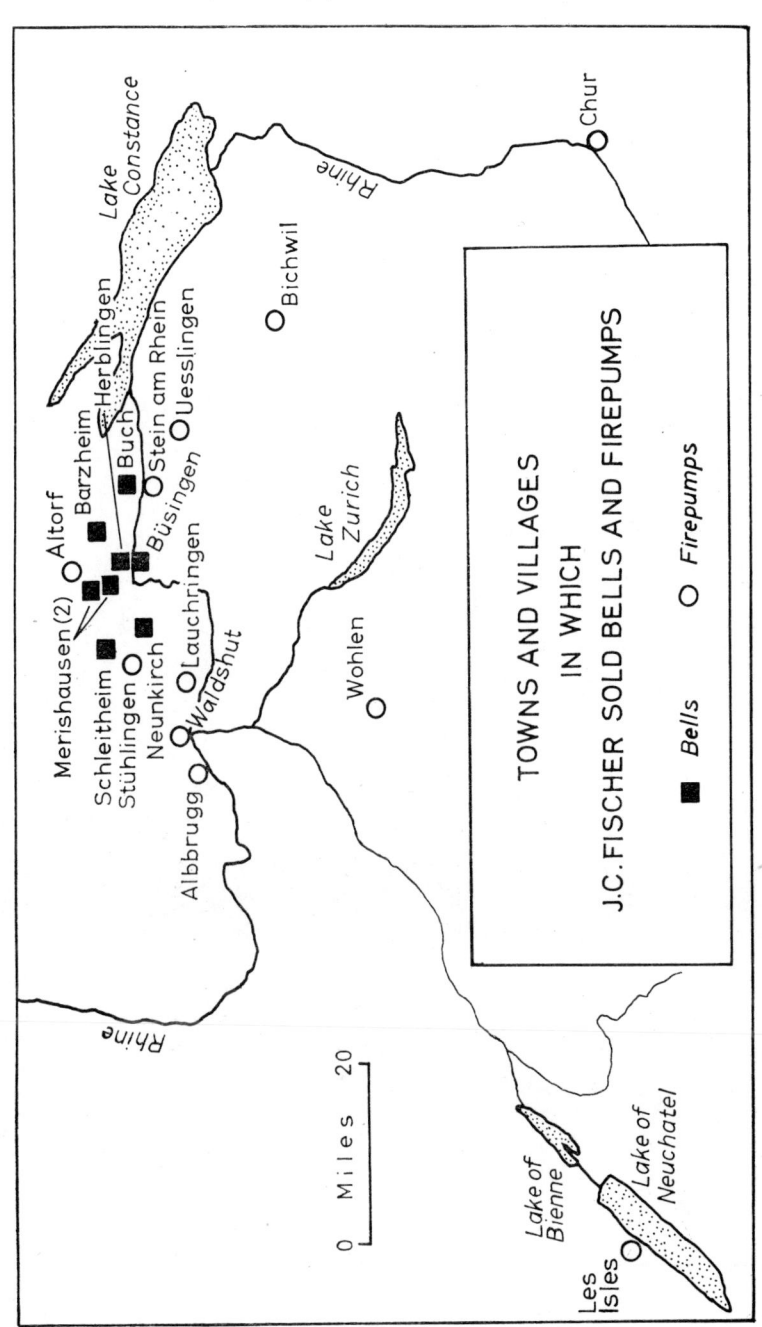

TOWNS AND VILLAGES
IN WHICH
J.C. FISCHER SOLD BELLS AND FIREPUMPS

■ *Bells*   ○ *Firepumps*

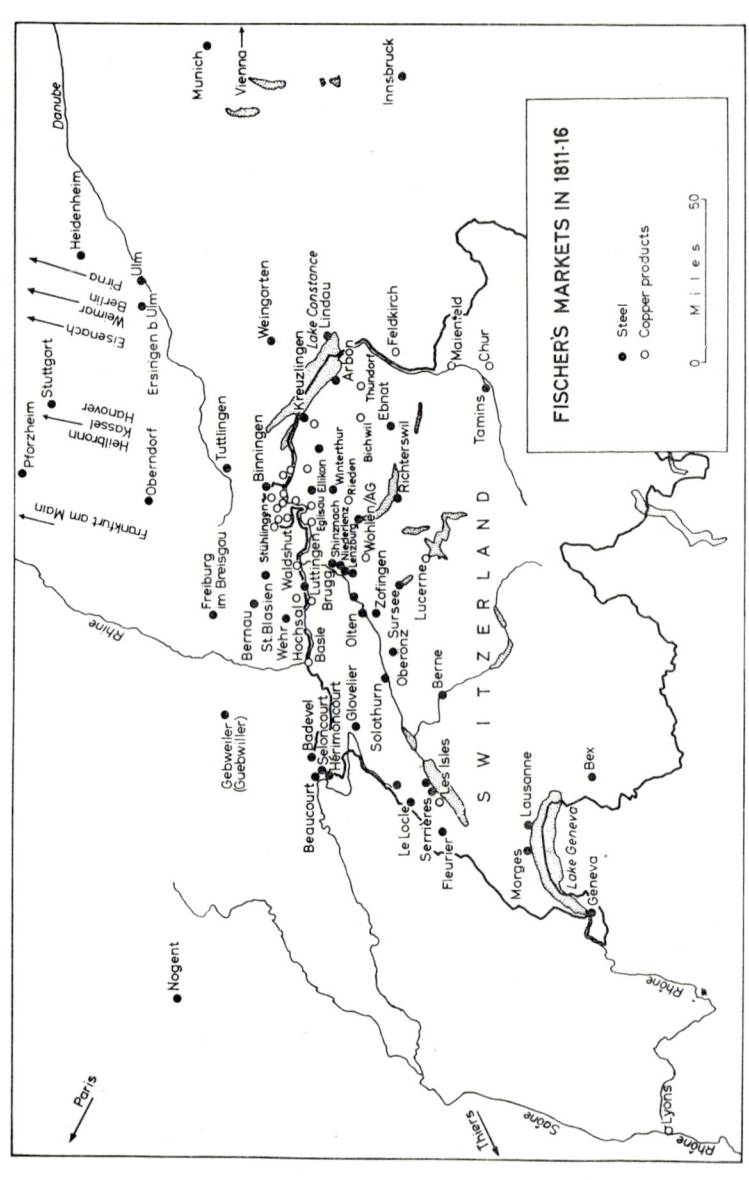

FISCHER'S MARKETS IN 1811-16

● Steel
○ Copper products

0   Miles   50

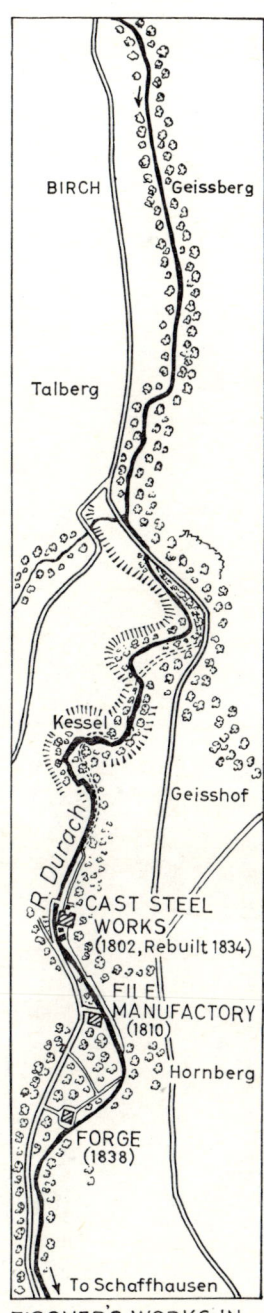

FISCHER'S WORKS IN
THE MÜHLENTAL, 1802-54

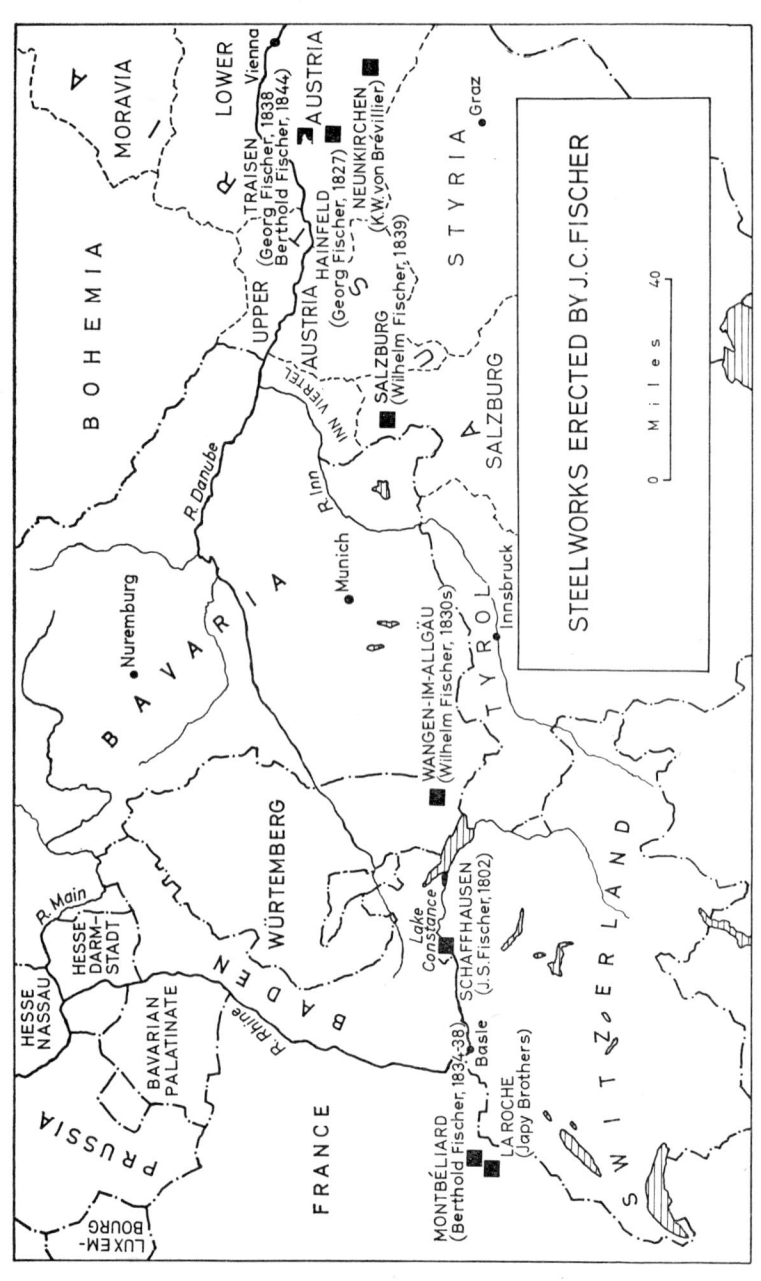

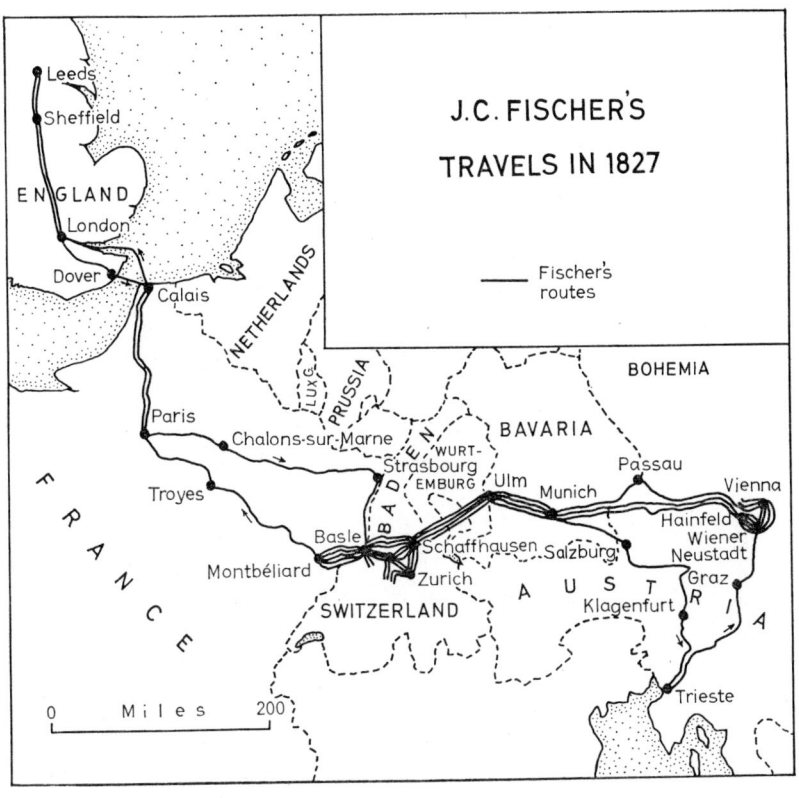

J.C. FISCHER'S

TRAVELS IN 1827

Fischer's
routes

LOHN

Clay quarries

Iron ore mines operated
by J.C. Fischer in 1810-50
as Director of Mines

0   Feet   1000

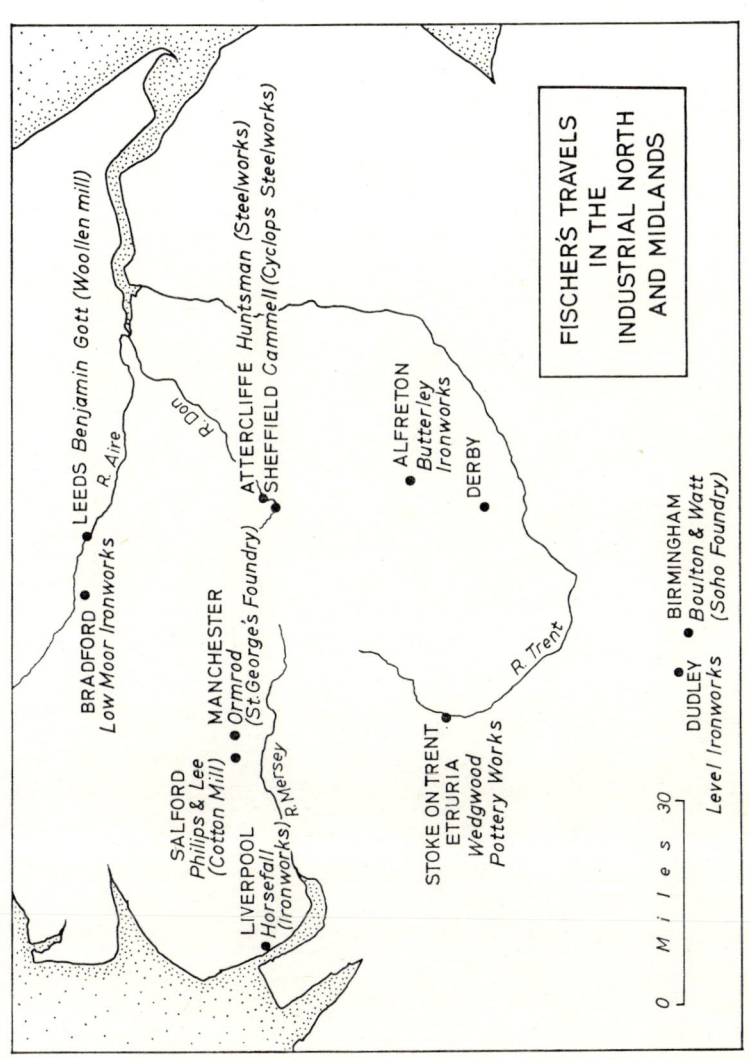

FISCHER'S TRAVELS
IN THE
INDUSTRIAL NORTH
AND MIDLANDS

LEEDS *Benjamin Gott (Woollen mill)*

R. Aire

R. Don

ATTERCLIFFE *Huntsman (Steelworks)*
SHEFFIELD *Cammell (Cyclops Steelworks)*

ALFRETON
Butterley Ironworks

DERBY

BRADFORD
Low Moor Ironworks

MANCHESTER
Ormrod
(St.George's Foundry)

SALFORD
Philips & Lee
(Cotton Mill)

LIVERPOOL
Horsefall
(Ironworks)

R. Mersey

R. Trent

BIRMINGHAM
Boulton & Watt
(Soho Foundry)

DUDLEY
Level Ironworks

STOKE ON TRENT
ETRURIA
Wedgwood
Pottery Works

0   Miles   30

Bibliography

Ackermann, E. and Meier, W. *Dreissig Jahre Aktiengesellschaft der Eisen-und Stahlwerke, vormals Georg Fischer Schaffhausen, 1896-1926* (1926).

Aschinger, F. (ed.). *Hundertfünfzig Jahre Georg Fischer Werke 1802-1952* (1952).

Bodmer, W. *Die Entwicklung der schweizerischen Textilwirtschaft im Rahmen der übrigen Industrien und Wirtschaftszweige* (1960).

Boesch, H. *Die Unternehmungen von Johann Conrad Fischer* (Neujahrsblatt herausgegeben von der Naturforschenden Gesellschaft Schaffhausen auf das Jahr 1952).

Boesch, H. and Schib, K. *Beiträge zur Geschichte der schweizerischen Eisengiessereien* (1960).

Feldhaus, F. M. 'Zwei technologische Reisen nach England, 1814 und 1825' (*Geschichtsblätter für Technik und Gewerbe*, Vol. V, 1918).

Fischer, Wolfram, 'Drei Schweizer Pioniere der Industrie' (*Tradition*, 1958).

Gnade, R. *The Metallurgist Johann Conrad Fischer, 1773-1854, and his Relations with Britain*, (1947).

Hauser, A. *Schweizerische Wirtschafts- und Sozialgeschichte von den Anfängen bis zur Gegenwart* (1961).

Peter, Charlotte, 'Hans Caspar Escher 1775-1859' (in *Schweizer Pioniere der Wirtschaft und Technik*, Vol. VI, 1956).

Pfister, H. 'Entwicklung der Industrie der Stadt Schaffenhausen' (in *Festschrift der Stadt Schaffhausen zur Bundesfeier*, 1901).

Puschnig, R. 'Ein Tag im Hause Erzherzog Johanns' (*Zeitschrift des Historischen Vereins für Steiermark*, Vol. L, 1959, pp. 71-91).

Rappard, W. E. *La Révolution industrielle et les origines de la protection legale du travail en Suisse* (1914).

Schib, Karl. (ed.). *Johann Conrad Fischer 1773-1854: Tagebücher*, (1951).

Schib, Karl. *Geschichte der Stadt Schaffhausen* (1946).

Schib, K. and Gnade, R. *Johann Conrad Fischer 1773-1954* (1954).

Schib, Karl. 'Heinrich Zschokke als Biograph des Schaffhauser Erfinders J. C. Fischer' (*Festgabe Otto Mittler*, 1960, pp. 242-60).

Schudel, B. *Johann Conrad Fischer. Ein Schweizer Pionier der Stahlindustrie 1773-1854* (Schaffhausen, 1921).

Vogel, Otto. 'Johann Conrad Fischer und die englische Tempergiesserei' (*Stahl und Eisen*, vol. XL, 1920, pp. 869-72).

Waldvogel, W. *Les relations économiques entre la Grande Bretagne et la Suisse* (1922).

Manuscripts in the Fischer Archives

1. Correspondence Journal 1811–17. The original manuscript is in the municipal Museum zu Allerheiligen. There is a copy in the Fischer Archives.

2. Notebook (*Schreibkalender*), 1827. This notebook includes an account of Fischer's meeting with the Archduke Johann on Sunday, June 24, 1827 and notes of his journey to England from September 17 to October 14, 1827. Both the original manuscript and a typed copy are preserved in the Fischer Archives.

3. Notebook, 1834: original manuscript.

4. Notebook, 1838: original manuscript.

5. Notebook, 1854: original manuscript.

Index

This index of persons, firms and places excludes names that occur frequently such as J. C. Fischer, Schaffhausen, Mühlental, Austria, Switzerland, England and London.